WHAT'S FOR DINNER?

OUR FOOD, OUR CHOICES, OUR PLANET

JILL GRIFFITHS

T&H

First published in Australia in 2023
by Thames & Hudson Australia Pty Ltd
11 Central Boulevard, Portside Business Park
Port Melbourne, Victoria 3207
ABN: 72 004 751 964

thamesandhudson.com.au

The information contained in this book is for general information purposes only and is not intended to constitute professional dietary or medical advice.

26 25 24 23   5 4 3 2 1

Thames & Hudson Australia wishes to acknowledge that Aboriginal and Torres Strait Islander people are the first storytellers of this nation and the traditional custodians of the land on which we live and work. We acknowledge their continuing culture and pay respect to Elders past, present and future.

ISBN 978-1-760-76316-9
ISBN 978-1-760-76319-0 (ebook)

A catalogue record for this book is available from the National Library of Australia

Cover design: Design by Committee
Typesetting: Cannon Typesetting
Editing: Fay Helfenbaum

Printed and bound in Australia by McPherson's Printing Group

MIX
Paper | Supporting responsible forestry
FSC
www.fsc.org FSC® C001695

FSC® is dedicated to the promotion of responsible forest management worldwide. This book is made of material from FSC®-certified forests and other controlled sources.

WHAT'S FOR DINNER?

OUR FOOD, OUR CHOICES, OUR PLANET

JILL GRIFFITHS

T&H

First published in Australia in 2023
by Thames & Hudson Australia Pty Ltd
11 Central Boulevard, Portside Business Park
Port Melbourne, Victoria 3207
ABN: 72 004 751 964

thamesandhudson.com.au

The information contained in this book is for general information purposes only and is not
intended to constitute professional dietary or medical advice.

26 25 24 23   5 4 3 2 1

Thames & Hudson Australia wishes to acknowledge that Aboriginal and Torres Strait Islander
people are the first storytellers of this nation and the traditional custodians of the land on
which we live and work. We acknowledge their continuing culture and pay respect to Elders
past, present and future.

ISBN 978-1-760-76316-9
ISBN 978-1-760-76319-0 (ebook)

A catalogue record for this
book is available from the
NATIONAL LIBRARY OF AUSTRALIA
National Library of Australia

Every effort has been made to trace accurate ownership of copyrighted text and visual materials
used in this book. Errors or omissions will be corrected in subsequent editions, provided
notification is sent to the publisher.

Cover design: Design by Committee
Typesetting: Cannon Typesetting
Editing: Fay Helfenbaum

Printed and bound in Australia by McPherson's Printing Group

MIX
Paper | Supporting
responsible forestry
FSC
www.fsc.org   FSC® C001695

FSC® is dedicated to the promotion of responsible forest management
worldwide. This book is made of material from FSC®-certified forests
and other controlled sources.

Contents

'Eating is an agricultural act.'
Wendell Berry

Seventy-five – Twelve – Five

'WHAT WOULD YOU like for dinner?' I hear myself asking my kids as I stack breakfast dishes and wipe the kitchen bench. My mother used to ask the same question and it always frustrated me that she expected me to think of dinner first thing in the morning. Now I understand she was planning the day ahead, and that meant she was also thinking about food because meals don't turn up on tables without forethought and work.

As a child I never thought much about what I was eating. I got on with the business of being a child and, for the most part (forgetting the usual whinging and fussiness), ate what was dished up. Mum did the cooking and my family, like many people of Anglo-Saxon descent in 1970s Australia, mostly ate 'meat and three veg' – mutton chops, mashed potato, peas and carrots; or perhaps beans or cabbage or cauliflower. Occasionally it was steak instead of mutton, sometimes pork, especially during the years when Dad indulged his long-held desire to be a farmer and kept pigs at a farm just outside the country town where we lived. Sometimes the meat was roasted and the potatoes brown and juicy from cooking in the pan with the meat, all served with lashings of gravy. Once a week there were sausages.

From time to time we had chicken, but not often. In summer it would be cold meat and salad – lettuce, tomato, cucumber, carrot. It was functional food. Economical. Simple. Made from what was available. Nothing fancy.

As an adult, I began to question what I was eating almost as soon as it was my responsibility to fill the fridge and pantry. Initially, my questions focused on cost and how to survive within my modest means as a university student. The lessons of that time were to favour basic ingredients, seasonality and making things from scratch.

I was a biology undergraduate and my studies made me begin to wonder about the way our food nourished us (and where and why it failed to do so). I quickly came to value nutrition and fresh food. I wondered where our food systems fitted in with the broader environment; how farms fit into the Australian landscape. I had grown up in the Western Australian wheatbelt hearing farmers talk about the spread of salt across their paddocks. Yet it was only when I got to university that I began to understand the links between land clearing and salinity, and to question the way we farm this continent's ancient soils.

I became concerned about the role of animals in agriculture. I took to ranting about livestock farming, which was somewhat ironic given my happy escape from the city was my uncle's farm (he ran beef cattle at the time and I never considered his cattle mistreated in any way). I tried vegetarianism as a possible answer to my environmental and animal welfare concerns and mostly stuck to it for the better part of a decade.

I have gone through stages of ordering weekly boxes of seasonal, organic vegetables delivered to my door. Then cancelled my subscription when I began to wonder whether it really was worth the extra money to buy organic, or when faced with an over-abundance of things that were already prevalent in my garden. At times I have tried to buy all local produce, caught up in the idea that food miles matter above all else, only to give up when I realised the 'local' bananas in Perth travel almost 1000 kilometres south from Carnarvon. Besides, I was never going to give up drinking tea and the leaves cross oceans to get to my teapot.

Some years ago, a Saturday morning farmers' market started up within walking distance of my suburban Perth home. There is a lot about it that I like. The produce is fresh and seasonal, mostly sold by the people who grow it. I like knowing where my food comes from; I am forever seeking that elusive connection to place and food is a tangible aspect of that. But I have to admit that I baulk at some of the farmers' market prices. Like most people, I'm conscious of price when I shop for food, even if I feel guilty about it because I know how hard it can be for growers to make a profit. Working in science communication with agricultural researchers gave me an insight into just how much farmers are squeezed by profit margins and gripped by the vagaries of nature. My job afforded me the privilege of meeting and talking to many farmers finding innovative ways to remain sustainable and profitable. It's work that is invisible from the supermarket aisles, tempting though it is to think that's where food comes from. It's not, of course, but supermarkets do feature in my family's food shopping.

I also grow a few veggies in my yard and have some chooks. Keeping chooks and growing food are near constants in my life – when I was growing up we always had chooks and a productive garden, and for most of my adult life I have kept chooks and grown veggies where possible (and in a few places where it looked almost impossible). It simply makes sense to me to do so.

While it's easy enough to grow a bit of lettuce and a few herbs, they alone won't sustain a family. People need protein and calories. In *Out of the Scientist's Garden*, agricultural researcher Richard Stirzaker analyses the reality of backyard self-sufficiency, looking in detail at the calories needed to sustain a family and the difficulties of producing them in a backyard. Potatoes offer potential for supplying the required calories, Stirzaker suggests, but his analysis of just how many potatoes need to be grown is daunting. The feasibility of growing a cereal crop in a backyard simply isn't there, let alone harvesting and processing it. We rely on farmers, and farms, for our daily sustenance.

I've always had a soft spot for farmers. My maternal grandparents were dairy and beef farmers and I spent my childhood among wheat and sheep farmers. To this day, I believe my love of winter rain was kindled as a child when watching the sheer joy of the local farmers when good rain fell. Their success or otherwise is held so much in the grip of the weather but urbanites are largely immune from knowing or feeling it. Drought in the wheatbelt sends farmers bankrupt but doesn't affect the price of a loaf of bread in the city. How can that be? Occasionally a cyclone in Queensland will briefly push up the price of bananas in the southern cities, but mostly city dwellers are protected from the difficulties of food production. There is a disconnect between the economics of agriculture and the economics of food consumption. Even as public discussions about food and environment become more common, I keep thinking something is lacking, some underlying bedrock of truth and connection. It seems we as a society are less aware that the food we eat comes from the earth, regardless of what we eat. As American farmer and poet Wendell Berry put it, 'Eating is an agricultural act.' But we deny that reality every time we demand unseasonal produce or reach for conveniently pre-prepared food with a long list of industrial ingredients.

In a bid to better understand, I started deeply questioning the food I choose to put on the table and how I make those decisions. I questioned the food system that makes that food available. I questioned the diet and health books that push us towards this or that fad.

I questioned the call to eat less meat and the rise of veganism and what it means for farming and the environment, even as I continued to wrangle with my own meat eating. I questioned what it means to have food traded internationally as a commodity, and what 'food miles' really mean. I questioned the use of synthetic chemicals in growing food and whether we would be better off without them. I wondered what impact the push for paddock-to-plate traceability has on farmers.

In the midst of seeking answers, I stumbled across a startling fact: 75 per cent of the world's food comes from just twelve plant species and five animal species. I learned the list by heart: the plants – wheat, sugar, maize, rice, potatoes, soybeans, cassava, tomatoes, bananas, onions, apples, grapes; and the animals – cattle, chickens, pigs, goats and sheep. The lack of diversity in this list alarms the biologist in me, while the consumer in me, faced with the plethora of foodstuffs cramming the supermarket shelves, cannot quite comprehend it. Is it really true? Does that abundance come from such a narrow range? What are these things and where do they come from? What about the other 25 per cent of our food? What about the people who produce our food? Who is really feeding us? The answers raise yet more questions. So I go looking for deeper, more satisfying answers to the question of what's for dinner.

Some plants –
Six of the twelve

CHAPTER 1

Tomatoes

S CRAWLED ON MY shopping list, somewhere between cheese and
soap, are the words 'tinned tomatoes'. Sounds simple enough, but
as I stand before the shelves the choices are mind boggling. Crushed,
whole or chopped? With added herbs or without? Organic or not?
Australian or imported? I ignore the cheaper price of some of the
imported cans in favour of buying Australian and select a tin of non-
organic, Australian-grown chopped tomatoes with no added herbs.
That's my go-to. It's a basic staple that sits on the bottom shelf of my
pantry and gets restocked as soon as the supply dwindles. But I realise
I know very little about where and how tomatoes are grown and
processed and by whom. Am I making the best choice? How should
I make the judgement?

Chefs sing the praises of Italian tinned tomatoes – many of
them who otherwise focus on Australian produce apparently prefer
imported ones. Tomatoes have come to be associated with Italy and
Italian cuisine but they originate in South and Central America.
It was probably Mexicans who first domesticated tomatoes. Spanish
explorers took them back to Europe and, like so many things, they
spread around the world with European colonists.

These days, Italy processes around 5.5 million tonnes of tomatoes annually and in some southern areas of the country up to 89 per cent of the tomatoes end up in cans. Worldwide, tomatoes are big business; about 40 million tonnes of tomatoes are processed globally each year. In Australia, tomatoes come in second only to their potato cousins as the most important vegetable crop. (I say cousins because they are from the same plant family – the Solanaceae or potato family, also called the nightshades. It's a big family that includes eggplants, capsicums and chillies. Also worth noting is that all of these 'vegetables', except potatoes, are actually fruit, botanically speaking, because they are the fleshy containers for seeds. But we call them veggies because that's how we use them.)

The Australian tomato harvest is around 426,000 tonnes and has a value of roughly $645 million. Almost half of that is grown in Echuca, Victoria by a little-known Japanese company called Kagome. Troy Hudgson, Marketing and Business Development Manager for Kagome, tells me the company is a household brand in Japan but few Australians have heard of it because in Australia it operates business-to-business, supplying processed tomato products to the companies that put products on our shelves. 'We produce about 15,000 tonnes of product that goes into foodservice,' Hudgson says. (Foodservice refers to restaurants, cafes, hospital and school cafeterias, and catering companies. To put it another way, it's the food that doesn't get prepared in people's homes.) 'The rest goes to brands – your pasta sauces, tomato sauces, pizza sauces,' Hudgson continues. 'Some of our tomato products go to Japan, South-East Asia and New Zealand, but 80 per cent of it is consumed in Australia.' Kagome also grows and processes carrots, beetroot, apples and garlic, most of which go to Japan. 'We process the freshest fruit and vegetables,' Hudgson says. He explains to me that around 97 per cent of the tomatoes end up in the cans, but the remaining 3 per cent is not entirely wasted. 'We dry that into a powder and sell that too. In the past it has gone to animal feed, and carrot wastage currently goes to animal feed. We are now installing a drying machine to create a new product and reduce the waste from tomatoes even further.' It all sounds impressively efficient.

The other big player in Australian tomatoes is SPC, which is the company behind the tinned tomatoes that sit on the shelves wearing the SPC and Ardmona labels. The company also owns the Goulburn Valley label, which markets fruit products. Their website says their tomatoes are grown on farms in the Goulburn Valley, New South Wales and are 'produced in clean, green conditions under strict food safety standards and they're picked and packed within 24 hours to lock in all the natural goodness.' SPC processes about 50,000 tonnes of tomatoes a year, but some of the Ardmona tomato products contain Kagome tomatoes.

Sometimes I think I should try to grow enough tomatoes to bottle my own. I figure I go through around two 400-gram tins a week – let's call it a hundred a year, roughly. According to Italian research, it takes 833 grams of tomatoes to fill a 400-gram can, a figure that includes wastage during the canning process. An American study found it takes 1.6 kilograms of fresh tomatoes to make one kilogram of canned tomatoes; that is, 640 grams fresh for a 400-gram tin. Which may mean American canned tomatoes are more watery than Italian canned tomatoes, or it may mean American canneries are more efficient. I don't know. I'm not sure if I would be more or less wasteful than a cannery, but for the purpose of this exercise, let's say I am making thick, gloopy, bottled tomatoes that any Italian would be happy to put in their favourite pasta sauce. That means I need to grow about 83 kilograms of tomatoes to bottle the equivalent of my hundred cans.

I do a bit of research in gardening books and on internet sites and decide it's reasonable for me to expect to get about 10 kilograms of fruit per plant, at least in theory. That means I would need eight or nine plants. Let's call it ten; given that my figures are already rubbery, I may as well make them simple to calculate. Ten tomato plants sounds achievable (although that is only replacing the tinned tomatoes and not the bottles of passata and tomato sauce, nor the jars of tomato paste, and fresh tomatoes).

The efficiency of the whole enterprise depends on a few factors. How much time would it take and how do I value my time? What about water and fertiliser? What about the energy used to bottle the tomatoes? If I'm serious about this analysis, I should also look at resources used to make the tools I'm using. It's all getting very complicated and I still haven't answered my original question as to whether it's better, environmentally speaking, to opt for imported Italian tinned tomatoes or the local Australian product.

When in doubt, ask an expert. I contact Dr Brad Ridoutt, a CSIRO researcher who specialises in life cycle sustainability assessment in the agriculture and food sectors. Scientists like Ridoutt use life cycle assessment (LCA) to understand the environmental impact of a product through its entire life cycle, including extracting and processing raw materials, manufacturing, distributing, packaging, use, recycling, and final disposal. With so many variables it's complicated, but they crunch numbers and come up with useful comparisons.

Ridoutt tells me he hasn't done direct comparisons of Italian and Australian tinned tomatoes but says that if all other things are equal, products travelling further will have a higher carbon footprint. 'Though bear in mind that sea freight is a relatively less GHG [greenhouse gas] emission–intensive form of transportation,' he says. 'The issue is that, typically, not everything else is equal, which makes it a complex scenario to compare.'

It's precisely because all other things are rarely equal that it is so hard to drill down to clear-cut answers. As an example, Ridoutt and his colleagues looked at the trade-offs between carbon footprint and water use when assessing the environmental impact of producing fresh tomatoes for a Sydney market. Only about 8 per cent of the fresh tomatoes sold in Sydney are produced locally (which was defined as within 25 kilometres), with most of the rest coming from other parts of Australia. The researchers investigated different production systems used to meet the demand, and the impacts of each. They looked at water and carbon because neither factor alone tells us the overall environmental impact. Even looking at just two potential impacts of one product delivered to one market did not deliver a definitive number that said 'this is good and this is bad'. The tomatoes' footprints depended on the season and the type of production system. They found the carbon footprint per kilogram of tomatoes ranged from 0.39 to 1.97 kilograms CO_2e (carbon dioxide equivalent, which is the measure scientists use to calculate and compare the amount of carbon emitted by a particular activity). The water footprint ranged from 5 to 53 litres. They are fairly large ranges.

The study concluded that local tomatoes produced in an unheated greenhouse had the lowest overall impact. But in the Sydney climate, tomatoes can only be grown this way for five months of the year. If Sydneysiders want fresh tomatoes year round, heated greenhouses could be used to produce them locally or they could be grown in Queensland and transported south. Both of these options carried a higher environmental footprint than the local, seasonal tomatoes, but the Queensland tomatoes had lower impact than those grown in the heated greenhouse in Sydney. So, eating local did have a lower impact, but only if it was local *and* in season. As much as eating local has become a catchcry of environmental responsibility, it is more nuanced than simply choosing the produce grown closest to our homes.

A different study looked more closely at the whole 'eat local' message. Does it improve food security and climate resilience? Is it the best way for consumers to reduce their environmental impact? These questions are not as simple as they at first seem. The researchers urged caution in making comparisons because of the difficulties in putting one study beside another, and in determining the relative importance of different factors. I think it's worth remembering that specialist sustainability researchers spend careers trying to get to the bottom of these questions. To expect a two-word slogan to contain the answer is unrealistic. The 'eat local' study concluded that it is open to debate how well eating locally performs environmentally when a range of factors are considered. As in the Sydney fresh tomatoes study, even seemingly simple comparisons can be fraught. How something is grown, packaged and transported makes a difference to its overall environmental impact. As does how it is stored and how much ends up being wasted. Wrapping something in plastic creates an environmental impact, but may improve its shelf life and prevent waste, which would reduce its impact. Which makes it very complicated.

There are always trade-offs between the resources available to grow particular foods and the location of the people who want to eat them. Water is a serious consideration in many locations. Temperature is more important in others. Growing tomatoes and other vegetables in an open field is not the same as growing them in a heated greenhouse. Fresh food that requires rapid refrigerated transport is one thing; dried food travelling by train or ship is something entirely different. I think the take-home message is that local *seasonal* produce will generally win out, but possibly not always. Simplifying that message to 'eat local', as we so often hear, doesn't always work.

Eating locally is not new. In the past, people ate what could be grown nearby in any given season. Surplus produce was stored or preserved for the hungry times. We no longer live like that. Most of us want lettuce and tomatoes all year round but there are few locations where it is possible to grow them locally year round, certainly not outside. They either need to be grown in greenhouses at least some of the time or transported from faraway fields where they will grow in the 'off' seasons.

I'm still not sure where all this leaves my decision about buying Australian or Italian tinned tomatoes. I think it probably means that the environmental aspects are so hard to negotiate that it's reasonable to make a choice based on other considerations. As in, which do I prefer the taste of and how much does it matter to me to support Australian growers (even if the company doing the processing is not Australian). I favour buying Australian as a rule.

Australia is a net producer of food – we export more than we import – and Aussie farmers produce around 90 per cent of what we eat. Yet imported products are often cheaper (due to cheaper labour, economies of scale and different regulations), which puts pressure on domestic producers. I think that from the perspective of national food security it makes sense for us to have a thriving agricultural sector. I'm not advocating for tariffs to protect our farmers, because I don't understand enough about economics and international trade to have an informed opinion about that, but I do think as a matter of principle that where we can and do grow food the Australian option deserves support. I opt to make that support personal and buy Australian, putting my money where my mouth is. Literally.

There is, of course, the option I suggested earlier of growing my own tomatoes. After all, you don't get much more local than your own garden and if I can use environmentally-friendly gardening methods then maybe it's the best option. Tomatoes are a reasonably easy crop to grow. My father used to grow mountains of the things. All summer long they would line the window sills of our house ripening out of harm's way from bugs. The scent of chopped tomatoes and onions being turned into jars of tomato relish would fill the kitchen. (My Aunty Rosie's recipe, adopted by Mum.) I too have had my seasons of abundance with tomatoes, when I've proudly thrust buckets-full on visitors and made tomato relish and tomato chutney and bottles of passata. But this past summer, my tomatoes have been blighted by wilt and ravaged by heat.

As much as it disappoints me to have so few tomatoes from my garden, it's not a disaster for me. I have tinned tomatoes in the cupboard (chopped, Australian grown, no added herbs) and there are shelves of them in the shops, despite the Covid pandemic. There are bright red tomatoes in the vegetable section at the supermarket and down at the farmers' market. I can choose truss, Roma, heirloom (zebra, striped, yellow), cherry, grape, hydroponic, organic, Western Australian grown, Australian grown. I can buy fresh tomatoes, dried tomatoes, tinned tomatoes, tomato sauce, tomato paste, passata, sugo, relish, chutney, and jam. Even without growing them, I have access to as many tomatoes as I could care to eat, whenever I choose to eat them. The price, quality and quantity of the fresh ones fluctuate a bit with the season, but they are always available. If tomatoes are my desire, I can sate it easily, despite the wilting bushes in my garden.

But what if the season's tomato harvest from my garden was my tomato supply for the year? This year my family and I would have had a dozen or so full-sized tomatoes, each needing a few bug holes cut out before they were edible, and half a dozen small bowls of cherry tomatoes. In the midst of shops full of bounty, it's easy to forget that food production can be precarious.

————

Often, early on summer mornings, I sit in my garden and write, the scent of basil washing over me from where I brushed past it. I listen to bees buzzing in the rosemary and on the cucumbers. I love it. I like my little garden and I like growing veggies. I'm in good company cultivating a home vegetable garden. The Australia Institute reported that 52 per cent of Australian households grow some of their own food and a further 13 per cent intended to start at the time of the survey. That was before Covid. At the start of the pandemic demand for seeds and seedlings was reported as being up to 1800 per cent higher, year on year, in some places. Nurseries sold out as everyone frantically planted a few veggies to prevent starvation when the shops ran out of food. Fortunately, the shops haven't run out of food; supply chains have been challenged at times, but have remained generally reliable.

The idea of growing vegetables at home to ease people through a time of crisis is not new. Far from it. The Victory Gardens movement of the Second World War saw governments in several countries, including Australia, encourage people to grow their own fruits and vegetables to help supply food. Before that there was the War Garden or Liberty Garden of the First World War, which was the same idea. As Australian author Peter Timms writes in *Australia's Quarter Acre*, 'For centuries, the vegetable garden and home orchard were simply a matter of necessity [...] We tend to forget that, throughout human history, gardening has very often been a matter of life and death.' In these modern times of plenty, can home gardens make a valuable contribution to household food requirements? I already quoted Richard Stirzaker's take on how difficult it is to grow enough food to meet all of our energy requirements, but what if we concentrate on vegetables?

Dr Sumita Ghosh from the University of Technology Sydney researches urban resilience. She used the New South Wales regional city of Dubbo as a case study for the urban agriculture potential of home gardens in residential areas. Ghosh looked at how urban plots could be cultivated and concluded that, with the available land, home gardens could supply up to 84.3 per cent of the residents' annual 'dietary vegetable demand' if most of the available space was used, while even with a much less intensive usage, almost a quarter of these veggies could be grown at home. She reported that the potential of home gardens to grow food depended on many factors, such as plot sizes and available productive land, along with related social, cultural and economic factors. Ghosh also cites other research that found urban home gardens encouraged dietary diversity, improved micro-nutrient deficiencies, and increased children's consumption of fruits and vegetables. Ghosh writes that according to a household survey undertaken by the Australian Bureau of Statistics in 1992, New South Wales backyards grew 70.4 kilograms of vegetables on average. The most popular vegetable grown was – you guessed it – tomatoes!

In a survey of Hobart household vegetable gardeners, University of Tasmania geographers Distinguished Professor Jamie Kirkpatrick and Associate Professor Aidan Davison found domestic food production supplied 38 per cent of the vegetables gardeners ate at home. Kirkpatrick and Davison reported that participants were motivated to grow vegetables for pleasure, better health and food access, and to promote social change.

The 'better health' motivation is interesting to investigate a little further. It's often said that the nutritive value of the fruit and vegetables available to us commercially has declined in recent decades. Canadian food researcher Dr Robin J Marles investigated whether there was any validity in this idea. Marles drilled down to find the sources of some widely touted claims and found the underlying data was generally absent or not comparable. But he found there was a grain of truth in the idea that modern vegetables and fruit are lower in minerals and vitamins than they were fifty years ago. This has mainly occurred due to a dilution effect, where yield has been increased by increasing the starch, sugar and fibre of new varieties without also increasing micronutrients. Overall, the changes were of no real consequence in terms of dietary consumption; even seemingly large decreases in the percentages of some micronutrients amount to very little change in real terms when the actual figures are analysed. Take copper for example, which is needed in trace amounts in our diets. Declines of up to 81 per cent in the copper content of some fruit and vegetables have been reported. Now that sounds alarming. But here's the punchline: throughout seasons and varieties, the actual content of copper in vegetables ranges by 1555 per cent and in fruit by a whopping 26,000 per cent. So a change of 81 per cent is meaningless in comparison. Put bluntly, if people aren't getting adequate intakes of vitamins and minerals in their modern diet, it's because they're not eating enough fruit and vegetables, not because mineral levels have changed.

If growing your own makes you eat more fruit and vegetables (and indications are that it does), then it probably will have a positive impact on your health (aside from the associated benefits of getting outside and exercising while doing the work).

Then there's another study from environmental scientists at the University of Adelaide. What if all the lawn in urban gardens was converted to growing vegetables, the researchers asked, would that enable cities to be self-sufficient? Isobel Hume, Professor Timothy Cavagnaro and Dr David Summers set about answering this question by looking at the land available in Adelaide, South Australia. They crunched some numbers around expected yields and the amount of vegetables the Dieticians Association of Australia recommends we all eat (five serves a day) and concluded that, if yields equivalent to those obtained in commercial vegetable gardens could be harvested, over three quarters of households in the study area had enough space to be self-sufficient in veggies. If high yields could be obtained, under a quarter of the existing lawn area would be needed. The researchers pointed out that their study didn't include people who live in apartments, but suggested street verges and rooftops could be explored as an option for apartment-dwellers.

Hume, Cavagnaro and Summers write that home-grown vegetables are a plausible way to provide vegetables in an urban setting and the approach could reduce greenhouse gas emissions. They cite earlier research that showed home-grown vegetables save 2.10 kilograms CO_2e (carbon dioxide equivalent) for every kilogram of vegetables consumed. At the time they did the study, over 1.2 million people were calling Adelaide home. Each of them, according to the Dieticians Association of Australia, should consume 137 kilograms of fresh vegetables annually. Based on these figures, if everyone in Adelaide consumed all the vegetables they should, according to the dieticians, and they grew them all themselves, it would prevent 345.24 million kilograms of CO_2e entering the atmosphere every year. That's not insignificant. But it's also a lot of gardening. The researchers suggest it would take twenty minutes a day for a household to do this.

There is, of course, the uncomfortable fact that if everyone did that, the people who currently grow, transport and sell vegetables for a living would be out of work. It would be a significant disruption, even if it is, in many ways, a return to days of old. I suppose there's an argument that there would be other work in providing the seeds, seedlings and fertiliser needed for all these home gardeners. The truth is, it's a utopian ideal to suggest we would all go back to growing all our own veggies (or perhaps it's a dystopian view that it would be necessary). It does seem, though, that the evidence suggests growing some veggies in our gardens can be a useful contribution, to our diets (people with vegetable gardens eat more veg), to our overall health (it's good for us to get outside), and to how heavily we tread on the planet (by reducing carbon dioxide emissions). But it's still worth keeping in mind that environmental impact is not all about carbon emissions. It's also about resources, especially water and fertiliser. A home garden might or might not use these as efficiently as a commercial enterprise.

My veggie garden isn't a matter of life and death, or not mine at least; the snails and caterpillars may have a different view. My garden is small. The main part takes up about 8 square metres of what was once lawn. I have eight half wine barrels and some big pots I plant with veggies, plus some small fruit trees and lots of herbs in areas most people would probably plant ornamental shrubs. Overall, it doesn't produce a lot, really nothing more than a token contribution to my family's meals. But it provides me with great pleasure and a sense of connection to place and seasons, and something else that is even less tangible. It provides a demonstration. It demonstrates how damned hard it can be to produce food. There are bugs. Rats sneak in and chew the oranges just as I'm about to pick them. The sun shines too strongly and heat wilts everything. It rains too much. Or not at all. The wind blows. The dog digs. I'm glad I don't need my garden to feed my family. But I'll continue to potter and grow things, partly because I feel it's a good thing to do, partly because I enjoy it, and also because I like to be reminded to be thankful. I'm grateful to the farmers who produce the bounty we eat and for all that happens to get it to us.

CHAPTER 2

Wheat

THE DAY AFTER my final high school exam, I started work on the wheat bin at a small town not far from where I lived in rural Western Australia. The bin was the central location where surrounding farmers would bring their truckloads of grain, mostly wheat, but also barley, oats and lupins. The bins and associated silos dominated the wheatbelt towns; each town had a grain receival point and some 'towns' had little else, just a few associated shacks and a white-lettered dark-green sign announcing the town's name.

My job that summer of 1982–3 was as sampler, a position I had qualified for on a one-day training course a month earlier. At the course, I'd satisfied the powers that be I could tell the difference between wheat and barley grains, and could pick out oats and find mustard seeds among them. I could identify a weevil. I knew how to gauge the weight of the grains. And in doing all that, could classify and certify the quality of the grain.

I was the first stop for farmers delivering grain. My shed was a metal box on stilts – corrugated iron walls and roof, chequer-plate iron floor, industrial steel steps leading up from the bitumen below. It was possible to step straight off the shed's 'balcony' onto the back of a truck. This was required, and I would step out armed with the sampling spear – a one-and-a-half-metre-long hollow metal shaft. When twisted, the outer sleeve of the spear opened from the bottom to the top, filling its centre with a sample of grain drawn from across the depth of the load. On each truck, I was to take three spears-full, tipping the contents into a bucket and mixing them. I would then draw a smaller sample to be tested on the basic instruments inside my metal-box laboratory-on-stilts.

When I stepped into the Kununoppin wheat bin sampling shed in December 1982, I think I was the first female sampler to take that position; as far as I know, I was the first woman to work on any bin in the local area. There was a line of trucks queued up waiting for the bin to open. I knew most of them: I'd grown up in the district and the population was sparse, social occasions few and sporting events between local towns almost compulsory. Everyone knew everyone.

I was self-conscious in my short shorts and tee-shirt, my blue water container sloshing its 2 litres of Staminade and ice blocks as I walked up, climbed the steps and took my place. (Now you won't see anyone at grain receival points in shorts and tee-shirts. Long sleeves and long trousers with high visibility colours and reflective bands are de rigueur in these workplace safety days, as are boots and broad-brimmed hats. Women's roles on the bins are now many and varied, and grain sampling is automated. Sampling and weighbridge sheds are air conditioned. But I digress.)

At 7 o'clock on the dot on my first day, the site foreman came and opened the gate. The bin was open. The first truck pulled up along-side the sampling shed. The farmer had already rolled the tarpaulin back off the load and I stepped out of my shoes and across the narrow gap onto the truck, spear and bucket in hand. My feet sank into the golden grain. It trickled between my toes and prickled my ankles. I stabbed the spear down into the grain and slowly twisted it open, listening to the tinkle of grain filling the spear. I twisted it closed, then pulled the full spear from the wheat and emptied it into the bucket. I repeated the process twice more. With my bucket of wheat in hand, I stepped back across onto the shed balcony and slipped back into my shoes. At the bench in the shed, I measured the requisite amount of grain, weighed it, sieved it, checked it for weed seeds (not too many) and weevils (none!) and foreign material such as sticks and stones (none). I pronounced it clean 'A' grade wheat, filled out the form in duplicate, signed it, put one copy in the file and gave the other to the farmer. He nodded his appreciation and drove off to the weighbridge, where the truck would be weighed. From there he would drive down and dump the grain at the receival point, before coming back to be reweighed on the way out, so the weighbridge officer could calculate the amount of wheat delivered. This weight, coupled with my grading of the grain's quality, determined how much the farmer would be paid for the load.

Truck after truck after truck. All day long. Some days the bin was open for receivals for twelve hours. Some days only ten and rarely eight. I sampled every truckload of grain that came in. It was hot, dusty, dirty work. The air temperature regularly rose above 40 degrees Celsius – and that was the official temperature taken in the shade. In the blazing sun on the back of the trucks it was higher and in my hotbox sampling shed, higher again. I often saw the mercury in the little thermometer on my bench creep up to 47 degrees Celsius.

At times, it was simply too hot. The brittle air crackled and even the tough eucalypts by the side of the road wilted, their long slender leaves hanging downwards to hide from the direct glare of the sun. A fire ban would be enforced, preventing harvesting until the temperature dropped. Receivals would slow to a trickle as farmers would only be able to empty the on-farm storage they had previously filled, rather than harvesting more grain from the rippling paddocks.

Combine harvesters, the machines each worth as much as a suburban house, would stand idle, the swath of stubble behind them, the full seed heads before them, waiting for the temperature to drop before their great diesel engines could roar back to life. The weighbridge officer and I would sit in the shade under my shed, drinking water and chewing ice blocks as we watched the ants and galahs steal grains of spilled wheat.

The weighbridge officer was a university student. 'The thing I don't get,' he said, looking across the road to the paddock of wheat shimmering in the heat haze beyond, 'is what happens to all this wheat?'*

'What do you mean?' I asked.

'There's so much of it!' he said. 'Tons and tons and tons of it. And that's just here. Think about that across the wheatbelt. Millions of tons. Why on earth do we need so much?'

'Um, do you eat bread?' I asked. 'And biscuits and cake and spaghetti?'

'Yes, but all the people in Perth wouldn't eat the amount that we've received here. Probably not all the people in Australia. So why do we need to grow so much? Where does it go? What happens to it? It can't all be made into bread, surely.'

I'd never thought about it like that. I'd grown up in a town set in the midst of thousands upon thousands of hectares of wheat fields, paddocks that stretched to the horizon and beyond. Paddocks that changed through the seasons from barren baked brown at the end of summer to rich ploughed earth when the autumn rains fell, to bright green as the crops sprouted, to a golden harvest, then to pale

---

* This and other conversations from my childhood and early adult life are recounted as I remember them in essence and are not intended to be word-for-word recollections of what was said, but they do portray events that happened.

straw stubble and around again. The seasons dictated the colour of the landscape and the activities of the farmers. Growing wheat was what people did. I'd never thought about the quantity of it, other than to understand through some kind of osmosis whether or not it was a good year or a poor one, a variation determined by the rainfall that shaped the mood of the community as well as its wealth. But this city boy had a point; where did all this wheat go?

The year I first worked on the wheat bins was 1982. The Australian national wheat harvest that year was a touch under 9 million tonnes, of which around 2.7 million tonnes was produced in Western Australia. A small portion of that was delivered to the Kununoppin wheat bin and sampled by me. The apparent vastness of the wheat crop that surrounded that bin was a reality; in 1982 wheat was planted on about 4.3 million hectares of land across the Western Australian wheatbelt. In 2018, this had increased to about 4.9 million hectares, but that year the harvest was close to 10 million tonnes. Yes, you read that correctly. In the past four decades, there has been little change in the area of land in Western Australia planted to wheat. This has been true across Australia: the amount of land sown with wheat has remained relatively constant for decades. But the amount of grain harvested has dramatically increased (give or take a few years when drought has prevailed).

The Australian wheat harvest, most of which comes from Western Australia and New South Wales, is usually around 25 million tonnes, which accounts for 3.5 per cent of annual global production. The 700 or so million tonnes of wheat produced in the world provides around one fifth of the calories available for people to eat. Add to that tally the other two major grains – rice and maize – and we can account for 60 per cent of the world's food calories. An alarmingly large amount – somewhere between 760 million and a billion tonnes – of the world's grain also goes to feed livestock. We'll look at that a little more closely later, so hold onto that thought.

The vast majority of wheat grown in Australia relies on rainfall to germinate and grow – it is 'rainfed' rather than irrigated. In New South Wales there are areas where wheat is grown under irrigation, but the rest of Australia relies on rain falling on the wheat crops where they are planted. When rain doesn't fall, crops don't grow but farmers' overdrafts do. Rain has to fall at the right times and in the right quantities. Too much rain on growing crops can waterlog the soil and drown the roots. Rain at harvest is bad. Grain needs to be dry to reap. Rain on ripe grain may cause it to sprout in the seed head, which rapidly turns high-quality wheat into low-value animal feed. But in the Goldilocks zone of not too much and not too little but just the right amount of rain, wheat grows abundantly and farmers smile broadly.

For years I wrote articles for a national farming magazine and that gave me the privilege and the pleasure of talking to farmers across Australia on a regular basis. Invariably, we began by talking about the weather and my standard question was to ask for their average annual rainfall. In 2020, I swear every single farmer began their answer by saying words to the effect of, 'Well, we say our long-term average is around *this much*, but we don't see that very often these days. If we're talking the past twenty years, it's closer to *this much*.' The second 'this much' was always a lot less than the first. It's not exactly scientific, but anecdotally it suggests that farmers are concerned about changing rainfall. The data backs up the observation that the wheatbelt rainfall declined from the 1970s to the present, and had already declined by then. A graph of rainfall averages of the mid-20th century, late-20th century and early 21st century looks like descending steps.

At the same time that rainfall has declined, yields have increased. Australian farms have become more productive, which is strange when you consider the link between rainfall and grain growth. The increased productivity is thanks to a range of things, not least of which is a vast amount of research that has gone into developing better varieties of wheat, better methods of sowing, fertilising and growing, better machinery and better weed control. That's a lot of betters and that makes for a better harvest, despite the rainfall. Richard Stirzaker writes that in the 1950s, Australian paddocks produced enough grain to make about four slices of bread per square metre of wheat grown. By the turn of the century, according to Stirzaker, average yields were up to eight slices per square metre, with some farmers reaping double that amount. It continues to climb. These increased yields have come at a cost, and I'll come back to that because it's important.

The improvement in yields really took off in the 1950s and 1960s during the Green Revolution. American agronomist Dr Norman Borlaug is often called the father of the Green Revolution. He is credited with saving over a billion people from starvation and received the 1970 Nobel Peace Prize for his efforts. His genius was in leading research to create dwarfing varieties of grain plants, notably wheat, rice and corn, that put more effort into producing grain than into producing stems and leaves. This, along with improved agronomy (the science of growing agricultural plants) and increased fertiliser use, led to increased yields. But research didn't stop at that point and new varieties are constantly being developed. These days this research largely focuses on improving nutrient levels and creating varieties that cope with a range of environmental challenges.

———

CSIRO wheat breeder Dr Greg Rebetzke is one of many scientists working to develop new wheat varieties but when we first talk over the phone and he finds out I'm from Western Australia he wants to talk wine. He has a penchant for the shiraz wines grown in south-western Western Australia so we trade vineyard names before we get talking about wheat. Rebetzke is a pre-breeder; his job is to find the genetic material that can be passed on to commercial plant breeders to develop new varieties. He studies the genomes of old and over-seas varieties of wheat to find desirable traits. One of the projects Rebetzke has recently been involved in is developing wheat varieties with long coleoptiles.

A coleoptile is a sheath that protects the first leaf that grows out from the seed. That little shoot, along with its leaf, has to make it from wherever the seed was planted, up through the soil to the surface where it can bask in the sunlight and start to photosynthesise and thereby power the plant to grow. Most wheat varieties can push a coleoptile up from about 4 to 6 centimetres depth. Sow it too deep and it will run out of energy before it breaks the surface and the plant is doomed to shrivel and die.

'When the Green Revolution produced higher-yielding dwarfing varieties of wheat, they inadvertently selected varieties with shorter coleoptiles,' Rebetzke says. 'The Green Revolution dwarfing genes (*Rht-B1b* and *Rht-D1b*) are about the most important genes used globally in cropping. Their use permitted greater fertiliser use to enhance production and ensure global food security. Yet their poten-tial is greatest in more favourable environments. We saw these genes might be limiting potential in our rainfed, typically water-limited environments.' In other words, if you're planting wheat into moist soil where ongoing water availability is almost guaranteed, dwarfed wheats with short coleoptiles are fine. But that's not the situation in Australian wheat fields. Rain is unreliable and drought at the end of the growing season is common. Rebetzke and his team at CSIRO went looking for different genes with the desirable dwarfing and high-yielding characteristics of modern wheats, but with long coleoptiles and early leaf vigour to shade soil and suppress weeds. They found two dwarfing genes with commercial potential, and proceeded with caution. 'You have to be very careful when changing existing genetics and particularly genetics that changed global agriculture,' Rebetzke says.

So far, so good. Having done the early work, Rebetzke and the CSIRO team passed the genetics on to commercial breeders and new varieties with the new traits will soon be sown in Australian paddocks. They will give farmers more options regarding early sowing, which Rebetzke says will become increasingly important as climate change continues to increase variability with winter rainfall in Australia's grain growing regions.

Wheat breeding, and plant breeding in general, never reaches the final goal. There are always new challenges, like climate change or increasing salinity, and new demands, like a desire for higher protein or a more robust flavour, that require new varieties to be developed. Breeders respond to these challenges and goals by looking back as well as looking forward, so the varieties being grown when I was sampling wheat in the 1980s have been moved aside to make way for new, improved varieties. The way in which wheat is grown has also moved on.

The wheat I sampled in the 1982–83 harvest was almost certainly sown into ploughed earth, with heavy machines going around and around in ever diminishing circles until the whole paddock was covered.

But if you go out to the wheatbelt these days (and I urge you to do so) when autumn and the promise of winter rain hangs heavy in the air and the farmers drag their immense machinery from their colossal sheds, you probably won't see ploughs turning ever diminishing circles around paddocks. It's unlikely you will see much ploughed ground at all. There has been a quiet transformation in the broadacre paddocks of Australia, and elsewhere in the world, in the past few decades. It's called no-till or minimum till. Basically, farmers stopped ploughing before sowing. The benefits for soil conservation of not tilling (ploughing) are immense. With the stubble (the leftover stalks and stems from last year's crop) retained, the soil holds together and erosion is minimised. The soil also holds more moisture and carbon. These days, over 90 per cent of Western Australian grain farmers use a no-till system. Nationally, no-till is the most commonly used method of cropping, with around 80 per cent of cropping land receiving no cultivation other than at planting, when sharp knife-like 'points' cut slices through the soil into which the seeds are dropped.

There have been other revolutionary changes in the broadacre cropping paddocks. Precision equipment now allows farmers to plant grain in exact places, lined up by GPS to within millimetres – yes, within millimetres in those vast thousands of hectares. This equipment also ensures grain is planted at a predetermined depth to make sure the seed is in contact with as much soil moisture as the length of its coleoptile will allow. Rather than going round and round the paddocks, the machinery now goes up and down, autosteering sensors in the tractors lining up the lines of grain precisely, usually in the gap between the rows of stubble left from last year's crop. On many farms, particularly those with compaction-prone soils, this is coupled with 'controlled traffic farming' – CTF to those in the game – that lines up the wheel tracks for every piece of machinery that traverses the paddock, to prevent compaction across the entire paddock. When soil is compacted the soil particles are squashed together, leaving no space between. Air, water and roots can't penetrate compacted soils, so crop growth suffers.

Computerised recordings on harvesters produce yield maps showing grain production across the paddock. Soil testing and mapping link production to a whole suite of soil parameters – salinity, nutrients, acidity – and 'amendments', in the form of lime or nutrients, are added to improve yield. The Australian family broadacre cropping enterprise is high-tech and sophisticated. Grain growing these days is a combination of art and science, but mostly it's science. It's calculated decisions about yields and soils and plant varieties and weather forecasts and crop rotations and herbicides. Oh yes, did I not mention herbicides?

Herbicide use has increased drastically in cropping systems. Herbicides go with no-till farming a bit like the proverbial hand and glove and, like gloved hands, herbicides are somewhat out of fashion in many circles but considered essential in others. The thing is, if you don't plough the soil you don't have a chance to bury the weeds. In the old days, farmers would wait for the break of season – the first autumn rains – then head out on their tractors to plough the ground, turning the weeds that sprouted with the first rain back into the ground. They might do that a couple of times, letting weeds germinate and turning them back in, until finally getting a nice weed-free surface. Into this tilth, the crop would be planted. But if you don't turn the ground over, the weeds grow unhindered. In a no-dig garden you might smother the weeds with a layer of mulch, but it's pretty much impossible to find enough mulch to smother a 200-hectare paddock, let alone a 10,000-hectare farm. No-till agriculture has, in most instances, brought with it a high reliance on herbicides. That has increased yields but also comes with its own suite of problems.

One of the biggest is herbicide resistance. It's a simple enough problem to understand.

When weeds are sprayed with herbicide, not every weed is killed. The survivors live to produce seed. That seed grows into new weeds that have some resistance to the herbicide. When that generation is sprayed with the same herbicide, a larger proportion survive and they have increased tolerance to the herbicide. It's simple evolutionary theory in practice: survival of the fittest. It's the same process that leads to antibiotic-resistant pathogens.

As weeds become herbicide-resistant, crop growers need to use higher rates of herbicide and herbicides that contain different chemicals. The piles of empty drums mount up. Most farmers I speak to don't like using chemicals but see them as an essential tool in managing their farms and reaping a profit. They trust the testing of chemicals before they hit the market and the regulation of them by the relevant authorities. This is another topic I'll come back to later; there's a lot to say about agricultural chemicals.

Once harvested, the majority of Australian wheat – 70–80 per cent of it – is exported. Wheat is consistently Australia's tenth top export in terms of dollar value and generates about $5.5 to $6 billion annually. Most of this wheat goes to Asia and the Middle East, a bit goes south to New Zealand. The rest is consumed domestically. It goes into bread, biscuits, cakes, noodles, pasta, couscous and confectionary. Due to the scale of production, it's a relatively cheap ingredient so is often added to processed foods. It finds its way into our shops and homes and into our stomachs.

Wheat has been filling bellies for thousands of years – around 10,000 or 11,000 years. It was domesticated in the area of northern

Africa and the Middle East known as the Fertile Crescent, which today takes in Israel, Jordan, Lebanon, Syria, Turkey, Iran and Iraq. Wheat is a remarkably complex plant, with complex genetics; as University of Birmingham anthropologist Alice Roberts writes in *Tamed*, the 'protracted and complex history of domestication in wheat almost comes across like the plot-line of a romantic novel'. One of the consequences of wheat domestication is that the endosperm of the wheat grain became very much bigger. The endosperm is the bit inside a seed that stores the energy to power its germination (sending that seed leaf up to the surface in search of sunlight). In wheat, the endosperm is full of starch, with some vitamins, minerals, fats and oils thrown in. It is that starchy endosperm that we grind up to make flour. And it's that flour we eat.

I could walk down to the shop and buy a loaf of bread now, an artisan loaf, say, for $6, more or less. Up to $10 in some shops and with some marketing; $11 at the specialised bakery near my sister's house, which claims its sourdough starter is around thirty years old. A basic sliced loaf of white bread is cheaper, just a couple of dollars in a supermarket. With 26.2 per cent of the market share, Coles is the biggest retailer of bread in Australia, with Woolworths a close second at 25.8 per cent. In an average week, Australians spend $89.6 million on bread, made up of 11 million people spending around $8.20 each. Whichever way you cut the numbers, it's a lot of bread. Bread has formed, and continues to form, an important part of people's diets.

But bread consumption has fallen slightly in the past few decades. Between 1995 and 2018, average daily consumption dropped by 20 grams per person. This, according to dieticians Sara Grafenauer and Felicity Curtain, is because of people's concerns about gluten, sodium, sugar and overall carbohydrate levels in bread. Grafenauer and Curtain audited breads for sale in Australia in 2017 and their results are as comforting as a slice of hot buttered toast on a cold morning. Bread, they conclude, can readily provide all the whole grains recommended by dietary guidelines, along with a sizeable serve of protein and carbohydrates. Bread is an important source of essential nutrients such as thiamine, iodine and folic acid, which are routinely added to it. It's probably important to note the use of the word 'can', as in *can* provide recommended whole grains, because it seems unlikely that overly processed white bread would manage that.

My grandmother made bread and served it with every meal. At breakfast, she would lay the carefully cut slices of bread on the black metal trays in the oven of the wood stove to dry out a little before stabbing them with the sharp prongs of a toasting fork – made from fencing wire bent into shape – and hold them to the hot coals in the stove's fire box to make crisp, crunchy toast.

I regret never learning bread-making from Grandma. I wish I'd paid attention to how she kneaded it, the quantities of ingredients she used, the feel she had for its art and, most especially, the way she cultured the yeast. I don't know if she was given the original starter culture or made it from scratch. A quick Google search now reveals a bunch of pages explaining how to make a yeast starter from boiling a potato and leaving the water to ferment. Maybe that was the method Grandma used to make her yeast culture. In any case, she didn't buy yeast. She kept a brown bottle of yeast in a cupboard in the kitchen and that was what she used. That yeast along with water, flour and salt was all that went into her bread, of that I am fairly certain. It was a simple farmhouse loaf of the type that has been feeding people for thousands of years.

There was a time when all leavened breads were made from these sorts of yeasts, home cultured in liquid brews or sourdough starters. They use the yeasts and bacteria that occur naturally on the wheat or rye or in the local environment. A sourdough culture may contain more than fifty different species of bacteria, mostly various *Lactobacillus* species, and more than twenty different species of yeast, including *Saccharomyces* and *Candida*. For thousands of years bread was made without any knowledge of exactly what was causing the fermentation to occur. Then in the 1870s the French microbiologist Louis Pasteur developed techniques that enabled species of micro-organisms to be isolated and cultured. This led to the cultivation of baker's yeast, *Saccharomyces cerevisiae*. (It's the same species as brewer's yeast but a different strain; in early times, bakers got their yeast from brewers.)

As so often happens when things are simplified, we probably lost something in the process of moving towards the easier, more consistent bread produced using pure *S. cerevisiae* rather than the local, mixed wild cultures. Sourdough bread, which does not use this type of pure yeast, produces a lower glycaemic response than bread made with baker's yeast (so blood sugar remains more stable), has probiotic and antifungal properties, higher bioavailability of minerals and nutrients, and a few other desirable attributes. Basically, bread with more complexity is better for us.

Like a lot of people, at the start of the Covid pandemic I got a sourdough starter culture from a friend. It came as a sticky goo in a small plastic bag. I tipped it into a jar and added half a cup of flour and half a cup of water. When my culture was bubbling away, I proceeded to make bread. My first loaf of sourdough was as hard as a brick but unlike a brick was not useful for anything, except perhaps as a good example of how not to make sourdough.

I went internet browsing to look for a new recipe or some tips. I found a blog post of twelve common mistakes people make when baking sourdough. I'd made them all. I tried again. The second loaf had good flavour but was doughy and dense. I read more recipes. All tips pointed towards it being much easier to bake sourdough if you used a Dutch oven, so I ordered a Dutch oven online and waited for it to be delivered. In the meantime, I fed my sourdough culture and read recipes. The Dutch oven arrived – a beautiful red extravaganza with a cream enamelled interior. It's a weighty thing and I was glad it came with free postage, although the $148 price tag was making this a very expensive loaf of bread.

I found another sourdough recipe and set to work. Late Friday evening, I fed my culture. (I called it Marshall in honour of the friend who gave it to me – apparently, it's the thing to name sourdough starters.) The next morning, I began the work of actually making the bread, going through all those mysterious processes of autolysing, stretching and folding, rising, shaping, proofing, and finally baking. The yeasty, fruity smell of it filled the house. I left the baked loaf to cure on the bench, telling the kids they were not allowed to sample it yet. Finally, the time came to cut it. And there it was – a good crumb, textured, flavoursome and delicious. If I'm totally honest, it could have been cooked a tiny bit longer; the middle was a touch doughy. But it was a good loaf of bread. It had taken me all day to make, and that's not counting the hours of reading recipes and baking failed loaves before I finally got to one successful one.

With time and effort, I am confident I could get better at it but I'm a long way from having the skill and patience to keep our household in bread. Yet Grandma did just that for decades. I remind myself that she had little choice, at least in the early days of her homesteading.

There was no supermarket down the road for her to buy bread from, no freezer to store a couple of extra loaves. Sacks of flour and bags of salt collected by horse and cart were the extent of the external inputs to her loaves when she and Grandad were carving their farm from the karri forest in the 1930s. Now, with our lives dominated by convenience and abundance, it is easy to forget how recently scarcity and bloody hard work were kitchen companions to everyone. It's even easier to forget the effort that still goes into getting the food onto the supermarket shelves in the first place. Or the real price paid to put it there.

That wheat bin I first worked on was in Kununoppin, a small town in the Shire of Trayning in the central wheatbelt of Western Australia. I grew up in the town of Trayning. Wheat has been the main grain of farms around that area since European agriculture was introduced in the early 20th century. Before then, the land was covered by eucalypt woodland. For at least 45,000 years before the Europeans arrived the eucalypt woodland was Noongar country and the Noongar people maintain an ongoing connection to the land.

Making way for agriculture and creating the wheatbelt destroyed almost all of that woodland. The 'clearing line', where the grain belt gives way to the still-vegetated pastoral lands, is visible from satellites. Trees were felled to make way for wheat; a hard job with axe and horse and brute force. In the early days, with eyes firmly on the prize of clean European-style paddocks, the problems with removing perennial native vegetation from the landscape were initially not known and later ignored. Biodiversity loss was immediate and widespread but not generally considered important at the time. Land degradation – salinity, erosion, and soil acidity and sodicity – came later. They are now recognised problems, and not just in the Western Australian wheatbelt. Food production generally is now attributed as the largest cause of global environmental change. In agricultural land, these forms of degradation fall under the name of 'constraints' to productive farming and considerable effort is expended mitigating their consequences. It may seem ironic, but the very industry that created the problems changed, and continues to change, to deal with them. No-till is one such approach. Adding lime to redress acidity is another. Putting trees and other perennial vegetation back into landscapes is perhaps the most visible. The problems of land degradation were caused by the practices that built the cropping land of the wheatbelt and were generally in line with government policy at the time, but the cost of lost production and of repairing land degradation are largely borne by farmers today.

When the land in the Shire of Trayning was surveyed for European-style agriculture in 1907, the majority of the blocks were between 300 and 400 hectares, the area then considered necessary for a viable farm. As historian Reg Appleyard and farmer Don Couper write in their book *A History of Trayning*, 'a square mile of first class land would keep the farmer and his family in prosperous circumstances.' These days, a square mile of wheatbelt land would barely qualify as a hobby farm. Appleyard and Couper, referring to how the 'get big or get out' dictum saw farms rapidly expand in size, write that by the late 20th century 'increased grain output occurred on properties that were now ten times – or more – larger in acreage than they had been during settlement.' They give an example of a family who, in 2009 when Appleyard and Couper wrote their book, were farming an area 'comprising twenty-two original locations'. Farms get bigger, farm machinery gets bigger, input costs increase, profit margins get tighter. The 8-tonne trucks I sampled wheat from in the 1980s are now museum pieces, along with the hessian wheat bags and horse-carts that preceded them. Now wheat is carted in semi-trailers.

There's no more land to be had out there. The farms that get bigger do so by buying out neighbours. There were 13,106 farms in the Western Australian wheatbelt in 1970 but by 2013 it was down to 4941. The farmers who sell usually leave the district, most often headed to the city or bigger towns in search of work. The push for higher yields has screwed the profit margins ever tighter for farmers. The ones who survive do so by a combination of dogged determination, good agronomy, bank overdrafts and getting bigger. Plus a bit of good luck from time to time. And the occasional season of good rainfall.

As successful farmers buy out others, population declines. As population declines, towns shrink and services and shops disappear. Farms get bigger and towns get smaller. It's the same story with farmland all over the world, wherever farming produces commodities. The World Health Organization says that 2007 was the year in which the world shifted from being mostly rural to being mostly urban. Trayning is an easy example for me to use because it's where I grew up, not because it is unique in the story it tells.

When I started primary school in the early 1970s, Trayning had two primary schools but then the convent closed and the kids from there joined the rest of us at the state school. Today, Trayning Primary looks much the same as it did when I left. At least in essence. The basic three-classroom structure is unchanged, a ubiquitous design spread across rural Australia. Some extra buildings have been added – new ablution blocks, a library. A new playground. It's air-conditioned; it wasn't back in the day.

Despite these improvements, in so many ways that little school is a shadow of its former self. When my cohort left the school in 1977 there were about seventy kids enrolled. In 2021 there were thirteen. The shire population declined from 739 in 1976 to 394 in 2001. By the 2016 census, it was down to 133. The last meeting of the local football club, once a pillar of community excitement and activity, was held on 31 August 1993. I'm not a huge football fan but as I write that, I feel a heavy sadness. I well remember weaving royal blue and white crepe paper into arches for the local youths to burst through as they ran onto the ground for the grand final against their arch rivals from nearby Mukinbudin. Every town had a football club, cricket club, hockey club, basketball club, pony club, repertory club, Country Women's Association branch, Rural Youth club. These small organisations were the institutions upon which community was built.

In the 1970s, the town where I lived had two grocery shops, a butcher shop, a bakery (where the baker actually baked bread every day and jubilee twist once a week), a newsagent, a pub, a cafe, two or three machinery dealerships, a few mechanics, a stock and station agent, a bank, a tyre shop, a post office, three churches. You could buy fuel at the cafe and at the co-op or through a bulk retailer if you were on a farm. The co-op also had drapery and hardware sections. There were hundreds of other vibrant little towns like this scattered across the country.

The Trayning pub is still there. The post office is still there, now selling gifts and knick-knacks along with stamps. The co-op has gone. There are no banks. St Joseph's Catholic Church still has a service most Sundays but only a handful of people attend. The other two churches stand empty. There is no grocery shop in town. To buy groceries, locals travel almost an hour south-east to Merredin or over an hour and a half south-west to the larger town of Northam. You can't buy a loaf of bread in the town that was built around the wheat industry. An analysis of the 2021 Australian Census data showed

43 per cent of the houses in Trayning were vacant. When I was a kid, houses were regularly being built in town, or more often arriving pre-built on the back of very big trucks.

All of these things are linked. The yields from the paddocks. The research to create varieties that produce more with less. The way the land is farmed. The cost of the machinery. The herbicides sprayed. The size of the farms. The number of kids in rural schools. The disappearance of businesses in the towns. And the price we pay for bread and the abundance with which it sits on supermarket shelves. It's something I think about as I buy bread or flour or pasta. I check that it's made from Australian wheat and wonder about the anonymous farmer producing the commodities that are turned into the food we eat. I'm comfortable in my confidence that the vast majority of grain growers out there are doing the best they can to look after the environment and make a living, working with improved knowledge and understanding. I know they make a contribution to feeding the world that we can all take some pride in. But I also know it's not perfect, that change is ongoing and necessary. I like it when I find a story on the packet about the farmer who grew the grain; the QR codes that give a personal insight to paste over the anonymity. I'm happy to pay a bit more for a shorter supply chain that bypasses the commodity market and puts more in the individual farmer's pocket. But I don't live on bread alone.

CHAPTER 3

Potatoes

BOILED, MASHED, BAKED, roasted, French fries, chips; sprinkled with salt or lathered with butter or cheese or gravy. So many options for cooking and serving potatoes. My favourite is centimetre-thick slices of potato brushed with olive oil and grilled on the barbecue, about eight to ten minutes on each side, long enough for char lines to appear on the crisp outside and for the inside to be hot and soft and delicious. Serve immediately with a good mayonnaise and whatever else you fancy.

Potatoes are a remarkably nutritious staple, eaten by many cultures through many centuries after spreading across the world from their Andean origins. Along with the cereal grains, they have provided bulk calories and fibre to millions of people for millennia.

Potatoes have been a staple in Australia since the early days of colonisation, replacing without forethought the indigenous tuberous yams. (I'll come back to that in a later chapter.) Hort Innovation, a not-for-profit research and development organisation for the Australian horticulture industry, reported that in the year ending June 2021, there were enough potatoes produced in Australia for everyone here to eat 18 kilograms of fresh potatoes that year. Despite this, potato consumption in Australia has declined in recent decades. It dropped by 20 per cent between 1995 and 2012. (Conversely, potato consumption in Africa and Asia is increasing, up by about 70 per cent between 1961 and 2013.) The falling consumption of potatoes in Australia and other Western cultures is likely due to potatoes having developed a reputation as being little more than a carbohydrate source and thus associated with weight gain (in the same way bread has). Like many food myths, there seems little data to back this; potatoes are perhaps being maligned not for any inherent qualities but rather because of the way we process and eat them – more for their associates than themselves.

A 2016 survey found Australian consumers believed potatoes are 'versatile, convenient, good value for money and delicious' but those same consumers had limited knowledge of the nutrient composition of potatoes and associated them negatively with carbohydrates. That made me wonder, just what *is* the nutritional composition of potatoes? Like the people surveyed, I think of potatoes as being starchy rather than vitamin and mineral laden. But it turns out potatoes are loaded with minerals and vitamins, most notably vitamins C and B6, as well as potassium, magnesium, and iron. They come into their own in the B group vitamins and have more potassium than bananas. A US study found they provide Americans with 5 per cent of their magnesium. They don't have a lot of iron but the good thing is that what they do have is highly available – meaning that if you eat potatoes, the iron you consume is readily used by your body. Potatoes also bust a myth about plant protein. As University of Utah nutritionist Dr Katherine Beals writes, 'It is a common misconception that plant proteins are missing or lacking one or more essential amino acid. In fact, potatoes contain all nine essential amino acids and, thus, are a "complete" protein.' Although the ratios of amino acids in potatoes are not as balanced (in terms of human nutrition) as they are in meat, the protein in potatoes is also highly bioavailable – more so than legumes, that other highly prized source of plant protein. Potatoes are stacking up pretty well on the nutrient front. But what about that pesky carbohydrate load?

There's no getting away from the reality that potatoes are a starchy vegetable. Despite the vitamins, minerals and protein, carbohydrate is the main nutrient they contain. If you take the water out of potatoes, about three quarters of what remains is carbohydrate. But don't take them off your shopping list just yet. The starch in potatoes is mostly two types of carbohydrate: amylopectin and amylose in about equal proportions. But only mostly. There's also a small proportion of resistant starch, so called because it 'resists' being broken down by enzymes in the gut and passes through to the large intestine relatively intact. Once there, it serves as food for all sorts of good bacteria that do good things for gut health. (Resistant starch is also one of the things that makes wholemeal sourdough bread a healthier option than yeasted white bread.)

Potatoes have been associated with lowered blood pressure and reduced incidence of stroke, possibly because of their high potassium level. They contain phytochemicals and antioxidants that have been linked with reducing some cancers and general inflammation. Those phytochemicals include lutein and zeaxanthin, which protect and improve eyesight and may help to reduce macular degeneration. And potato peels have been shown to improve cholesterol concentrations, at least in rats, so it's best not to peel them. Potatoes are low in fat (unless you smother them with butter or deep fry them) and a potato with its skin contains as much fibre as many wholegrain breads and pastas. They are, of course, gluten free, which, if you are coeliac or gluten intolerant, makes them a good satiating option. But you will have to make your own chips from scratch; processed potatoes are generally not gluten free due to additives.

Despite all of this, potatoes are still fattening, right, on account of all those carbs? Well, probably not. According to Beals, previous studies linking potatoes with obesity were flawed. One of the main ones did not actually count total calories consumed by participants in the study, which seems a bit of an oversight to say the least. As Beals says, potatoes have been singled out as being fattening even though most studies show weight gain is generally due to a range of lifestyle and dietary factors rather than single foods. Potatoes seem to get a bad rap quite often. Again in the US, University of Minnesota nutritionists Janet King and Joanne Slavin point out the conflicting advice American dietary guidelines give on potatoes. On one hand, the advice is to reduce the intake of fried white potatoes to reduce solid fat intake, while on the other hand, the same dietary guidelines advise 'increasing the intake of vegetables, particularly those that provide substantial amounts of the [four] shortfall nutrients (dietary fiber, potassium, vitamin D, and calcium).' Maybe fried potatoes aren't the best option for consuming vegetables but, as we saw before, potatoes contain more potassium per standard serving than any other vegetable, which means eating potatoes can increase potassium intake. No wonder people get confused.

It looks to me as if potatoes deserve a place on our plates. Just don't eat too many of them, because too much of anything is rarely a good idea. Everything in moderation, as is said. And watch how they are cooked; potatoes may be low in fat but if you fry them in oil they no longer are. Perhaps unfortunately, that's what happens to most potatoes. Around two thirds of the potatoes grown in Australia are turned into potato crisps, hash browns, potato gems, French fries or chips before we buy them. Our waistlines and hearts would likely thank us if we bought fresh potatoes and cooked them with less fat and salt, rather than opting for the pre-packaged options.

———

Even though you probably could survive on little more than potatoes, you would be unlikely to thrive. Diversity in diets is a good thing, and not just from a nutrition perspective. This was well illustrated in the mid-1800s in Ireland. Potatoes were introduced to Ireland in the 1700s and by the 1800s about a third of the population relied on them as their staple food. Until the potato crop failed. History tells us what a tragedy that was. Around a million people died during the Irish Potato Famine. A further million fled Ireland in search of a decent meal.

One of the reasons why the Irish potato crop failed so miserably was because all the potatoes grown in Ireland in the 19th century were the same variety: the Irish Lumper. The lack of diversity meant that when disease struck, all the potatoes were equally vulnerable – there wasn't a pocket of something slightly different with resistance to the pathogen. All the potatoes turned to mush in the fields and gardens. Tragic as it was, the Irish Potato Famine is a lesson and salient reminder not to focus overly on one crop. There is strength and resilience in diversity; diversity within a crop and diversity between crops. Unfortunately, it's not a lesson we have learned particularly well.

As consumers we tend to expect our foods to look and taste the same each time we eat them. We demand consistency. Modern agriculture has been remarkably good at meeting that demand, aided by supply chains that reward consistency and penalise diversity.

When big buyers, such as supermarkets, food processors or fast-food franchises, demand particular varieties or specifications, it pushes the entire production for that item in a particular direction. McDonald's fries are a classic example in the modern food system.

McDonald's has almost a thousand restaurants in Australia and over 14,000 restaurants in the US. Worldwide, there are more than 36,000 McDonald's in 119 countries. That's a lot of purchasing power. So much that, according to the Idaho Farm Bureau Federation, new potato varieties are unlikely to be grown commercially unless they meet McDonald's specifications. It doesn't matter if they offer promise in other ways; selling to McDonald's is the make-or-break deal.

In Europe in 2018, unusually hot and dry conditions meant potatoes were smaller than normal, which was a problem for potato growers supplying McDonald's because McDonald's fries have to be a particular length. Shorter fries don't fit the machinery and packaging specifications in the outlets, which meant the machines needed to be recalibrated so the potatoes could still be used.

McDonald's didn't create this problem of uniformity, but their sheer size makes it obvious. The demand for consistency and shift away from diversity has happened, and continues to happen, time and again in our food systems. There are thousands of types of potatoes, but in the shops near me, I'm lucky if there are four varieties available. Yet even as I feel like ranting about that, I tend to buy the same variety every time I shop, so I'm part of the problem. As consumers, we tend to want some assurances when we buy things; we want to know what they taste like and how to prepare them. Buying different varieties comes with a risk – what if that variety of potato doesn't make the creamy mash I'm after? Rushing around the supermarket, I reach for what I know.

The disease that led to the Irish Potato Famine is called late blight. It is caused by a pathogen known scientifically as *Phytophthora infestans*. It's still around and it's still a problem, although not (so far) here in

Australia. Worldwide, it remains one of the worst diseases of potatoes. Preventing the recurrence of a modern-day disaster along the lines of the Irish Potato Famine is one of the biggest drivers of pesticide use in the world. Still, it's estimated that costs and losses due to late blight may take 16 per cent of all global potato production.

It's not just late blight. There are loads of things that threaten potato crops. Along with the various blights, there are other fungal diseases and insects, nematodes and weeds. Mostly they are beaten with a chemical arsenal. Even here in Australia, where potato growers are untroubled by late blight, a smorgasbord of chemicals is used to keep the potato plants pest-free. By the time a cut potato tuber is dropped into the furrow to grow a new potato plant, seven different pesticides have already been sprayed on the tuber or the ground in preparation, Simon Moltoni told me. Moltoni grew potatoes and raised beef on the rich loamy soils near Pemberton, Western Australia, until he left the farm for a corporate life in the city. He is now CEO of the industry body WA Potatoes. He says there are advantages to city life but he clearly misses being a farmer. Still, his passion for potatoes shines through. ('Chips or mash?' I ask him. 'Both!' he laughs.)

'After germination, through the life of the crop, the plants are sprayed as necessary,' Moltoni says. 'Fungicides, herbicides, insecticides.' It seems there are a lot of things other than people that want to eat potatoes. Moltoni is not overly bothered by the amount of chemical used on potato fields. 'In Australia, we have very good regulations around agricultural chemicals,' he says. 'There are strict requirements before anything is approved for use and there are residue limits that are tested.'

In Australia, the use and control of agricultural chemicals is regulated by the Australian Pesticides and Veterinary Medicines Authority (APVMA). They're the ones who decide whether an agvet (as in agricultural and veterinary) chemical can be used in Australia and, if so, under what circumstances, for what purposes, by whom, when and where. They also regularly review existing rules and regulations in light of new or changed evidence. But they are not the only ones involved in the agvet chemical regulation scene. They work with various state and territory government departments. The maximum residue limits of agvet chemicals allowed in food are set by Food Standards Australia New Zealand (FSANZ), who are also responsible for other standards relating to food. State and territory government agencies monitor food to ensure the standards, including maximum residue limits, are met. This doesn't mean that there are never any residual agvet chemicals in our food, but it means that levels should be well within safety limits.

Each year, the Australian Department of Agriculture, Water and the Environment conducts the National Residue Survey. Basically, it takes samples of a range of foodstuffs and tests them for the presence of a pile of different agvet chemicals they could contain. It's been done every year since 1992. In the 2020–21 survey, sixteen out of twenty foods tested had 100 per cent compliance with residue limits. Of the four that didn't achieve the perfect score, all scored over 99 per cent, to give an average overall compliance rate of 99.85 per cent. According to that testing, our farmers are doing the right thing and our food is very safe.

An annual list called 'The Dirty Dozen' frequently makes the news. It's a list put together by an American NGO called the Environmental Working Group as part of its annual assessment of chemical residues in food sold in America. When asked by *SBS News Australia* whether the list is relevant to Australia, Lorraine Haase of FSANZ said it wasn't relevant at all. 'In Australia, we use different herbicides and pesticides and we set very strict limits on residue limits, as well as the minimum time between spraying a crop and harvesting, to minimise any impact,' Haase was reported as saying. SBS added that 'limits affect organic and conventional farming because, as Haase points out, organic farms use pesticides, too. Some of them use the very same pesticides found in conventional farms.'

'What about growing potatoes organically, with no pesticides?' I ask Moltoni.

'Sure, you can do that,' he replies. 'You just have to accept much lower yields and the occasional scabby looking potatoes. If the big retailers and consumers accepted that, we could cut down the amount of chemicals.' (I feel I've been here before; we're back to that demand for uniformity and perfection; perhaps we need to change our attitudes.) Moltoni says the environment and the farmers would be the beneficiaries of reduced chemicals; but consumers would pay with higher prices and lower-quality produce. Given the low levels of residues in our produce anyway, it's unlikely it would make much difference to the amount of agvet chemical residues we consume via our food, which is already very small. Moltoni also says the chemicals used now are much better than in the early days.

The early days he's referring to are the 1950s, 60s and 70s when heavy-hitting organochlorine pesticides were used on crops. The organochlorines, such as DDT, heptachlor and dieldrin, persisted in the soil and accumulated up food chains. In the south-west of Western Australia, the story of organochlorine residues is enmeshed with beef exports. Farmers, like the Moltoni family, grew potatoes in rotation with pasture for beef cattle. 'One year of potatoes, three years of pasture,' Moltoni says. 'That's how we did it.' The pasture phase enabled the ground to rest before the next potato crop. During the potato phase, organochlorine pesticides were used to control insect pests, such as black beetle, which can devastate potato crops.

The problem was that the beef cattle consumed the pesticide residues in the soil as they grazed. Organochlorines are fat soluble, so they accumulated in the cattle's fat. It all hit the fan, so to speak, when standard testing of exported beef showed levels of dieldrin and DDT above acceptable levels. The US refused to take Australian beef. A huge program of soil testing and quarantining was put in place. It wasn't just about potato farming. Pesticides, especially heptachlor, used to control Argentine ants and termites, were also implicated. Hundreds of hectares of farmland across the south-west was designated as unfit to be grazed by livestock intended for human consumption. (Free-range chickens were a particular problem because they ingest a lot of soil as they scratch and peck about looking for seeds and grubs.) Blue gums were planted on much of the contaminated land to take it out of food production. The use of organochlorines was banned. It took a long time for the beef and potato farmers to recover. Some didn't; as in, they went broke.

Organochlorines do eventually break down. Microbial action in the soil splits the bonds that hold the chemicals together. Sunlight and rain do their work, especially if the affected soil is ploughed and exposed to sunlight. There are still areas where livestock enterprises are restricted due to organochlorine residues, but a lot of the previously quarantined areas are back in agricultural production. The problem is not exactly solved, but it has diminished. But how serious a problem was it really? Newspaper headlines at the time screamed disaster but were likely overblown. An inquiry ordered by the then Western Australian Minister for Agriculture, Monty House, concluded it was something to investigate and improve rather than panic about. But it seems there's a lasting legacy of fear around pesticides of all types. It plays into a wider consumer distrust of agricultural chemicals.

The story of the damage organochlorine pesticides wrought on natural systems was famously told by Rachel Carson in *Silent Spring*.

It's a book I first read when I was an undergraduate biology student in the 1980s, when I was doing a unit in pollutants and toxicology. It became hard to eat anything. My paranoia about chemicals – 'nasty chemicals' – in food was paramount. I sought out organic vegetables, which was surprisingly difficult and alarmingly expensive in the 1980s – it's easy to forget how much our food choices have expanded in recent decades. My views have tempered over the years, partly, I suppose, because of my exposure to conventional farmers who repeatedly say they would go out of business without agvet chemicals; that they would be swamped by weeds and insects and pestilence; that crops would suffer, yields decline, retail prices hike. I also now have more trust in the science that assesses the merits and dangers of agricultural chemicals before they are released. More trust too in the regulators who set the residue levels and enforce them. More trust in the compliance of farmers who apply the chemicals.

Yet despite this temperance my trust is not complete. As much as I can see a valid role for pesticides in modern farming, I remain wary of the power and motivations of the agvet chemical companies; there's a lot of money to be made in selling pesticides. I am still drawn to the organic section of the vegetable stands. I am drawn to the small growers with their bulbs of organic garlic and grubby looking potatoes. In my own garden, I suffer the bugs and crop losses rather than buy pesticides in plastic bottles. I'm more inclined to mix up an old-fashioned soap-and-garlic spray than to buy an insecticide. If it doesn't work, so be it. I'm only talking about a few rows of veggies and I won't go broke or starve if they don't grow. I'm a hippie gardener at heart, even if my head is more pragmatic.

But there's something else at play for me too. I've heard enough entomologists talk about integrated pest management to be convinced that broadscale killing of insect pests is rarely the best answer, that waiting a short while will allow the predatory insects and mites to make their move. The predator numbers will build, the pest numbers will decline. There is still some loss with this approach, but natural systems tend to find a balance, if we let them. The trouble is we cannot always afford the time and losses to allow nature to find that balance, and it is not always where we want it to be. We also provide easy pickings for pests when we grow extensive monocultures of crop plants. That's a conundrum we need to manage. And, of course, it's not all about insects and pesticides. There are fungal diseases, weeds and nematodes. There is no end of threats to crops.

Then again, there is also the other collateral damage of broad-scale spraying of various biocides. When we wipe out insects, for example, we wipe out food sources for lizards and geckoes and birds and fish and marsupials. The ripples of our actions spread out into the surrounding environment, even if the immediate actions of the biocides are local. Newer, more targeted chemicals and management approaches can help reduce these impacts and they are being more widely adopted by growers. Integrated pest management is no longer the domain of the radical fringe; the most conventional of crop conferences will have multiple presentations on the topic. The same goes for integrated weed management. High-tech equipment that identifies weeds and targets herbicide spraying is becoming more readily available. It drastically reduces the amount of herbicide sprayed, thus also reducing the cost to the grower. I suspect (or maybe I just hope) the pendulum is swinging away from agriculture finding the entire answer in adding expensive chemicals, even though a lot of agvet chemicals are in use and applying them is a major task for most farmers. Because a lot of the work involved in growing things is stopping other things from growing.

What about those farmers who spray the pesticides? If anyone is vulnerable to dangerous chemicals, it's the farmers who apply them. It's the person handling the chemicals who is most at risk. One of the most talked about issues in this regard is exposure to carcinogens. Pesticides are often implicated in this and many studies focus on them when assessing farmers' cancer risk. But there is a stack of other potential carcinogens farmers may be exposed to, depending on the type of farming they do. Things such as fuels, engine exhausts, organic solvents, crystalline silica, metals, wood dust and sunlight. It's a long list. It seems surprising then, that farmers as a group have been found to have a lower risk of cancer overall than the general population.

Unfortunately, the same can't be said for mental health issues. Australian agricultural workers have twice the suicide rate of any other employed worker. Studies in the US and Norway have found farmers have the highest levels of depression and anxiety when compared with all other occupations. Potential reasons for this are many and include that farming has traditionally been 'more physically demanding, involving longer work hours, with a reduced likelihood to seek respite or vacations off farm, and is more socially and spatially isolating than other occupations.' Other aspects of farming life, such as financial instability and isolation, can affect mental health. And so can exposure to chemicals. There is evidence that some agricultural chemicals can affect brain chemistry, leading to psychological distress. There appears to be a link between poor mental health and chronic low-dose exposure to pesticides.

Then there is acute toxicity. That is, the effect of being exposed to a dangerous amount of a pesticide. This can happen when a farmer has direct contact with treated crops or soil while they are sowing crops or spraying for insects or weeds, or while tending animals. It can also happen through accidental spillage. However it occurs, pesticide poisoning is considered an important occupational health problem in farmers and farm workers globally. Worldwide, it kills an estimated 200,000 people annually, mostly in developing countries.

I don't really like the idea that someone is exposed to all of that on my behalf, that someone sprays chemicals on crops so I can have a cheap, scab-free potato. I do understand that it is, to some extent, the farmer's choice. I complicate the story in my own mind by also not wanting to tell a farmer how best to do their job; I'm not qualified to do that. Really, if a farmer thinks their best option for staying in business and producing good-quality food is to apply agvet chemicals, who am I to judge? But aren't they in some way producing something in response to my demands? So surely it is responsible of me to temper those demands, to not insist on perfect, cheap produce at every turn?

Moltoni told me that when he was farming, he always did all the spraying himself. He didn't want to expose his staff to any potential danger. He also didn't have the time and inclination to go through the rigmarole of teaching short-term casual staff how to safely mix, handle and apply chemicals. Safe handling of chemicals is critical to minimising farmers' exposure.

Moltoni thinks genetic modification has a role to play in reducing the chemical load sprayed on potatoes. In the US they grow genetically modified (GM) potatoes. A gene from a type of bacteria called *Bacterium thuringiensis* – Bt for short – has been inserted into the genome of the modified potatoes. (As a quick aside, GM – genetically modified – organisms are differentiated from traditionally bred plants and animals in the way they are developed. Rather than taking the traditional approach of crossing two parents together and seeing what arises, genetic modification uses biotechnology to directly modify or remove a gene, or to transfer a gene from one organism to another.

More about this later when we look at canola, the major GM food crop currently grown in Australia.)

Bt is a bacterium that produces a toxin that kills caterpillars. Bt toxin is regularly used as an insecticide, including in organic farming systems. When the Bt gene is inserted into a plant, the plant produces Bt toxin for itself. There's nothing unusual in a plant producing something that discourages or kills something that wants to eat it; that's what a large proportion of phytochemicals do. (They make plants poisonous or bitter to discourage things from eating them). Any potato grower, conventional or organic, can spray their potatoes with a pesticide containing Bt toxin. But, at the moment, if the Bt gene is inserted into the potato plant, no potato growers in Australia can grow them. We have extremely tight regulations for GM techniques being used for most agricultural purposes. Any fresh potatoes you buy in Australia today will not be genetically modified because they can't be grown here and we don't import fresh potatoes. But that does not mean there aren't products containing genetically modified potatoes for sale in Australia. There are. We import processed potatoes, including frozen products, and some of these could be genetically modified. It seems a double standard to say our growers can't grow them but our eaters can eat them.

I'm sticking with fresh Australian potatoes, not because I have any qualms about eating genetically modified potatoes, but because I prefer to support Aussie farmers and I also avoid processed foods. Although there are certainly some processed foods I enjoy. Did someone say cake?

CHAPTER 4

Sugar

W<small>E ARE DESIGNED</small> to seek sweetness. If you take the long view of history, sweetness has usually been hard to come by: it meant plucking the ripest fruits, braving the sting of bees or sucking the drop of nectar from a flower. It was rare, tantalising, hard to obtain. It provided much-needed calories and brain fuel.

The human brain is powered by the simple sugar glucose. Our bodies evolved feedback mechanisms that give us pleasure when we eat sugar – sweet foods trigger the release of dopamine, a feel-good brain chemical. This mechanism exists even in people who aren't necessarily sweet tooths; it's a deeply embedded mammalian system. It goes further. Dopamine promotes learning and encourages us to seek more of the foods that provide us with that feel-good hit. The more we eat sugar, the more we want sugar. That was okay when sweet foods were hard to come by; it was more than okay, a sweet tooth was advantageous. It helped our ancestors to eat the right things, to avoid unripe or rotten food, to ensure that their bodies had enough fuel to burn, and their brains were functioning correctly. It doesn't serve us so well now, but our craving for sweetness is so deep that sugar consistently ranks in the top three or four biggest crops in the world. The value of its annual production is topped only by maize, wheat and rice, which provide much needed protein and nutrients along with calories. Sugar is pure energy.

In 2020, the global sugar industry was valued at US$56 billion, down from over US$99 billion in 2012. Sugar is grown on 13 million hectares throughout the world. That's an area about twice the size of Tasmania. Total commercial world production of sugar is over 50 million tonnes, which may not sound huge on a global scale, but 50 million tonnes of sugar is about 250 billion cups. That's a lot, especially taking into consideration that sugar is not the only source of sweetness we cultivate. By volume though, sugar cane outweighs any other crop, both globally and in Australia. We really do like it sweet.

The world's refined sugar comes from a couple of sources, notably sugar cane and sugar beets. Most sugar – 80 per cent of globally traded sugar – comes from sugar cane, a tropical grass probably of South-East Asian origin. As with other species with a long history of human use, it's not easy to pinpoint exactly where sugar was first domesticated, but plant remnants and DNA evidence point to New Guinea. Sugar cane may have been domesticated there 10,000 years ago. The first evidence of it being processed into the crystals we know so well today comes from India about 2500 years ago. From there it spread, used for a long time as a condiment, similar to the way we use spices today. Ultimately, our sweet tooth got the better of us.

Worldwide, sugar cane distribution is restricted to tropical and sub-tropical environments. It likes sunshine and warmth and water. It doesn't like the cold. It arrived in Australia with the First Fleet in 1788 but the Australian sugar industry didn't really kick off until 1862, when a sugar cane plantation was established near Brisbane and Australia's first commercial sugar mill was built. Before widespread mechanisation, cane growing and harvesting was labour intensive. The problem of lack of cheap labour brought about by the end of the convict era was 'solved' by 'bringing' people, mostly men but also some women, from islands across Melanesia, from Vanuatu to the Solomon Islands. Between 1863 and 1904, more than 62,000 contracts were issued to so-called 'Kanakas' to work in the Australian sugar industry. 'Kanakas' is now recognised as a derogatory term, derived from the Hawaiian word for bush people and implying inferiority. Their descendants are now called Australian South Sea Islanders (ASSI). According to historian Emeritus Professor Clive Moore it is hard to put an exact figure on how many ASSI came to work on Australian sugar plantations because it was a 'circular migration, usually over three or more years.' He says 'large numbers also returned to their home islands, and some of them came to Australia on two or more occasions.' Although not actually called slaves, the ASSI were pretty close to it – indentured labour is the term used. They were paid about a third of the wages of European workers and over a quarter died prematurely in Australia after exposure to diseases, such as measles, to which they had no immunity. The whole story is made worse by the forced deportation of around 10,000 ASSI under the Pacific Island Labourers Act of 1901, which brought the scheme to an abrupt end. The jobs went to white labourers, in what was a precursor to the infamous White Australia Policy.

The sugar industry founded on ASSI labour continues today but has moved on to become highly mechanised. In Australia, all our sugar comes from sugar cane grown on a 2100-kilometre strip of coastline between Mossman, in far north Queensland, and Grafton, in northern New South Wales. In that coastal strip, over 3000 farmers grow around 380,000 hectares of sugar cane. In a typical year, they produce over 30 million tonnes of sugar cane. In 2018–19, sugar cane was the eighteenth most valuable agricultural crop in Australia, making up 1.7 per cent of the total value of our agricultural sector. Eighty per cent of the sugar produced in Australia is exported as raw bulk sugar, making Australia the second-largest exporter of raw sugar in the world.

Cane growing in Australia begins at the end of the wet season when billets – small sections of sugar cane stem – are placed horizontally in furrows and lightly covered with earth. Cane plants sprout from the nodes on the billets. The cane grows for about thirteen months until it is harvested. Sugar is extracted from the stems of sugar cane, so the whole plant above the ground is cut for harvest. The roots and stolons (the parts from which new shoots grow) are left in the ground to regrow. Some growers get three harvests from a planting, some get four or five. After the final harvest, the ground is ploughed and left fallow for the summer, or sown with a crop of soybeans or mung beans, before the process begins again when summer rains have finished and the ground is dry enough to traverse. Controlled traffic systems, similar to that used in the wheatbelt, provide hard wheel tracks across paddocks and enable machinery onto ground sooner after rain.

Cane growing runs into conflict at harvest time. For years, cane has been burned before harvest. That sounds counterintuitive but, as canegrower David Cox explained to me, the idea is to remove the leafy 'trash' from the valuable stems to facilitate harvesting. Cox has been growing sugar cane in the Burdekin region of Queensland for more than three decades. Like others in the Burdekin, he still burns his cane, even though the process has been phased out in most other cane growing areas. 'We don't burn it because we like to, we burn it because we have to,' Cox says. 'I hate the black ash that drifts over the district from the cane fires, but when you have the high-yielding irrigated crops like we have up here, then you have to burn it.' He says that while it is possible to cut the cane without burning, you just can't separate the cane billets from the trash, resulting in enormous cane loss. He says Burdekin growers are looking for an alternative but haven't come up with a cost-effective solution yet. While he agrees the ash is annoying, he dismisses any concerns over greenhouse gas emissions. 'The amount of carbon that goes up in smoke is exactly the same amount as the amount of carbon that was absorbed by the cane as it grew those leaves,' he says. He has a point. He adds that when the cane is processed the leftover trash, called bagasse, is burned to power the mill and produce electricity. 'One way or another, it gets burned,' he says.

The other contentious issue with cane growing is nitrogen; specifically, nitrogen being washed from cane fields into the ocean and affecting the Great Barrier Reef. The 2017 Scientific Consensus Statement on Land Use Impacts on Great Barrier Reef Water Quality and Ecosystem Condition says the amount of nitrogen entering the reef ecosystem has greatly increased with land use change in the catchments. It's not all about sugar cane, but clearing and modifying coastal habitats for farming is part of the problem. Urban, industrial and island development, along with illegal fishing activities, all play a role as well. Exactly how much nitrogen runoff has increased depends on the form of nitrogen being measured and where along the coast measurements are taken. It ranges from a 1.2-fold increase up to a six-fold increase.

Excess nitrogen (and phosphorus) running off from farmland is a problem for ecosystems, especially marine and other aquatic ecosystems, because it throws things out of balance. It promotes algal growth, which can smother other organisms and deplete the amount of oxygen in the water. This process, called eutrophication, isn't limited to nutrient runoff from cane fields into Barrier Reef waters; it's a widespread problem. It can occur when more nitrogen is applied as fertiliser than the crops are able to use. Better-matching of nitrogen application and crop use is one way to help solve it, but is not always as easy as it sounds. Farmers don't want to starve their crops of nitrogen; nitrogen-starved crops won't thrive and that affects yields and income. On the other hand, farmers don't want to waste nitrogen, because it isn't cheap. (And they get hammered by people saying they are wrecking the environment when fertiliser run-off is implicated in ecosystem decline.)

Once cut, sugar cane must be quickly processed so the sugars don't break down. Extensive rail networks have been built through the cane fields to facilitate this. The cut cane is taken to mills and crushed to extract the juice, which is concentrated and processed to extract the pure sugar crystals. As the sugar is concentrated up the processing line, so too is the sugar industry. There are over 3000 farmers grow-ing sugar cane in Australia, but there are only twenty-four processing mills, which are operated by eight companies. A step further along the process there are only three sugar refineries in Australia, two of which are owned by one company.

The basic split of the Australian sugar industry is that the domestic supply comes from New South Wales and the sugar from Queensland is exported. About 40 per cent of the domestic supply is sold through supermarkets directly to consumers and about 20 per cent goes to wholesalers. The remainder goes to 'other markets' to be incorporated into food and drink. Sugar is high on the list of ingredients used in processed foods because it's cheap and consumers like it. Adding sugar is an easy way to make things taste good and provide mouthfeel, that sensory quality of food in the mouth that contributes so much to whether we like something or not.

In this way, sugar sneaks into a lot of foods where people don't expect to find it and we tend to eat too much of it. The World Health Organization says we should only consume about five teaspoons of added sugar a day – 25 grams to be precise – or no more than 5 per cent of our total calories. Current average Australian daily consumption is closer to 13 teaspoons. The key word there is 'average'. In some groups it's much higher – twenty teaspoons a day for teenage boys and seventeen for Aboriginal and Torres Strait Islander people. And obviously the variation among individuals within different groups is significant.

Despite these high consumption figures, Australians are eating less sugar now than we did a few decades ago. The public health campaigns imploring us to cut our sugar consumption seem to be working. If we, as a nation, keep going on the current downward trajectory, we'll get down to the recommended daily intake in another forty years. That sounds like slow progress but reducing sugar consumption must be a good thing for our waistlines and general health, surely? Well, maybe not.

Dr Alan W Barclay from the Australian Diabetes Society and Professor Jennie Brand-Miller, University of Sydney, identified a phenomenon they call 'the Australian Paradox' – our sugar consumption has declined at the same time as our weights have increased. (Incidentally, Brand-Miller is the person who created the glycaemic index, which tells us what happens to our blood sugar when we eat different foods.) In their 2011 study, Barclay and Brand-Miller looked back over data from the previous thirty years. Over that period,

Barclay and Brand-Miller report, there has been a 'consistent and substantial decline' in sugar consumption by Australians but, at the same time, obesity rates have tripled. It's not the sugar making us fat. Nor is it making us unhealthy: Barclay and Brand-Miller report 'no significant associations between intakes of sugars and health status, including body fatness, BMI and blood pressure.'

Perhaps we've oversimplified things. Cutting back on sugar is not going to reduce weight if total calories aren't reduced. Barclay and Brand-Miller point out that the increase in total calories consumed by Australians has been almost exclusively due to increased fat consumption. They refer to the 'sugar fat seesaw', where reducing sugar consumption leads to increased fat consumption, and vice versa. 'Logic tells us that an inappropriately high intake of any energy source (alcohol, fat, protein, starch or sugar) will result in weight gain.' They say that lowering 'the sugar content of foods may be counterproductive for weight management if there is replacement of sugars with refined or high glycaemic index starches, saturated fats or alcohol.' These simple things always seem to be more complicated when we delve into them.

Another aspect of the whole sugary food debate isn't so much about the sugar itself but rather about the types of foods that a lot of sugar gets put into, especially the so-called industrialised or ultra-processed food. Not exactly a sexy title and it's debatable whether it deserves to be categorised as food at all. The ingredients begin as food, but are then processed way beyond recognition. Ultra-processed products are the fastest-growing category of 'food' (maybe 'things we eat' is better terminology here). In their excellent book, *Eat Like the Animals*, research biologists Professor David Raubenheimer and Professor

Stephen J Simpson suggest using the term 'ultra-processed products' rather than food because these products are 'industrial creations'. Raubenheimer and Simpson write that the manufacture of these products 'begins in large machines that separate whole foods into their components, such as starch, sugars, fats, oils, protein, and fiber'.

Of course, processing food is not new and nor is it necessarily bad. Some processing is positively helpful – cooking itself is a form of processing, as are old techniques of drying and other forms of preserving food such as bottling. It's a question of the degree of processing and what happens to the food along the way. The term 'ultra-processed' comes from the NOVA system, which is a way of categorising food according to its level of processing that is widely used by scientists. (NOVA is not an acronym, it simply means new but in this context is generally written in all caps.) It recognises four levels of food processing. NOVA 1 foods are unprocessed (or natural) foods. These are the edible parts of plants or food from animals, and also fungi, algae and water. NOVA 2 refers to processed culinary ingredients, such as oils, butter, lard, sugar and salt. NOVA 3 are processed foods made by adding salt, oil, sugar or other substances from NOVA 2 to NOVA 1 foods. Think canned veggies and bottled fruit, ham, bacon, pastrami, and smoked fish, most freshly baked breads and simple cheeses. NOVA 4 is where we step away from food and into industrial products. These are the ultra-processed foods typically created by industrial techniques and processes. They are 'formulations of ingredients, mostly of exclusive industrial use'. The list of these products is long: 'carbonated soft drinks; sweet, fatty or salty packaged snacks; candies (confectionery); mass produced packaged breads and buns, cookies (biscuits), pastries, cakes and cake mixes; margarine and other spreads; sweetened breakfast "cereals" and fruit yoghurt and "energy" drinks; pre-prepared meat, cheese, pasta and pizza dishes; poultry and fish "nuggets" and "sticks";

sausages, burgers, hot dogs and other reconstituted meat products; powdered and packaged "instant" soups, noodles and desserts; baby formula; and many other types of product.' I find it interesting that so many things on this NOVA 4 list are mimics and replacements for foods in lower categories – mass-produced cakes for a home-baked cake made from flour, eggs, sugar and milk; chicken nuggets for a piece of chicken; baby formula for breastmilk. I suspect this tricks us into believing all cake or chicken or baby food is equivalent, but that's not true.

Most processed food consumed in Australia is made by a handful of transnational corporations and sold in the big supermarkets. Junk food is big business. It's a $104.2 billion industry in Australia. This is the largest segment of Australia's food and grocery industry. In 2018, 61 per cent of packaged foods for sale were NOVA 4 products. A walk down the aisles of a supermarket browsing product labels will confirm that frightening figure, at least anecdotally.

Raubenheimer and Simpson say ultra-processed products have 'nothing to do with improving human diets but rather with making products more efficient to produce or more appealing to consumers'. There is nothing inherently wrong with an industrially produced substance. Many industrially produced substances are identical to those produced naturally, and just because something is naturally produced does not in itself make a substance benign – there are plenty of natural toxins out there. But, and this is a big but, we have now introduced into our food system a smorgasbord of new chemicals in mixtures and at quantities that we have not evolved to consume. Some of these chemicals are harmless, some of them are possibly dangerous, and some are almost certainly nasty.

And Raubenheimer and Simpson have a bigger fear than this 'lottery of toxicity', as they call it. Their fear is that these products are deliberately designed to ensure we eat them in large quantities.

All the manufacturers of ultra-processed foods want a share of our stomachs. And I think it's fair to say they would like to expand our stomachs so they can have a bigger share. Of course, they don't say this. They talk about moderation and things being part of an overall balanced diet and discretion and treats. But have you ever opened a packet of potato chips and just eaten one? I certainly haven't. Those salty, sweet, umami flavours hit right in on our long-ago-programmed appetites. One is never enough. The manufacturers know this. They design the products to play on that very fact.

There is another aspect to these foods, which in diets fall into the category of discretionary foods; discretionary as in we don't really need them. (And would generally be better off health-wise without them, or at least severely limiting them.) Research into Australian diets has shown that these 'extras' have a significant impact on the overall environmental footprint of our food consumption.

One aspect of the environmental impact of food is the amount of land it takes to grow it. This is referred to as the 'cropland footprint'. Recent estimates suggest that, globally, about 1.9 billion hectares is occupied by cropland. That's around 14 per cent of the world's ice-free land. This might not sound like a huge percentage but experts say the planetary boundary for cropland (that is, the amount of land the world could devote to crops without having potentially irreversible earth system changes) is 15 per cent, so we are getting very close. If it goes beyond that we run the risk of sudden abrupt changes in earth systems, such as the atmosphere, biosphere and geosphere. Which is all a bit scary, especially as, worldwide, cropland is continuing to expand, most notably into tropical biodiverse regions.

Not all land is of equal value, but research into the impact of Australian diets calculated the average adult Australian's cropland footprint is greater than what is considered sustainable. Basically, on average, we're using too much cropland. But there are wide variations – young men have a higher dietary cropland footprint than older women, for example. This is partly explained by calorie intake; just watch a young man eat (or try to keep food in a house where one lives!) to understand this. Or at the other end of the scale, watch an elderly aunt pick at the small meal she has been served for lunch. I speak from experience in both these observations. These sorts of differences are to be expected due to differences in life stage and energy requirements, but that's not to let us all off the hook.

Overall, the research found that around 45 per cent of the differences in individual dietary footprints was due to energy intake. The second biggest influence was discretionary foods, which the researchers defined as 'energy-dense and nutrient-poor foods high in saturated fat, added sugars and/or salt, and alcohol.' These foods accounted for about a third of the difference in cropland footprint. So almost half of Australians could reduce the environmental impact of their diets by eating less junk. It would also likely reduce the number of overweight and obese Australians and reduce the disease burden caused, at least in part, by poor diet (less than one in ten Australians eat the recommended amount of vegetables). The 2017–18 Australian Bureau of Statistics' National Health Survey found just over two thirds of Australian adults were overweight or obese. Two in three! That was an increase of about 4 percentage points from the previous survey in 2014–15. At that rate, there will be more than 18 million overweight or obese Australians by 2030.

Food for thought indeed.

I wrote earlier about how we are designed to seek sweetness. However, it is not sweetness that controls our appetite and tells us when to stop eating. That switch is in the hands of protein. In an illuminating series of experiments, beginning with locusts and going on through flies, mice, orangutans and ultimately to people, Raubenheimer and Simpson (the biologists mentioned earlier as the authors of *Eat Like the Animals*) along with a string of colleagues, showed that all of us keep eating until our pre-programmed desire for protein is satisfied. In humans, that dial is set somewhere between 15 and 20 per cent of total calorie intake. In a carbohydrate- and fat-rich world, we unconsciously overeat trying to satisfy our innate desire to balance protein. Ultra-processed foods are typically lower in protein, fibre and micronutrients, while being high in fats, refined carbohydrates (sugars!), and flavour enhancers – the exact things that are likely to cause us to overeat. The link here is borne out by research. In a detailed examination of a huge dataset on the diets of Americans, a very tight correlation was found between the increase in the proportion of ultra-processed food in the diet, a decrease in the percentage of protein in those foods, and an increase in the number of calories.

The Food and Agriculture Organization of the United Nations says over-reliance on processed foods, especially energy-dense foods high in sugar, fat and salt, is gradually displacing home-prepared meals and the consumption of fresh fruit and vegetables in typical diets. Sugar is part of that problem, but it's not all down to sugar. On its own, sugar falls into NOVA category 2. It's a culinary ingredient. It's the bad company it keeps that is the problem. So watch where the sugar is sneaking into your diet and moderate it. I'm happy to add sugar to a home-made cake, but these days I tend to leave the manufactured biscuits on the supermarket shelf. I have a bit of a sweet tooth, but I remind myself that this sweet tooth arose in our ancestors to make us reach for the sweetest, ripest, juiciest fruit.

CHAPTER 5

Apples

A BIG BOX OF apples sat tucked behind the front door. Jonathans. Dad said they were the best. Sweet, red and crunchy: we were allowed to eat one whenever we wanted. I must have been nine or ten years old. In my memory, the box of apples appeared every autumn thereafter but maybe it was only once and the experience of it burned deeply. A whole box of apples. Pure abundance. Mum perhaps shook her head and wondered at the excess. That was the way they played the roles, Dad prone to excess, Mum living by the motto of 'I hate waste'. The last apples left in the box were the crinkled, scabby, marked ones. Mum, of course, chopped them up and made apple jelly.

Mum said the best apples grew on a tree at her parents' farm. It was a tree of indeterminant origin, apparently grown from the seed of an apple core dropped by the fence. It grew big, pale-red apples that gave a satisfying crunch when bitten into and held their shape when cooked. A versatile apple, with a touch of mystery due to its origins.

Apple seeds readily sprout, given moisture and warmth, but they don't necessarily grow into good apple-producing trees. Apples have complex genetics and their seeds do not grow into a tree that will produce apples like the one from which they came. Some will produce inedible fruit and others might barely fruit at all. The chances of getting something delicious are said to be about one in 50,000.

Apples, like many tree fruits, are commercially (and usually domestically) grown from grafted trees. To do this, a cutting from a tree that produces desirable fruit is taped to a stem with stronger roots (called a rootstock stem). The plant mends the join and a new tree is born. It will grow the same fruit and leaves as the tree from which the grafted twig was taken. There's nothing new in this for apples. The cultivation of sweet apples probably arose in China around 4000 years ago when grafting techniques were being developed.

Like all domesticated plants and animals, apples came from wild relatives. There are between twenty-five and forty-seven *Malus* species currently recognised by plant scientists. Clearly there's some disagreement between the scientists as to exactly where the lines should be drawn between what constitutes one apple species and what constitutes another. Suffice to say, apples have a lot of wild relatives, with a huge amount of genetic diversity.

Most of the vast number of genes in the apples we eat today come from a wild apple (*Malus sieversii*) that still forms forests of huge apple trees in the Tian Shan Mountains. The Heavenly Mountains, as the name translates, lie across Kazakhstan, Kyrgyzstan and the Chinese province of Xinjiang, and are reportedly as beautiful as the name suggests. The apple forests themselves – and we're talking forests of apple trees, not just forests with a few scattered apple trees among other species – cloak the mountainsides. The apple trees grow up to 20 metres tall and their fruit varies in size from marbles to softballs, and in colour from red to yellow to green to purple.

Apples travelled west through the Middle East and on to Europe. From Europe, they journeyed across the world with colonisation. They came to Australia with the First Fleet and have been grown here ever since. According to the industry body Apple and Pear Australia Limited, 99.7 per cent of apples on the shelves in Australian shops are grown in Australian orchards. The small number of imported apples comes from New Zealand, China and the US, subject to strict quarantine measures to prevent introducing pests and diseases. In 2020–21, there were over 500 commercial apple orchards in Australia and they produced 262,966 tonnes of apples. About 1 to 2 per cent of Australian-grown apples are exported and we eat the rest; roughly 10 kilograms of apples per person per year. That's only an apple a week on average, not the proverbial apple a day long held to keep the doctor away.

In 2015, a team of researchers from the University of Michigan School of Nursing decided to see if there was any truth in the old saying. They found that people who ate an apple a day did visit the doctor fewer times than people who didn't eat an apple every day, but it wasn't just down to apple eating. Other lifestyle factors complicated the results and they found they could not conclude cause and effect. On the other hand, the researchers' finding that people who eat an apple a day are slightly less likely to take prescription medication was found to be robust. They concluded that eating an apple a day – and it has to be a fresh apple, eaten raw – won't keep the doctor away but it may help keep the pharmacist at bay.

While it is the grafted stem that controls the type of apples a tree produces, the size and growth characteristics of the tree itself are determined by the rootstock. There are about ten to twelve different rootstocks used in Australian apple growing. The little dwarf apple trees in my suburban garden are little dwarves because they are on dwarfing rootstock. The trees, barely more than a metre tall, grow full-size apples. Well, they would, if the parrots didn't swoop in and nick them before they ripen.

Apple rootstock are grown by a process of layering; branches are laid down horizontally along a furrow and covered with earth. They send stems upwards and roots downwards. Sections with a single stem are cut off and these cuttings form the basis of the new trees. The stems are trimmed back and a cutting from the desired tree is grafted on. Grafting is a way of ensuring trees grow true to type, a way of making sure varieties are preserved. But, of course, new varieties are also bred and produced. Sometimes deliberately but sometimes accidentally, in the way of my grandparents' tree. Apples like these are called 'chance' apples – they grow by chance. I learned this talking to Jon Doust, a Western Australian writer and apple enthusiast. When we met, Doust was writing a book about the Pink Lady apple.* 'It's a fascinating story,' he says.

Doust tells me he grew up under an apple tree on the family farm in Bridgetown, Western Australia, once the heart of apple growing in the state. The cold winter nights are perfect for aiding fruit set: that is, the turning of flowers to fruit. Apples need a period of chilling to set fruit so don't fruit well, if at all, in areas without a chilly period. You won't find apples in the tropics. In temperate regions with cool or cold autumns, they grow almost everywhere. Apples are the most widely grown temperate fruit in the world.

Despite the Pink Lady being the focus of Doust's book, Granny Smiths are his favourite apple. For a time, Granny Smiths were the mainstay of the Australian apple industry, which was largely based on exporting Grannies to the United Kingdom. (That phrase really needs to be read in context.) The export market disappeared when the UK joined the European Union and, for a time, Australian apple orchards

---

* To be published by Fremantle Press in 2023

were ripped from the ground. It was a tough time to be an Australian apple grower.

Doust is not impressed with the hard, green Granny Smiths for sale in shops. 'Granny Smiths are ideally left on the tree to ripen,' he says. 'When ready to eat they blush with yellow.' I ask him if he grows them in his garden and he says he has just planted one, partly because they're great pollinators and he has a couple of chance apple seedlings he is keen to see pollinated and produce fruit that have never been seen before. Apples usually need the pollen from a different apple to produce fruit. When Doust says Granny Smiths are good pollinators, he means their pollen works to form fruit on many other apple varieties. There are many types of fruit that require this sort of cross-pollination between varieties. Fruits that don't need this are referred to as self-pollinators. Generally speaking, planting a single tree of a fruit variety that needs cross-pollinating will bring you no joy unless there is a suitable cross-pollinator in someone else's garden nearby. Without that, you need to plant something yourself to ensure cross-pollination.

Granny Smith is another chance apple, just like my grandparents' apple and Lady Williams, an apple deeply relevant to Doust's story of the Pink Lady. The original Lady Williams still grows beside the farmhouse on Boronia Farm in Donnybrook, Western Australia. The story goes that, when the Williams family was building the house in 1935, the apple tree grew up as a young seedling. Eventually it fruited and the fruit was like no other apple. It is now thought that the Lady Williams was born of Granny Smith and Jonathan parents, but that's not known for sure. Others suggest it is more likely to be a cross between Granny Smith and Rokewood. Regardless of its parentage, the Lady Williams was, and remains, crucial to apple breeding in Western Australia. It is a parent of the popular commercial apples Cripps Pink (marketed in Australia as Pink Lady) and Cripps Red (marketed in Australia as Sundowner but known as Joya in Europe). The Cripps in the names is for John Cripps AO, an apple breeder who worked with the Western Australian agricultural department for many years.

Cripps was born in England in 1927 and died in Australia in 2022. He migrated to Australia when he was twenty-eight to take a job at the Western Australian Department of Agriculture. In 1973, he officially began an apple breeding program at Manjimup, Western Australia, although he had already been crossing apple varieties and raising seedlings for a long time. 'In 1959 I did do some cross-pollination and raised a few seedlings, but the superintendent of horticulture said he didn't want apple seedlings on the research station because they made the place look untidy,' Cripps said in an interview with Karen George, recorded for the Apple and Pear Oral History Project. When he finally got the go-ahead to embark on an apple breeding project, Cripps was told he could do it as long as it didn't interfere with what was considered to be his more important work with rootstocks, soil management and 'that sort of thing'.

'The chances of success were very slim,' Cripps said. 'You had to have a large population to select from.' Cripps chose to focus his breeding efforts on crossing Golden Delicious (because it is sweet, thin skinned and crops heavily) with Lady Williams (because it is a hard apple that stores well and was a local variety).

When apple breeders want to make a particular cross, they take pollen from one parent flower and insert it into the unopened flower of the other parent. A bag is then placed over the flower so that when it opens and goes about its business of turning from flower to fruit, no busy little bee gets in there carrying pollen from another flower and messing up the purity of the cross. Cripps' apple breeding efforts produced around 108,000 seedlings, almost all from crossing Lady Williams and Golden Delicious.

Apple breeding is a slow process. It took ten years for Cripps to get the first apples to taste. Then, as the trees were fruiting, Cripps and his colleagues would walk up and down among the seedlings tasting apples for three or four months of the year. Cripps said there were 'all sorts of apples. Most of them were completely inedible. Too sour. Too hard. But you had to try them all. You didn't know what you were going to get.'

Ironically, the first time Cripps tasted the apple that would go on to become known as Pink Lady, it came out of cold storage. When that particular apple was picked, Cripps was on long-service leave travelling in Europe. While he was away, the apple breeding technicians picked the apples and put them straight into cold storage for Cripps to taste upon his return. 'It came out of store in good condition,' Cripps said. From those apple samples, he also selected the apple variety that would be marketed as Sundowner or Joya. Cripps thought he had found two varieties that would be useful, local commercial varieties. He didn't realise he'd found an apple that would gain worldwide acceptance and fame.

'The program was more successful than I expected. I didn't think it [Pink Lady] would be grown in fifteen countries and sold in thirty-one,' he said. 'I'm pleased it's been so successful and so many people enjoy eating it.'

The program that produced the Pink Lady is still going and is proudly touted by the Western Australian Department of Primary Industries and Regional Development as the only government apple breeding program in Australia. It is now called the Australian National Apple Breeding Program (ANABP) and will, according to project leader Steele Jacob, commercialise several more varieties in coming years. They are working to develop a new pink apple and a yellow one similar to Golden Delicious, which bruises easily so has fallen out of favour with growers, supermarkets and consumers. Jacob took me on a tour of the program's apple orchard.

We stop by a few trees planted on the side of an internal road at the research station. 'That's the original Pink Lady tree,' Jacob says as we stand in the drizzle. 'We transplanted it here from its original location in the Perth Hills and, fortunately, it survived.' It's an unremarkable tree to look at and it would be easy to pass it without a second glance, which somehow makes its role in the apple world all the more remarkable. I carry the wonder with me as I get back in the car and we drive on past seedling trials of various ages. There are thousands upon thousands of seedling trees, some with fruit and some that haven't yet fruited at all. 'We have 40,000–50,000 trees in the ground at any one time,' Jacob says. 'They're grown from seed and we keep them growing until they start fruiting and we can start tasting them. Some get culled as soon as they are tasted. Some go on for further testing.' Each year they make new crosses, grow new seedlings, looking for that elusive tree that will produce something worthwhile.

The rain eases and we get out of the car and walk along the rows. Jacob encourages me to pick and taste a few, just like the apple breeders do. I bite into a tiny red fruit the size of a cherry. And quickly spit it out again. So bitter. A huge apple, more the size of a rockmelon, catches my eye. 'You can try it if you like,' Jacob says, 'But I don't recommend it. It's awful.' I point to another, reddish-pink and more 'apple-sized'. Jacob shrugs, 'Ah, it's okay. It's just a jara,' he says. 'A jara?' I ask. 'Yes, a JARA – Just Another Red Apple. Nothing special.' Jacob isn't interested in breeding just another red apple; he's looking for the special one, the one that has outstanding flavour and colour. I ask him why it matters, why we need new varieties. He explains that it's partly about marketing but it's also about keeping qualities and finding a way to maintain supply all year. 'Now we are also looking at climate,' Jacob says. 'If climate change reduces chill hours that could be a problem for apple production. We are also looking for improved drought and heat tolerance.'

He picks a dark red fruit and bites into it, then shows me the way the reddish-pink from the outside is veined into the creamy-pink flesh. 'I'd like to find a red-fleshed apple,' he says. 'This one's not bad. It's hard to find a red-fleshed apple that's edible.'

The first apple out of the Australian National Apple Breeding Program is already in the shops, seasonally at least. It's a cross between Royal Gala and Cripps Red. It was first created in 1992 but it wasn't until 2014 that the first trees were commercialised and released to growers. The apples produced by the tree are a distinctive burgundy colour, high in potentially health-giving antioxidants and slow to brown when cut. You might have eaten one. I have. They come from a tree called ANABP 01, which is I guess what can happen when you let scientists name things. Fortunately, the marketing people got involved and the apples appear in shops under the more alluring name of Bravo – provided they meet strict quality testing. Not every apple picked from an ANABP 01 tree gets to shout Bravo from the fruit stand, just like not all apples picked from Cripps Red trees sit on the supermarket shelf as Pink Ladies.

'Every Bravo apple is tested and photographed in the packing shed,' Jacob says. The Bravo name is trademarked, which means the

ANABP 01 apples that don't meet the criteria are still sold, but they don't wear a Bravo sticker. The trees are protected by Plant Breeder's Rights, which are a bit like patents or licences for plants. Jacob says the marketing and quality criteria surrounding licensed fruit like Bravo protect growers and consumers. 'It means growers get paid well for their best fruit and also that consumers know exactly what they are getting when they buy a branded apple.' The owners of the rights to different varieties also dictate where it can be grown and sold, which helps ensure licensed varieties are grown in the most suitable areas. It's also a way of ensuring those who develop new varieties get paid for doing so. But it does add an extra cost to the whole process.

Pink Lady was the first trademarked apple, and perhaps the first trademarked fruit, grown in the world, although its branding wasn't done as well as it might have been. John Cripps reckoned the mishandling of the Plant Breeder's Rights for Pink Lady probably cost the Western Australian government about $1.5 million. It's no wonder they were so careful about getting it right with Bravo. For every Bravo apple sold anywhere in the world, regardless of where it is grown, a little bit of money trickles back to the apple breeding program. The same principle applies to other branded apples, such as Jazz. But in that case, the money trickles to New Zealand, because Jazz is a Kiwi apple, as is Gala. And Kanzi is Belgian. (That doesn't mean the apples of those varieties that we buy in Australia are grown in those countries; the trickle of money is about the licensing.)

Apple grower Harvey Giblett says people are always looking for the next apple variety. 'It's like cars,' he tells me as we sit in his office at Newton Orchards, Manjimup, not far from the apple breeding orchard I visited with Jacob. 'You've already got one but you want a better one, a new one.' (Giblett's car of choice is a dual cab ute – bright apple-red, of course.) 'The apple industry is a bit like that. Everyone knows about apples, but to keep the consumer interested I believe that new varieties are important.' He says that in the almost-sixty years he's been involved in the apple industry, the most important varieties have been Pink Lady and Gala. 'Very few apples stack up to the Pink Lady,' he says. 'It's very rare to have a bad Pink Lady. It's still growing in status. I think it's destined, at some point, to be number one apple in the world.' Giblett says that while there are many new apple varieties bred, it's not often that something distinctively different comes along. 'Supermarkets want to reduce the number of varieties they have on the shelves, so they're not particularly interested in new varieties unless it's something outstanding,' he says. 'Bravo is one of those.'

Bravo first hit the market in 2016 and rapidly grew in popularity due to its uniqueness, aided by clever marketing. Its high flavonoid levels appealed to health-conscious consumers. (Flavenoids are a large group of plant chemicals that are beneficial for human health. They include anti-inflammatories and antioxidants, and can help boost immune function.) In 2021, around a million Bravo apples were sold in Australia and in high-end markets in Dubai, Singapore and Hong Kong. As I said before, only the perfect apples make the grade.

Dr Johanna Christensen says the pursuit of the flawless apple 'seems to be the only constant in the history of orcharding, because even as all other aspects change, the aim to produce large quantities of top-quality apples has remained the same since the beginnings of colonial orcharding.' Christensen knows a thing or two about Australian apple history. She fell into a PhD on the topic at the University of Melbourne after coming across a remarkable collection of wax fruit and vegetables in Melbourne Museum. There are 124 apples in the collection, mostly created between 1873 and 1885. 'They are life-size, beautiful and deceptively real,' Christensen says. 'The curator told me that once, when left lying on an office desk overnight, one of the models had bite marks in it the next day.'

Christensen's real interest in the wax models was for the stories they tell about Australian apple growing, especially in Victoria. She says that while they tell of success, diversity and continuous change, they are also a legacy of the settler vision for productivity, wealth and export success. 'The apple models are the poster-child of the government's aspiration for productivity,' Christensen says. 'But that narrative stands in stark contrast to the stories of present-day growers.' During her PhD studies, Christensen interviewed many Victorian apple orchardists. She says their stories are largely of a struggle for survival.

'From the mid-twentieth century, urban sprawl overtook the orchards on the eastern outskirts of Melbourne,' Christensen says. 'Previously the orchards were a traditional spring-time attraction where urban families went on weekend outings to marvel at the sea of apple blossoms. Now these areas are residential suburbs with only street names to remind visitors of the early orchardists and the former apple industry in that area. Many of the orchards moved further east into the Yarra Valley, which continues as one of the big orcharding areas in Victoria in the twenty-first century. However, the Yarra Valley and many of the other orcharding areas are now competing with new land uses such as residential development or vineyards.' The engulfing of good agricultural land with suburbia is a problem on city fringes throughout the world. Patterns of human settlement are such that cities have grown around fertile river valleys, so a lot of potentially productive land now lies buried beneath concrete. One researcher told me he reckons the day will come when we tear down suburban houses and rip up streets to regain access to the fertile ground beneath.

An apple grower interviewed by Christensen describes the conflict between new residents and orchardists: 'People that come and
live in our areas, again that urban pressure, they say "oh I don't like
the look of that net" [...] People say they want farming to happen in
green wedges but they want farming to be this idyllic thing that they
might have seen in a story book.'

Christensen explains that in the early 20th century apple trees
were planted at a density of around 100 trees per hectare, whereas
today's orchards hold up to 6000 trees per hectare, and in some cases
up to 10,000. She tells me that optimal tree spacing, as recommended
by the Australian government, consists of 4-metre spacing between
the rows and 1-metre spacing between trees (4 × 1 metres), which is
shifting towards 3 × 0.5-metre spacing in more intensive orchards.
'These intensive production systems do not look like the older images
of apple orchards that linger in the tourism and branding imaginar-
ies,' Christensen says. 'By contrast, this intensive production is a
factory farming equivalent. Its beauty is in its utility and function.'

Apple growers seek to grow lots of apples that will sell at a good
price. Giblett says he targets picking 60 tonnes per hectare from his
orchards. 'We aim for 80 per cent pack out of that,' he says. 'Some
of the leftover 20 per cent goes to the "odd bunch" line and the rest
goes to processing – either juice, pie apples or cider.' The odd bunch
line he refers to is the supermarkets' way of marketing small, mis-
shapen or slightly damaged fruit. It's an important step in reducing
food waste.

Think about selecting apples in the shop – you almost certainly
go for the apples that are the size and colour you like best. I know
I do. I don't like them to be too big. Nor too small. I prefer them
to be red, unless I'm intending to cook with them, in which case
I usually choose Granny Smiths. I tend to leave the ones that are
bruised or scabby. Every apple we pick up and buy sends a market

signal. Jacob says market research has shown that if a consumer has a bad experience with an apple, it can take up to eight weeks to go back for another try. Christensen says the search for perfection is reflected in the practices adopted by apple growers. 'Embedded, but often hidden, in the chase for the faultless apples are the countless technological steps taken to ensure a picture-perfect outcome,' she says. 'The social, cultural and environmental side effects of this quest are mostly rendered invisible to the consumer's eye.'

Christensen says the biggest consideration for apple growers when they select varieties to grow is the type of market they supply, not physical suitability or personal preference. She says the aim is for red, crisp, sweet and heavy bearing. 'Breeding programs also influence variety selection and growers are keen to be up-to-date with the newest cultivars entering the market, which, more often than not, are licensed varieties.

'Growers who supply to the mainstream retailers end up in what is described as a "lock-in trap" because they are limited to growing only those few varieties that the supermarkets consider desirable; and in combination with the demand for high quantities and quality, growers are forced into adopting techno-scientific solutions to keep up with the intense production regime. Market demand and technologies reinforce each other, creating an ever-increasing productivity spiral. The direction is downward, because each decision to become more efficient and commit to further investment into technology, in turn, constrains future options.'

One of the things that struck me in my discussion with Giblett was his commitment to the apple industry and his town, and his desire to be a good employer and citizen beyond any labels. I asked him about growing apples organically and environmental considerations. He said he thought it was partly a generational thing, with younger people demanding more attention be paid to how things are done. 'As an industry, we need to get on top of environmental things,' he says. 'We need to look at our carbon footprint, especially from refrigeration and storage. Chemical use, too.'

For a while, Giblett's company, Newton Brothers, cultivated a small block of organic apples. That is, until they became infected with apple scab. Giblett sprayed the trees, killing the apple scab but losing the organic certification in the process. 'We could have left them and in a few years the apple scab would have probably sorted itself out,' he says. 'There was a neighbouring orchard nearby. There's not a lot of apple scab around here and I didn't want us to be responsible for infecting the neighbour's orchard. If there hadn't been a neighbour, I probably would have left it,' Giblett says. His comments left me pondering the complexity of decisions that superficially seem so simple; spraying or not spraying on his own land was deeply tied to broader considerations about and responsibilities to the industry. As shoppers choosing produce from a supermarket shelf, such things are entirely beyond our reach.

Growing apples is a long-term commitment. Giblett tells me it can cost up to $100,000 per hectare to plant a modern apple orchard, with no return for four years. During those years, the trees need watering, pruning and fertilising. All while waiting for the first harvest, which the grower hopes will hit the spot with the market. Giblett says an apple orchard gives about twenty harvests before production drops off to a level that is not commercially sustainable. The cycle then begins again, with those old trees removed and new ones established. Despite the cost of establishing orchards, Giblett says 60 per cent of his costs are labour – picking, pruning and thinning are among the annual jobs of growing apples and getting them to market. He says that presents a challenge when 'everyone has the perception that fresh fruit and veg should be cheap'. When I look at apples for sale in the shops and think about all it has taken to get them there, it seems to me they are cheap. Perhaps too cheap.

Christensen says that some of the apple growers she interviewed commented that in the past there was a broader range of varieties grown to extend the season in the absence of good refrigeration. 'While the number of varieties grown seems to be on the rise again, due to newer breeds and strains coming onto the market more rapidly because of advances in breeding practices, only some growers seem receptive to them,' she says. 'The cost associated with taking on a licensed variety represents a barrier for some growers.' In her thesis, she quotes 'Steve', a fifth-generation orchardist from Harcourt, Victoria: 'We have stuck with the original Pink Ladies. Probably because you have to pay for all those varieties, too, that's the other thing… because they all have royalties and things on them, patents and things …'

But Christensen says other growers see the future of their orchards as depending on and needing to anticipate future market trends, and on being up to date with new licensed cultivars. 'Growing licensed varieties also offers security, as the marketing is predominantly controlled by those who hold the rights to the cultivar and less by the retail chains,' she says. She leaves it to 'Todd', a sixth-generation grower from the Yarra Valley, Victoria to explain: 'I actually think they [licensed varieties] are better […] Because with the license varieties, I believe it is one of the only ways that you can take the supermarkets' dominance out of it. […] [If you] create the dialogue between the grower and marketer and the consumer and the consumer is demanding it, then you have taken the power of the chain out of it.'

Christensen says all the orchardists she spoke to confirmed that eventually the market dictates what they grow. 'Those who supply the mainstream retailers choose different varieties to those who sell at farmers' markets, and again different to those having an alternate use for their apples (i.e. cider). For example an organic grower said that the ultimate aim for her is to have an even spread of varieties throughout the season. And although this is ultimately again to satisfy market demand, the farmers' markets she sells at demand a different product range to the large-scale supermarket chains. She wants varieties that ripen consecutively, ideally with a nice range of things that ripen in small quantities that she can sell each week.'

Christensen says there is an implicit acceptance among growers that market demand drives their orcharding business practices. 'There is a saying that it is unwise to put all your eggs (or apples!) in one basket as it creates a risk of losing them all at once,' she says. 'However, this is exactly what is happening. Technologies have enabled growers to become more efficient by growing fewer varieties and perfecting the practice of how to grow them. Technologies have been used to overcome physical anxieties associated with pests and diseases, but today's growers told me a story that indicates that pests are increasing and even the best technologies are insufficient or too expensive. There is a great risk associated with current growing practices, which, despite being realised by some growers, appears to be essentially accepted throughout the industry.'

Worrying about the changes in apples wrought by technology is not new. Way back in 1862, American naturalist Henry David Thoreau lamented: 'I doubt if so extensive orchards are set out to-day in my town as there were a century ago … Now that they have grafted trees, and pay a price for them, they collect them into a plat by their houses, and fence them in …'. Thoreau preferred the 'old orchards of ungrafted apple-trees … so irregularly planted; sometimes two trees standing close together; and the rows so devious that you would think that they not only had grown while the owner was sleeping, but had been set out by him in a somnambulic state.' He had 'no faith in the selected lists of pomological gentlemen' and claimed the named varieties of the time 'commonly turn out very tame and forgettable'. But he also admitted that many of the wild apples need to be eaten out in woods while walking because 'what is sour in the house a bracing walk makes sweet'.

Indeed, it is that search for sweetness that drives the likes of Cripps and Jacob to search among their seedlings for the next Pink Lady or Bravo. Something that will provide growers with sweet, red, delicious fruit on heavy-bearing trees. Something that you and I won't be able to walk past when we see them for sale in the shops.

CHAPTER 6

Soy

F RESH SOY MILK sits in the dairy section at the shops, but is it
really milk? Maybe it should be called something else. My copy
of the *Macquarie Dictionary* gives the first definition of milk as 'an
opaque white or bluish white liquid secreted by the mammary glands
of female mammals, serving for the nourishment of their young, and,
in the case of the cow and some other animals, used by humans for
food or as a source of dairy products.' It's a pretty long definition,
but doesn't give any reason to have the word milk on the label of soy
milk. But wait, the Macquarie has more to say: 'any liquid resembling
this, as the liquid within a coconut, the juice or sap (latex) of certain
plants, or various pharmaceutical preparations.' So maybe soy milk
really is milk after all.

The question as to whether or not non-dairy products should be
called by dairy names is not new. In 1930, a Queensland newspaper,
the *Nambour Chronicle and North Coast Advertiser*, reported the
emergence of a new product that threatened to be a 'rival to butter'.
This new product was 'highly nutritive and palatable' and also kept
'indefinitely' and would not turn rancid. The paper reported that the

Department of Agriculture had pushed back on the product being labelled and sold as butter and so it was marketed as a paste – peanut paste. Butter was a name reserved for the churned cream product, in Queensland at least. The article suggested that not only was this new product a threat to our understanding of what butter is, the manufacture of butter substitutes, including margarine, should be stopped to protect the dairy industry.

The Australian dairy industry wasn't ruined by the arrival of peanut paste, even though the word butter has now slipped onto labels across the country. It seems it was only ever a regionalism – Queensland, South Australia and Western Australia originally insisted the name be peanut paste but it was probably peanut butter elsewhere from the start. Similarly, soy milk hasn't ruined the dairy industry, but industry body Dairy Australia says the use of the word milk in the increasing number of dairy alternatives can cause confusion. 'Many of these products do not resemble cow's milk from a nutritional perspective and therefore [have] the potential to confuse consumers.' Dairy Australia points out the guidelines that govern food labelling are under review (in 2022) and says they are 'encouraging a holistic review of the topic including labelling definitions of milk'. At the time of writing, Australian food standards dictate prescribed names such as 'milk' can be used on other (non-dairy) foods provided context is given. Soy milk can be called soy milk as long as the soy part of the label is clear. For now.

According to *ABC News* an Australian Government Senate Inquiry in February 2022 recommended animal descriptors should not be used to describe products that don't come from animals. It's not just about milk; it's also about plant-derived meat substitutes. In 2022, the ABC reported a Senate Inquiry recommendation to establish a regulatory framework for labelling plant-based protein products and 'a national standard be developed to restrict the use of "meat category brands" to animal protein products'. There is some disingenuity in this. Going back to my *Macquarie Dictionary*, the second definition of meat (after the first one that says it is the flesh of animals used for food) says it is food in general. But it is certainly confusing because the first definition, that meat is animal flesh, is widely used and accepted.

The ABC reported that Senator Susan McDonald, who led the Senate Inquiry, recommended the emerging plant-protein industry be supported, pointing out that Australian pulse (legume) and vegetable farmers 'can tap into the plant-protein market, so it makes no sense for people to frame this inquiry as somehow wanting to cripple that industry or attack vegans and vegetarians. All we're suggesting is that, like margarine makers did by choosing a name that didn't contain butter, plant protein marketers come up with ways to promote their products without trading on animal names and imagery.'

Whether soy milk is or is not milk is, to a certain degree at least, a moot point. In any case, a lot of it gets drunk. In 2016, market research company Roy Morgan reported that just over 1.1 million Australians over the age of fourteen said they consumed at least one soy drink in any given seven-day period. That was slightly more than the number who consumed energy drinks, sports drinks, iced tea or breakfast drinks. They reported consumption of energy and sports drinks had dropped over the preceding four years, while consumption of soy drinks had increased. I suspect it would have increased again since their last survey.

Soy milk is made from the seeds of soybeans, a smallish annual plant that lends itself well to broadacre cropping, providing it gets plenty of water and sunshine. The plant is native to Asia and mostly grows in tropical and semi-tropical regions. Soybeans are a legume, so they add nitrogen to soil. More accurately, nitrogen-fixing bacteria form nodules on soybean plant roots, and those bacteria (rhizobia) fix nitrogen. From an agricultural perspective, legumes play an important role in crop rotations.

Rotating crops is as old as agriculture. Growing different crops in different years or different seasons gives soil a chance to rest from the demands of a particular plant. It provides a chance to control bugs and disease, traditionally by taking away their food source for a year or more. More recently, that control is most often afforded by chemicals. Crop rotation is still important though, because it enables different herbicides to be used in subsequent years. (Different crops vary in their susceptibility to various chemicals.) This helps prevent herbicide resistance developing. There is also still an important element of growing a 'break' crop to break up disease cycles.

Soybeans aren't the only legume grown in crop rotations to add nitrogen to the soil, but in areas where they are grown it is an important aspect of their cultivation. Nitrogen is a major plant nutrient, essential for building amino acids and proteins. Growing legumes in crop rotations was once the major way of increasing soil nitrogen for nitrogen-hungry crops, such as grains and leafy vegetables. Even before people understood the magic of bacterial nitrogen fixation, they understood it was beneficial to add a legume to garden or paddock rotations. (I do so in my own garden – dedicating a bed to peas or beans in one season and following them with leafy greens the next.)

In the early 20th century, industrially produced nitrogen became available and now nitrogen is most often applied as synthetic urea or ammonium. Abundant synthetic nitrogen is one of the things that fuelled the Green Revolution (the increased yields that came with dwarfing varieties and new agronomic practices in the 1950s and

1960s) and all that it brought with it. But synthetic nitrogen came – still comes – at a cost. In 2019, the world used more than 120 million tonnes of nitrogen fertiliser, of which only 74 million tonnes ended up in harvested products. That gap between those figures is down to a few factors. Some nitrogen remains in the soil and in parts of plants that are not harvested, the roots and leaves of grain crops for example. Some runs off into waterways where it causes pollution problems (such as sugar cane fertiliser runoff affecting the Great Barrier Reef). And some escapes to the atmosphere as nitrous oxide, which is a potent greenhouse gas. Nitrous oxide has about 300 times the global warming potential of carbon dioxide.

This wastage of nitrogen is partly because plants don't use nitrogen evenly throughout their growing cycle; there are periods of high nitrogen demand and periods of low nitrogen use. It can be hard to get onto paddocks when nitrogen is needed – the crop may be too tall, for example, or it may not be known exactly when peak demand is going to occur, or there may simply be other things that need doing around the farm at that particular time. Nitrogen can be a limiting factor; which means that if it is not available at the level the plant needs, the plant simply won't grow to its full potential, even if all other conditions are perfect. To counter this, farmers growing high-value crops may want to load up nitrogen early in the growing season. Except, of course, where it is very expensive or hard to get, which is especially the case in many developing countries.

In one of those clever, quirky things that happen in plant ecology, if soil nitrogen levels are high, plants won't let rhizobia form nodules on their roots. The plants will get their nitrogen straight from the soil, rather than 'paying' the rhizobia to get it for them. (Plants provide carbohydrates to the bacteria.) After a legume has been grown, the nitrogen fixed by the rhizobia tends to stay in the soil until other bacteria break it down and make it available for plants. I've spoken to farmers who say one year of growing a legume will give them enough soil nitrogen for two years of wheat crops. It saves them truckloads of synthetic nitrogen, and money, and also saves them worrying about getting out onto the paddocks to spread it. But still, it is only worth dedicating a paddock to a legume rotation if there is some sort of market for that crop, or livestock available to eat the pasture. (Hold that thought: it's an important thing to remember in the overall consideration of how good farms function.)

The importance of legumes in agriculture has led to them being widely cultivated, none more so than soy. It is now one of the big-hitting plant species as far as production goes, with total global production at 350 million tonnes. This is double what it was in 2000 and an astonishing thirteen times what it was in 1960. Soybeans are now grown across the world and for years the United States led world production. In 2020–21 it was overtaken by Brazil. This was not because the US reduced production but rather because Brazil increased production. There is an implication that the increase in Brazilian soy has caused forest to be cleared to grow it, therefore consuming soy is bad for the environment, and is directly responsible for clearing the Amazon rainforest. Whether or not this is actually the case is somewhat controversial. As we see with so many things like this, the reality is complicated and nuanced.

In a detailed analysis of global soy production, Our World in Data researchers Dr Hannah Ritchie and Dr Max Roser concluded that most deforestation in Amazonian rainforests is to create beef cattle pasture, but soy production plays a significant role. Ritchie and Roser research and write extensively on global food supply and associated issues. They point out that when you increase production it can only be done by increasing yield or increasing the amount of land used to grow a crop. In the case of soy: 'Since 1961 global yields increased by 150 per cent. But production increased by 1200 per cent. This means the area used to grow soy has more than quadrupled.' Ritchie and Roser write that Brazilian yields have increased dramatically, but so has the area planted. In part, this occurs when cropland pushes into pastured land and then forest is cleared to make new pasture. Like I said, it's complicated and not easy to tease out cause and effect. But in any case, is Brazilian (or American) soy production relevant to Australian consumers?

Soybeans won't grow everywhere in Australia. Most Australian soybeans are grown in Queensland and northern New South Wales, with smaller pockets across the New South Wales coastal hinterland into northern Victoria, and also in the Northern Territory and across into the Kimberley. This wide adaptation reflects the many varieties of soybeans that have been developed to grow in different environments, but they still won't grow everywhere. (Other legumes are used in crop rotations in broadacre farms elsewhere in Australia: lupins or chickpeas, for example.)

Australia is a relatively small player on the global soybean-growing scene, with a fraction over 44,000 tonnes produced in 2020. (To put this into perspective, in the same year, Brazil produced 138 *million* tonnes and the US produced 120 *million* tonnes.) We import soybeans into Australia and we also export them, which sounds bizarre but that's the way it is. In 2020, Australia exported $1.35 million worth of soy, with most of it going to Chinese Taipei, New Zealand, South Korea, India and Papua New Guinea. That same year, we imported $4.76 million worth of soy, with most of it coming from China, Canada, Austria, the US and the Netherlands. There's no escaping the reality that we are a player, albeit a small one, in the global soy market. Overall, soybeans are considered to be an important part of Australia's $2.5 billion oilseed industry. Yes, although they are a legume, in terms of agricultural commodities soybeans are classified as an oilseed, because soya oil is one of the major products extracted from them. They are used for human consumption but also for various industrial uses. Soy contains about 20 per cent oil. The stuff left behind when the beans are crushed to extract the oil is called soy meal. It's high in protein and carbohydrate and is usually fed to animals.

That's a crucial point in the whole soy story; most soy is not used to feed people directly. Less than a fifth of the soy produced in the world is turned into soy milk, tofu, edamame or oil for human food. More than three quarters of it goes into animal feed, mostly to feed the millions and millions of chickens and pigs raised for human consumption. There's an argument in favour of skipping the chicken and pig phases and eating the plants instead. It runs along the lines that if everyone in the world was vegetarian, we could drastically reduce the environmental impact of feeding the world. It's an idea that has captured the public imagination, and vegetarianism is on the rise in many wealthy countries, including Australia.

In 2012, only 9.7 per cent of Australians identified themselves as vegetarian. That figure rose to 11.2 per cent by 2014 and up to 12.1 per cent by 2019. That's almost two-and-a-half million people in total, or to put it another way, Australia had about 300,000 more vegetarians in 2019 than in 2014.

If people don't eat meat, they need to get high-quality protein from somewhere else. Soybeans are one option and have been eaten by people for thousands of years. They are ubiquitous in Asian cuisines. Whole beans, or even whole pods (like in the Japanese dish edamame), can be cooked and eaten. But often soybeans are processed into soy sauce, soya oil, soy milk or tofu.

Tofu is a relatively simple form of processed food. It fits into the NOVA 2 category. The soybeans are first soaked, crushed and strained. The resulting liquid is then cooked to produce soy milk, which is a stable emulsion of fats, liquid and protein (meaning the different components don't separate in the way oil and water do when you mix them together). The soy milk (yes, I'm calling it milk) is heated. Next, a coagulant, such as magnesium chloride or calcium sulphate, is added and this causes lumps (curd) to form in the liquid (whey). (Yes, curds and whey, just like Little Miss Muffet was eating when the spider scared her, except hers were probably made from cow's milk not soy milk.) The mixture is strained and the curds either pressed or not, depending on the type of tofu required.

It is thought that tofu was probably first eaten in China around 2000 years ago. Soy products gained popularity in Western countries during and after the Second World War as a cheap source of high-quality protein. They became increasingly popular in Australia during the second half of the 20th century and the Australian soybean industry arose during this time.

Of course, soy isn't the only way for vegetarians and vegans to obtain good quality protein from plant sources. There is a range of legumes, among other things. Lately, plant-based proteins, sometimes called plant-based meat or plant-based alternatives, get a lot of attention. Whatever we call them, some of these products are made from soy, but they can also be manufactured from other legumes, wheat and mycoprotein, which is extracted from a fungus. Environmental concerns, especially climate change, are often cited as reasons for consuming these alternatives instead of meat.

Looking at global figures for greenhouse gas emissions, growing beans generates around 0.65 kilograms CO_2e for every 100 grams of protein produced. If those beans are eaten as tofu, the emissions per 100 grams jump up to 1.6 kilograms CO_2e. The equivalent emissions from using animals to produce the protein are 6 kilograms CO_2e for chicken, 6.5 kilograms CO_2e for pork, 20 kilograms CO_2e for lamb and 25 kilograms CO_2e for beef. But remember, these are global figures and the only environmental factor being considered is greenhouse gas emissions. We will see in later chapters that the issue is, as usual, more complex than this, and we've also already established that looking at carbon emissions alone is not an adequate way of assessing overall environmental impact.

The government research organisation AgriFutures Australia commissioned a life cycle assessment (LCA) of plant-based alternatives to chicken as part of its chicken meat program. The study points out that plant-based alternatives and 'cultured meat companies are actively competing with traditional meat, using environmental credentials as a major point of difference'. It warns that most studies assessing the environmental performance of plant-based alternatives are conducted overseas, rather than in Australia, where manufacturing impacts may be different due to Australia's reliance on fossil fuels. The study also cautions that 'product comparisons must take into account nutritional factors, but this is often not done'. The researchers found some of the claims made about plant-based alternatives were not supported by available research; in some cases, the evidence contradicted the claims. They attribute this to the lack of Australian market context for the results and concluded that this implies 'consumers may be misinformed by these claims in the Australian market'.

Regardless of this, plant-based meat alternatives are a fairly big, and growing, market. CSIRO valued the Australian plant protein market at $150 million in 2019 but predicts it will reach around $4 billion by 2030, creating 6000 jobs. Additionally, CSIRO sees a future export market of over $2.5 billion. CSIRO is walking its talk as far as this industry goes; it was a founding joint venture partner in v2food, the company that has developed and marketed v2food sausages, burgers, mince and sauce. The burger in Hungry Jack's Rebel Whopper is a v2food burger. According to v2food's website, their products are plant-based meat. As they put it: 'With the help of the scientists at Australia's top research organisation, CSIRO, we've worked out how to take protein from legumes and turn it into something that looks, cooks and tastes like meat.' The packet label says the legumes used are soy. Not, at this stage, Australian soy, or not entirely – the label says it contains at least 65 per cent Australian ingredients. But what does it taste like? Only one way to find out.

At my local supermarket there's a selection of different plant-based meat alternatives, including the v2food offerings. I chose a packet of v2food burgers for my taste test. They promise to 'deliver on the flavour you love, with none of the cow'. They cooked up easily enough and I found the texture remarkably close to a beef burger patty. They tasted okay but a bit bland. The real surprise was how filling they were; at least as filling as an equivalent-sized beef patty. But I'm not sold.

I confess that I don't really get it. Maybe I'm just not the demographic the plant-based meat is aimed at. Although maybe I am; I'm a lapsed vegetarian and am concerned about what I eat and interested in where my food comes from and the impact it has. I'm more than happy to eat a lentil burger or stir-fried tofu or lentil dahl or bean tacos. I sometimes drink soy milk. But fake meat? It strikes me as an ultra-processed (NOVA 4) product I don't need, even if I want a vegetarian meal. I asked a few vegetarian friends what they thought. They were mostly ambivalent. Not exactly scientific, but nonetheless interesting. One, who is a vegan, surprised me by saying that she didn't like the fake meat because it reminded her too much of meat, which is perhaps ironic. I realise it may be just what some people are looking for – the taste of meat without the death of an animal – but I'm still sceptical about the whole deal.

There is something hidden between the words on the packages of fake meat – nutritional equivalence, or perhaps the lack thereof. Fake meat may 'cook, look and taste' like meat, but what about its nutritional value? An American study that investigated the effects of plant-based meat on human health and climate change found: 'Novel plant-based meat alternatives should arguably be treated as meat alternatives in terms of sensory experience, but not as true meat replacements in terms of nutrition.' The researchers write that mimicking 'animal foods using isolated plant proteins, fats, vitamins, and minerals likely underestimates the true nutritional complexity of whole foods in their natural state, which contain hundreds to thousands of nutrients that impact human health.' (Again, reason to focus our diets more on the NOVA 1, 2 and 3 categories and avoid or minimise NOVA 4.) The study notes possible concerns over the levels of iron, zinc, vitamin B12 and folate in many vegan diets (which is not the same as saying a vegan diet can't be healthy). It also points out a difference in the metabolism of plant-sourced proteins and animal-sourced proteins, suggesting that the plant-based meats are not a direct substitute for meat. Animal proteins have more balanced amino acids than plant proteins, and this affects what happens within muscles. The researchers say eating more plant protein, and making sure it comes from a variety of sources, can help overcome this issue. They conclude that consuming plant-based protein alternatives as part of an omnivorous diet is unlikely to cause problems and point out benefits of combining animal and plant foods. Although we can certainly get all of our protein from plant sources, ominivory has benefits. For example, the absorption of some forms of iron from plants is enhanced if meat is eaten at the same time.

Iron deficiency is one of the major nutrient deficiencies throughout the world, especially among children, adolescent girls and older people. Consuming meat is an easy way to obtain and absorb iron. And although too much meat can potentially damage cardiovascular health, those effects can be mitigated by plant foods. Another point in favour of eating a variety of plant and animal foods. Time, then, to take a closer look at the animals that provide the meat that most of us eat.

A few animals –
Four of the five

CHAPTER 7

Cattle

IN THE EARLY morning, with the grass wet from overnight dew
and my feet dry inside Wellington boots, I headed down the hill,
crossed the creek on the footbridge and walked around the straggling
cows. 'Get up girls, come on, up you go!' I shouted in mimicry of my
uncle. The cows were already moving, their udders large and ready to
be milked. I was in my happy place, school holidays on my maternal
grandparents' farm, bringing the cows in with Uncle Will. In those
days, early in my childhood, when my boots were short and the cows
seemed enormous, my grandparents and uncle milked a small herd
in a little dairy shed and separated the cream from the skim milk.
The cream was put into large cans and picked up by a truck three
times a week to be taken to the factory and churned into butter. It
was not refrigerated while it waited to be picked up. The skim milk
was carried in buckets up the hill from the dairy to the sties and fed
to the pigs. It was a simple farming system that was killed off in the
early 1970s when Australian dairy went through a major upheaval.
Britain joined the European Union and no longer wanted Australian
butter. I was too young to understand what had happened other than

knowing that the chug of the milking machine no longer punctuated daily life on the farm.

Grandad couldn't bear to part with his beloved dairy cows, so he gradually shifted the herd towards beef production by changing bulls – the Illawarra Shorthorn dairy bull was sold and replaced by a Black Angus beef bull. Beef cattle and dairy cattle are quite separate breeds, bred over many, many generations to focus on different products. Beef cattle, of course, produce milk, but not in the quantity that dairy cows do. Similarly, dairy cattle can be slaughtered for meat, with some dairy breeds having reputations for producing good meat, but they don't fatten and lay down muscle to the extent, nor at the speed, that beef cattle do. My grandparents had always fattened up the young steers (sterilised male cattle) and sold them for beef, but it was a sideline to their main game of producing cream. With their dairying enterprise gone, their cattle herd changed to reflect the new market they sought.

The other change on the farm was that the pigs were sold. Without the skim milk by-product, it was uneconomical to raise pigs. The farm went from a dairy and pig farm to a beef farm. A pillar of its diversity was lost. Still, there were cows in the paddocks, and the habit of walking around the herd each morning stayed with the family and remained a great way of burning the energy from visiting grand-children before breakfast. It's nostalgic for me to think back on those bucolic days, the long shadows cast by the cows in the early morning light, my uncle's endless patience with my gazillion questions. It's the classic storybook view of a farm, slow and peaceful, with names for the animals (there was even a cow called Jill, named after me!), and seemingly all the time in the world to take in the surroundings, the grass green and the trees tall.

Fast-forward about fifty years. I'm standing behind the glass wall of the viewing gallery overlooking Bannister Downs Dairy. Sue and

Mat Daubney own and run Bannister Downs in the tall timber country of Northcliffe, Western Australia. It's about 140 kilometres south-east of where my grandparents farmed. The viewing deck was built to accommodate hundreds of visitors but today it's just me and Sue Daubney. The plan was to have people come and watch the operations and sample the produce in the cafe at the end of the production line but Covid put that on hold. Daubney is fitting me in between meetings and discussions trying to establish an Asian export arrangement for Bannister Downs milk. She's wearing corporate high heels, not farm boots. 'It's all about scale,' Daubney says. 'If we could sell enough milk here in Western Australia, we wouldn't need the export market. But we can't get that level of sales here to get to the scale we need to make it all work.'

I can't quite get my head around this; Western Australia is not self-sufficient in dairy produce – milk, cheese, butter and yoghurt are imported from elsewhere in Australia and also from overseas, mostly New Zealand and Europe. Yet here is a Western Australian dairy farmer telling me she needs to go to international markets to maintain scale for profitability. I know I am oversimplifying in making this observation, but there's something about it that seems warped, if not plain wrong. I put the thought aside as Daubney talks me through their operations.

Daubney explains that one of the motivations for building the Creamery, as they call the building we are standing in, was to show people what dairy farming really looks like. She says the images people see of cows confined to muddy stalls just don't reflect Australian dairy, which is predominantly pasture based. Australian dairy cows usually receive some extra feed, but about two thirds of their nutrition comes from grazing pasture and pretty much all of them spend almost all of their lives living outside on pastures. Daubney also expresses surprise at the things people don't know. 'Like what?' I ask. She shrugs and says, 'That cows need to have a calf to produce milk. People often don't make the link between birth and lactation.'

Dairy cows generally have a calf every year. The calves are taken away from the cows soon after birth and the cow goes into the milking herd. A few months later, she will be put back into calf (that is, get pregnant again) and will remain in milk production until she is 'dried off' a couple of months before the next calf is born. After she calves, the cycle begins again. Many dairy cows will produce a calf annually for many years, although in some dairies they are kept milking for longer before being put into calf again, so may only have a calf every one-and-a-half to two years. What happens after her life as a milker depends on the farm. Most often they are slaughtered for meat. One Jersey cow at Bannister Downs, Mrs Grey, has recently retired to pasture at eighteen years of age.

As Daubney and I talk, a cow is scratching herself on a big, bristled brush that has been put there just for this purpose. It spins as she rubs herself against it. She is clearly enjoying herself, bending and twisting and pushing against the brush. Having been milked, she is on her way back out to graze pasture. In an adjoining yard, some of her herd-mates are standing waiting for the gate to open to admit them into the milking machine. They stand patiently, huge udders heavy with milk. Most are Friesians, those ubiquitous black-and-white animals that immediately come to mind when you think 'cow'. They are the most productive dairy cow in the world and account for just over four fifths of the Australian herd. The Daubneys also have Jerseys, which are pretty caramel-coloured cows with dishy faces and melt-your-heart brown eyes. Jerseys don't produce as much milk as Friesians, but their milk is noted for its high content of cream and protein. There are also a few Brown Swiss and Illawarra Shorthorns in the mix at Bannister Downs. The aim of this mixture of breeds is to produce milk with the desired fat and flavour.

The gate opens and a cow walks through and steps onto the platform of the state-of-the-art rotational robotic dairy. Yes, robotic. The cow's udder is sprayed with water to clean it and a robotic arm swings down and places the four cups on her four teats. The circular platform slowly rotates as the cows stand placidly chewing their cud. There are a few dozen cows on the platform at any one time. When a cow has been milked, the cups drop off, are cleaned and then made ready to go onto the next cow. The cows step off when the platform completes its rotation. From there, they walk over to a feeding station to have their ration, then a scratch if they so desire, before heading back out to the paddock. The cows come back in when their full udder tells them it's time. In non-robotic dairies, cows are usually milked twice a day; in robotic dairies, they may choose to be milked more often and can decide to come in two or three times a day – it's up to the cow.

Daubney tells me the robotic dairy was marketed to them as being great for the dairy farmer, freeing them from the twice-daily, every-day-of-the-year grind of milking, but she says the real beneficiaries have been the cows. 'When you are milking a herd of 600, the cows spend a lot of time standing around waiting to go in to be milked, because they all come into the dairy at once,' Daubney says. 'With the robotic dairy, they come in whenever they like throughout the day, so they spend less time waiting. We haven't had any cases of mastitis requiring treatment or intervention since we moved to the robotic dairy.'

Mastitis is a very painful infection and inflammation caused by too much milk accumulating in the udder (or breast). Preventing mastitis is one of the major reasons why calves are taken from dairy cows soon after birth; in the case of Bannister Downs, two days after birth. 'These cows produce 20 to 30 litres of milk a day,' Daubney says. 'A calf will only drink about 4 litres in a feed. The calves simply can't drink all the milk the cow produces, so we take them away from their mothers after they have had their colostrum and they live a lovely life with the other calves.' Daubney says it's much safer for the calves to be out of the milking herd, where they would be at risk of being crushed or having the cows fight over them. The calves are moved to a calf-rearing creche – there are a few of these spread around Bannister Downs farm to ensure they are not overstocked. (That is, the number of animals on the paddocks is consistent with the amount of feed available and the animals are not damaging the land.)

Daubney says the calves always have plenty of shelter and are mostly outdoors on grass in protected areas of the farm. 'They are initially fed warm milk – collected daily from our dairy herd, not reconstituted from powder – by hand until we are confident they are "good feeders". Then they are put with the other youngsters and attended to twice daily for feeding [milk], plus introduced to some grain, water and grass. They gradually eat and drink more of that until they are finally weaned from the milk at around three to four months, determined more on their size and growth rather than any specific age.'

At Bannister Downs, the male and female calves are treated the same, but this is not the case at all dairy farms. The industry body Dairy Australia says that on many Australian farms male calves (and unwanted female calves) are sent to saleyards or abattoirs at around five days of age. Dairy Australia says, 'Unfortunately, not all male calves can be reared for beef due to lack of market opportunity. In instances where other pathways are not viable, calves are euthanised at birth. Some farmers are also using sexed semen technology to help increase the number of female calves born that can be reared and reduce the number of male calves.' The fate of unwanted calves (also called poddy calves) is a controversial aspect of dairying and one that the RSPCA would like to see addressed. They encourage 'farmers to raise calves in a way that gives them a life worth living and gives consumers the confidence to buy higher welfare veal or beef'.

Regardless of what happens to them, taking very young calves from their mothers, although common practice, is a point of contention in the dairy industry. According to an article in *The Guardian*, there are now around 400 dairies in Australia and Europe that are leaving the calves with their mothers for longer, but this is not without controversy either. The article quotes Helen Browning, dairy farmer and CEO of organic trade body the (UK) Soil Association, as saying that she thinks it is more of an emotive issue than a welfare issue. (The distinction is an interesting one, and runs to the heart of how people perceive what is and isn't done with livestock. It's something I'll tease apart later.)

One of the British farmers quoted in *The Guardian* article says he almost gave up keeping the calves with their mothers in the first year because it was so difficult and seemed to be even harder for the cows and calves. *The Guardian* quotes him saying: 'We just couldn't get the cows away from the calves and into the milking parlour. For weeks we'd be dragging the cows in there.' The calves were found to grow quicker and have lower mortality rates, but they consumed a significant amount of milk from the cows. Amazingly, cows will also 'hold back' the fat in their milk for their calves. All mammals need to 'let down' milk to suckle their offspring, or to be milked. Some cows with calves at foot will not let down at all; others only let down to a certain degree, retaining a portion for their calves. The farmer quoted in *The Guardian* reckoned that, overall, the calves kept on their mothers consumed more than 2000 litres of milk each, at an estimated cost of

£500 (about $880). Those 2000 litres of milk the calf drank while it was with its mother are likely around a fifth of the cow's annual milk production, or a little more. The farmer was milking 125 cows. That increases the cost of production for the dairy, so they have to sell their milk at a higher price. Which means consumers have to pay more.

Regardless of the age at which it is done, cows and calves will complain about being separated; people's opinions differ as to whether it is better to separate early, before the mother–calf bond is well established, or later, when the calf is more grown. It's worthwhile looking at what science tells us. Veterinarian and animal welfare researcher Associate Professor David Beggs, from The University of Melbourne, has spent a lot of time and effort investigating the welfare of dairy cows. He says it is interesting to think about the experience of the cow and calf when they are separated. 'We know there is a maternal cow–calf bond and we know it gets stronger in time,' he says. 'I'm certain there is a negative experience when calves are separated but I'm not sure what it is. I don't think the cow is grieving for what might have been. I suspect, and this is only a suspicion, it is a desire to express behaviours.'

Beggs says all animals have desires to express certain behaviours, often in response to a certain stimulus. 'The stimulus for cows to express maternal behaviour is probably a calf,' he explains. 'If the calf is gone, it doesn't take long for the maternal behaviour to subside.' He says cows will bellow when the calves are first taken away, but not for long. Beggs doesn't think a cow mourns for her own particular calf; that is not the way he has observed their bond. He says there is ample evidence to support this, including that cows will readily foster another calf and frequently 'steal' each other's calves. 'I think it's probably best to separate them as early as possible,' Beggs says. He points out that industry best practice is considered to be separating about twelve hours after birth, which is partly to reduce the incidence of disease in the calves and partly to prevent mastitis in the cows. 'The sooner you do it, the sooner they are over it and the less time they show signs of distress,' he says. 'I think the worst thing you can do is leave them on for a week, and then take them away.'

It is not standard practice in Australia, but in many places around the world calves are separated at birth and put into hutches by themselves. 'I don't think that's ideal,' Beggs says. 'All animals have behaviour they would like to express. I think calves are motivated to have some sort of social behaviour.' Giving calves access to playmates and shelter is crucial for good welfare. Making sure the calves are fed cow's milk, rather than a substitute, for at least the first few months, also seems to be important, regardless of when they are separated.

When my grandparents were dairying, the calves were separated from the cows soon after birth but I can't remember exactly when. What I do remember is that watching the calves play together in the calf paddock was endlessly entertaining and feeding the calves was one of the best jobs. To get the little ones to drink, we would put our fingers into their mouths and they would latch on and suck our fingers. We would then gently lower our hands into the bucket of milk, which came straight from the milking shed. As the calves sucked our fingers, they would also suck up the milk, eventually learning to drink from the bucket without our fingers in their mouths. The calves would slurp and waggle their tails. It still makes me smile to think of it.

Bannister Downs sells a branded, premium product, more expensive than the bigger supermarket brands. As we talk during my visit, Daubney mentions that Murdoch University food scientist Dr Vicky Solah is investigating milk from Bannister Downs and other dairies.

Later, back in the city, I sit down with Solah. 'We're looking at different milks and profiling the different fatty acids and opioid peptides,' she says, adding that at this stage all the milks she is studying are commercially available dairy milks. I ask her if there is variation in milk depending on how it is produced. She says she thinks there is, but she's not sure exactly what it is yet. 'That's what we want to find out,' she says. 'If you look at the nutrient panel, there is no difference. The difference lies in the gaps, in the proportions of things not listed on the panels. The ratios of different acids and opioids, for example. That's what we are trying to understand.'

Solah says whole milk is good food full of good things, such as conjugated linoleic acid. Often referred to by the acronym CLA, this group of fatty acids has been shown to benefit heart health, reduce obesity and help fight cancer. Solah suggests consuming whole milk and full-fat Greek-style yoghurt, then adds that skim milk should never be fed to children. She rails against oat and rice milks, saying most mess with blood sugar levels because of their high glycaemic index. 'If a packaged food has more than six listed ingredients, it's highly processed and alarm bells should ring,' she says. She encourages people to get back to basics and opt for more natural, less processed foods. 'Cooking at home is a good idea.'

Bannister Downs milk sells for a bit over $2 a litre from my local shops. Some of the bigger brands are about that for a 2-litre plastic bottle. Daubney tells me that her husband Mat says their milk isn't expensive, it's just that other milk is too cheap. 'People aren't paying enough for it to be produced well,' she says. 'People want to look out into the paddock and see cows happily grazing on lush green grass and have absolutely everything looked after perfectly, and the workers paid premium wages. Mat says he can do all that, do it exactly as people want it to be done, but then the milk will be $5 a litre.

'We do what we can. The cows' welfare comes first. We don't push them. We're happy with them producing 20 to 30 litres a day each. We don't push them to the super-high levels of 60 litres a day that they go to in some of the production-focused dairies. All the push is on yield, yield, yield. We have to remember the cows in it. The cows are the start of it all.' Daubney says they focus on making the best products that they can and 'behaving like decent human beings and just hope that those over-arching principles will carry us forward in the long term.' I think it's a sentiment shared by a lot of good farmers and I hope, for all our sakes, it's enough.

The milk from the cows at Bannister Downs is piped directly to the processing room next door to the dairy. This room is high-tech. The milk travels through shiny stainless-steel pipes. Swish production lines peel the flattened, unfilled milk pouches (made of calcium carbonate, not plastic) off the reel, fill and seal them, then put them into boxes. 'We process our milk fresh from our cows within hours of milking,' Daubney says. (I can't help but think of the cream cans sitting unrefrigerated in my grandparents' dairy for two or three days before collection.) 'Our equipment is a bespoke design to achieve effective pasteurisation at a lower temperature,' she continues. 'It takes longer but we believe this creates the best-quality fresh milk.' The packaging, which Daubney describes as the most environmentally friendly they could find, is part of their ethos and may contribute to the taste of their milk, as it means there are no plasticisers leaching into it. (Plastic may contain up to 40 per cent plasticiser, which is added to increase flexibility. But it can also leach into food, especially if that food has a high fat content.)

Standing on the Bannister Downs viewing deck, I realise the milk comes into the building at one end in the cows and goes out the other end packaged ready for delivery and sale. The whole show is a strange mix of farmyard and high-tech factory. It's a slick and impressive operation, bankrolled by debt that Daubney says she and Mat try not to think about and a partnership with Australia's mining magnate and heiress Gina Rinehart. Not every dairy farmer has such a partner, nor the ambition or desire to create a branded product and undertake all the work that goes with it. But there are increasing numbers of such dairies popping up all over Australia, and I think they're worth supporting. Which isn't to say that the majority of dairy farmers, who supply the large dairy processors, aren't also doing their very best to produce the best milk they can. But the pressures of the supply chain can be crippling – just think back to the milk price wars we saw a few years back.

At that time, supermarkets were fighting for market share by dropping retail milk prices, in turn putting a price squeeze on farmers. Some dairies were pouring fresh milk down the drain. They had no choice but to milk the cows – or else they would have come down with mastitis and stopped producing milk – but the price being offered to the farmers wasn't enough to make it worthwhile freighting the milk off the farm. That's dire. It was a complicated situation, with farmers' cost of production rising due, in some regions, to drought. At the same time some milk producers were locked into long-term contracts with the big supermarkets. Ultimately, early in 2019, the supermarkets lifted the price of the milk on their shelves (from $1 to $1.10). But even that is very cheap milk, especially if we demand dairy farmers pay attention to all the animal welfare and land management issues we – and they – want addressed. I like the idea of supporting dairy farmers, and farmers in general, who have more control over their whole production cycle and I like the idea of a larger proportion of the money I spend on milk (and other products) going to the farmer.

The dairy farmers who sell milk 'at the farm gate', which means selling bulk whole milk straight from the farm to the larger dairy processors that collect milk in huge tankers, can only increase their income by producing more or cutting costs. They can't value-add or introduce extra product lines. They are price takers. It's the same dilemma that always presents to farmers who produce commodities. They sell their product at whatever price their processor will pay. They are the ones who produce the raw materials for the cheap food we expect to have available. Yet they still get pressured by the consumer to do everything 'right'.

But is it 'right' to be farming cattle in this day and age anyway? This is a question that has come to the fore largely since the release of the United Nations Food and Agriculture Organization (FAO) report *Livestock's Long Shadow* in 2006. That report dumped a large portion of the blame for greenhouse gas emissions squarely on livestock industries, particularly those involving ruminants – cows, sheep and goats.

Ruminants are so called because of the rumen, the first part of their four-part stomach system. The rumen is rich in bacteria that break down tough plant material; this is why ruminants can graze on plants that humans and other animals cannot eat. It is also because of these bacteria that ruminants belch methane, and methane is the potent greenhouse gas that puts livestock farming, especially cattle farming, in the spotlight when it comes to climate change. Mostly the focus has been on beef cattle, because most of the world's cattle are farmed for beef. But the basic biology of cattle is the same, whether they are kept for meat or milk.

In the normal course of their day, cattle (and other ruminants) consume their feed then lie down and 'ruminate' on it. The semi-digested food is brought back into the mouth, mixed with saliva and chewed. This is what cows are doing when they hang around in paddocks chewing their cud, their jaws working away; it's what the cows I watched being milked at Bannister Downs were doing. Along with the cud chewing, and the broader processes of ruminant digestion, goes burping. A lot of burping. And a lot of methane. Livestock are responsible for 37 per cent of anthropogenic methane emissions, most of which comes from cow burps. That was one of the facts that stirred things up when *Livestock's Long Shadow* was released, but it wasn't the only one. The report shook a big fist at livestock: 'The livestock sector emerges as one of the top two or three most significant contributors to the most serious environmental problems, at every scale from local to global,' the report stated. Biodiversity loss, air pollution, climate change, land degradation, water pollution, water shortage; livestock cops the blame for all. There were more alarming statistics about land use: grazing occupies 26 per cent of the world's ice-free land; livestock production accounts for 70 per cent of all agricultural land. (It's worth remembering that a lot of that land isn't suitable for cropping, or may be used for cropping and livestock, so it's not that if we removed livestock from farms we would only need 30 per cent of the current farmland.)

Livestock's Long Shadow made some concessions towards the importance of livestock to a lot of people around the world. Livestock are socially and politically significant and account for 40 per cent of agricultural GDP. Livestock industries employ 1.3 billion people and, critically, create livelihoods for one billion of the world's poor. One third of humanity's protein intake comes from livestock and livestock are a recognised way of alleviating malnourishment of impoverished people in the developing world. But the media storm that erupted after the report was released focused on cows and climate.

There was an understandable backlash from livestock industries and others at the claims made in the report. One statement in particular raised the ire of the livestock industries: the FAO attributed 18 per cent of global greenhouse gas emissions to the livestock sector and said this was a bigger share than the transport sector. But the way this comparison was calculated was misleading. While the entire life cycle of livestock products was taken into account and emissions calculated for every step of the way, the same wasn't done for transport. Only the so-called tailpipe emissions were considered, not the resources and emissions used to produce and dispose of vehicles. But the general idea that cows are killing the planet slipped into the mainstream consciousness.

FAO livestock scientists Anne Mottet and Henning Steinfeld have written that it is difficult and flawed to compare transport emissions and livestock emissions. They point out that, while people in wealthy countries have options to drive less and change their consumption patterns to reduce their emissions, there are 820 million people suffering from hunger, and livestock products provide important ways to alleviate their hunger. Mottet and Steinfeld have concerns that too much negative press about livestock farming could influence development plans and investment, which could exacerbate food insecurity among the world's poorest people.

Maybe that means people in wealthy countries, like us in Australia, who are more likely to be overfed than hungry, and who have more options available for what to eat (or not), should bypass the dairy and beef counters and opt for other protein sources, and leave the livestock products to people with fewer options. It's worth thinking about and it's definitely an idea with some appeal. The facts remain that cows burp methane, and methane is a potent greenhouse gas, and there are a lot of cattle in the world; about a billion. That's roughly one cow for every eight people on the planet. In Australia, there are 2.4 million dairy cattle and 21 million beef cattle. That's almost one beast per person, far higher than the global average. The obvious question is, why? Why are there so many Australian cattle?

Partly it's because we are a sparsely populated agricultural nation and export a lot of our agricultural products, including beef and dairy. But it's also because Australians eat a lot of beef; 23.4 kilograms per person on average in 2020, compared with a global average of 4.6 kilograms per person per year. That ranks us as the seventh-highest beef-consuming country in the world. (Americans eat around 30 kilograms each.) In recent years, red meat consumption in Australia has been steadily declining, although not everyone is reducing their consumption. (The red meat category puts lamb and goat in with beef.) Over the past ten years, about two thirds of Australian consumers have maintained their level of red meat consumption, 28 per cent of consumers have reduced their intake, and 9 per cent have increased the amount of red meat they are eating. So, are we eating too much? It depends who you ask and how they define too much.

The Australian Dietary Guidelines recommend consuming 455 grams of cooked red meat per week as part of a healthy diet, saying red meat is an important source of protein, iron, zinc and vitamins, especially B group vitamins. A quick calculation reveals 455 grams a week is 23.66 kilograms a year, which sounds like only a fraction more than the figure I just gave for our current average consumption. Except, one figure was for red meat and the other was for beef, which tips the scales towards us eating too much red meat overall. But there is also a slight discrepancy in the figures because of the word 'cooked' in the amount recommended in the dietary guidelines. Cooked meat weighs less than raw meat. Maybe we're not eating too much after all? (I did warn that these things can be confusing.)

A few years ago, the prestigious scientific journal *The Lancet* published a report that became very contentious. (What is it with these big-name reports that propose answers to all our woes?) I think in this case the controversy arose because of some of the numbers it came up with and the broad generalisations it made. Known as *The EAT-Lancet Report* it proposed a diet that would be able to provide healthy, sustainable food for everyone on the planet. It sought to address environmental concerns about food production while providing enough food and nutrients. It suggests about 2.5 kilograms of red meat per person per year. Which would suggest we are eating way, way too much. Time to skip the beef burger perhaps?

Richard Eckard is Professor of Sustainable Agriculture at The University of Melbourne. Eckard is something of an agricultural polymath, with experience in soils, plants, livestock, climate and carbon. His research and teaching focus on sustainable agriculture, especially carbon neutral agriculture and finding ways for agriculture to cope with changing climate. Eckard says there's no getting away from the fact that livestock methane is a big contributor to greenhouse gas emissions. 'But what that whole discussion misses is that twenty years ago we didn't know there was a problem,' he says. 'Ten years ago, we had opportunities to reduce methane by 10 to 20 per cent. As of next year, there'll be two technologies on the market that can reduce methane by 80 per cent. Follow that through. A bunch of options will emerge.'

The two technologies Eckard is talking about are Asparagopsis and 3-NOP. Despite both these sounding somewhat like they could be names for Star Wars characters, they are livestock feed supplements. Asparagopsis is a seaweed that, when fed to ruminants, can reduce methane emissions by 90 per cent. Yes, 90 per cent! The other, 3-NOP, is a commercial product that reduces ruminant methane emissions by over 40 per cent. That's a remarkable reduction. There's also a nice kickback in this for livestock farmers. Reducing methane emissions actually increases livestock productivity, because methane emissions are a productivity loss. If animals aren't burping methane into the atmosphere, they need to eat less to grow more. Even better, there are no adverse effects on animal health or product quality, and the changes in the rumen caused by the additives last not just for the animal's lifetime, but may be passed on to their offspring, provided they do not mix with non-treated animals. Wow.

The red meat industry body, Meat & Livestock Australia (MLA), is looking at how these technologies can be rolled out across the country to reduce animal emissions. The organisation has set an industry target to be carbon neutral by 2030. Dr Margaret Jewell, the MLA staffer tasked with leading the way to make this happen, says the target means that by 2030, Australian beef, lamb and goat production, including feedlotting and meat processing, will make no net release of greenhouse gas emissions into the atmosphere. Jewell says consuming the amount of red meat recommended by the Australian Dietary Guidelines is sustainable and healthy. 'People should actually feel very happy that they're eating red meat and it's good for them and good for the environment as well,' she says. I get a sense that Jewell is frustrated that people don't seem to be getting the message about how well Australian farmers are doing and the improvements to sustainability that have already been made. It's an echo of a frustration I hear from many farmers and researchers.

'We have made improvements in emissions intensity over time,' Jewell says, referring to the carbon emissions per kilogram of meat produced. This figure has come down because of improvements in animal diets and feed conversion, which is a measure of how much an animal needs to eat to grow a certain amount. Part of that is due to improved genetics in the animals raised, part of it is due to improved pasture varieties, and some of it is about better farm management. 'It essentially means that we're selling animals at the same live weights, but at a younger age,' Jewell says. 'And it means that we're achieving those sale weights in a shorter period of time. So, animals are out in paddocks producing methane for a shorter period of time.' Of course, that also means the animals have shorter lives. Whether or not that matters is an individual opinion. I once heard an animal scientist who had been involved in an international project with some subsistence farmers tell the story of encouraging them to slaughter animals at a younger age to reduce their environmental impact, both in terms of methane emissions and land degradation through over-grazing. The farmers wouldn't do it because their cultural values were that the animals should have long lives. But most animal welfare scientists will say that the age at which an animal dies doesn't matter anywhere near as much as the way in which it dies.

I ask Eckard if we should all stop eating red meat to save the planet. 'Right now, if you want to reduce your personal greenhouse gas emissions, reducing your red meat consumption will help,' Eckard says. 'Having said that, the idea that reducing your personal footprint will save the planet is a big fallacy.' I ask him what he means and he throws back a simple calculation. 'Well, only around 8 per cent of the world's population has any say in what they eat,' he says. He talks me through his reasoning. 'Only 16 per cent of the world's population earns more than US$20 a day and if you are living on less than that, you really don't have much say in what you are eating. You're just trying to survive. So, say half of those 16 per cent really have autonomy over their food consumption. That's 8 per cent. In reality, it's probably more like 1 to 2 per cent. Just the rich people in the developed world. You and I are in that. For most people, they're eating what they can.

'But if you are in that 1 to 2 per cent, and you decide to be vegetarian to save the planet, then it's going to make two thirds of no difference to global emissions. We have the technology, either now or emerging, to completely cut the methane emissions from ruminants so it's not even a question.' Eckard believes that over the next decade or so, Asparagopsis, 3-NOP and other similar feed additives and feeding strategies will be rolled out across the rangelands and livestock pastures of Australia and the world. He also says livestock will remain an important part of farming systems in many areas, especially in the developing world. The *EAT-Lancet Report* also says this, pointing out the important role of animal products in regions where people suffer from undernutrition and malnutrition. Eckard says, 'Through most of Sub-Saharan Africa, livestock are critical to people who live in subsistence agriculture.' He's talking about small-holder farmers who produce food for themselves to eat but little more than that; a literal hand-to-mouth existence. Eckard says there's no way we can go into those systems and tell people to get rid of their livestock, because livestock are the way they are able to buffer crop failures. He also says suggesting getting rid of livestock ignores that we can use emerging technologies to prevent methane emissions.

Eckard also points out that if you look at any farming systems from a holistic perspective, removing grazing animals does not make sense. 'A mixed farming system will always be more resilient and sustainable, economically and environmentally,' he says. 'We're now putting all these chemicals into cropping systems to try to get production up, but what we need to be doing is putting pasture phases back into the rotations.' Pasture phases enable breaks in disease cycles, improve soil carbon and, if the pasture includes legumes, can add nitrogen, as I mentioned earlier.

American research suggests that beef raised on well-managed pasture, where lands are allowed to properly recover after a period of grazing, may sequester more carbon in the soil than the cattle emit as methane. The American study highlighted the differences in environmental impact from different ways of raising beef cattle. It found that meat alternatives may have lower impacts when compared with feedlot-finished beef – that is, when the cattle spend at least the last few months of their lives in yards eating grain and other concentrated foodstuffs. But when cattle are raised on well-managed pasture, the plants fix at least as much carbon as the cows emit, if not more. They say that well-managed grazing lands may be better carbon sinks than forests, especially in dry environments. It's worth noting that most Australian beef cattle spend most, if not all, of their lives at pasture – they are 'grass fed'. But the American researchers also added a word of caution, because not all pasture-based cattle grazing is well managed. And when it's not well managed or regenerative, grass-fed beef can have a higher footprint than some feedlots. Once again, it all gets complex and nuanced. And there's a word that appeared in that last sentence that deserves closer investigation – regenerative.

I find it hard not to get excited about the idea of regenerative agriculture – regen ag or regen, as it gets called. The term itself sounds like it must be a good thing, with its implication that it is a form of agriculture that regenerates. It's an idea treated with enthusiasm bordering on evangelism among its devoted advocates, who say it is a step beyond being sustainable. But it's not without its detractors, who range from dismissive to damning.

In Australia, the clarion call to regenerative agriculture came with the 2017 publication of *Call of the Reed Warbler* by Charles Massy. It's a weighty tome of a book but early on Massy, a farmer and academic, defines what he means: 'An ecologically and socially enhancing agriculture – what I call "regenerative agriculture" – can reverse this harmful carbon-emitting signature of industrial agriculture. It can do this via various methods, but all are based around revegetation and inculcating healthy, living soils (that is, soil containing plants, insects, bacteria, fungi and other organisms).' Despite this sounding like a virtuous aim, regenerative remains a somewhat controversial term in many farming circles. It can be divisive. One of the loudest criticisms of regenerative agriculture is that, despite Massy's clarity, its definitions tend to be slippery and there are no formal certification schemes by which consumers and others can identify regenerative farmers and their produce. Regenerative farmers tend to be self-identified; if someone says they are a regenerative farmer, then it's hard to say they are not. And it seems that farmers who don't identify with the term think those who do are judging them for pursuing conventional approaches. There could be some truth in this.

I once sat next to a leading farmer at a regenerative agriculture conference. I asked him if he called himself a regenerative farmer. He scoffed. 'No,' he said. I ran through a list of defining regenerative practices that a speaker had just mentioned on stage – minimum till, soil testing, integrated pest management, integrated weed management, biodiverse plantings and shelterbelts, erosion control, crop rotation – and asked if he used any of those practices. He did. All of them. 'But isn't that regenerative farming?' I asked. 'Nah,' he said, 'I'm not a regenerative farmer. I'm just trying to be a good farmer.'

I found it curious that he so adamantly didn't want to be identified as regenerative, but I've heard the same sentiment from other good, conventional farmers since.

Christie Stewart from Wide Open Agriculture tells me regenerative farming is about a mindset rather than action. Listed on the Australian Stock Exchange, Wide Open Agriculture markets itself as 'Australia's leading regenerative agriculture company'. They define regenerative agriculture as 'a system of farming principles and practices that increases biodiversity, enriches soils, improves water quality, and enhances ecosystem services. It aims to capture carbon in soil and aboveground biomass, reversing current global trends of atmospheric accumulation. At the same time, it offers increased yields, resilience to climate instability, and higher health and vitality for farming and grazing communities.' Like I said, it's hard not to get excited when you put it like that. I have heard soil scientists dispute some claims made about regenerative farmers' achievements in increasing soil carbon, though. The argument goes that soil carbon is part of a cycle and in many agro-ecological systems it is largely determined by water availability (that is, rain) and soil pH, with more acidic soils holding more carbon. It's another of those complex issues that researchers devote lifetimes to studying, so it's hard for the rest of us to get our heads around, or for writers to explain fully in a few sentences.

Stewart works directly with farmers who are moving towards regenerative farming and basing their work on Wide Open Agriculture's defined principles. 'The difference we perceive between regenerative and conventional farming is in the farmer's mindset,' she says. 'We want to support the uptake of regenerative farming, and we believe that each farmer is at their own point along a "regenerative journey" – whether they have just started implementing zero till this season, or if they have been farming that way for the past twenty years.' Stewart says regenerative agriculture also takes in traditional agronomy, but rather than looking at how one thing may be out of balance in the soil and correcting it, takes a more holistic approach. She says it's about looking at the whole farm as an ecosystem.

From what I've seen, I think it's fair to say regenerative farmers look beyond immediate yield to a bigger-picture view of what is happening on their farm. Stuart McAlpine is one such farmer (and is also a director of Wide Open Agriculture). He says he has always been comfortable with the idea of diverting financial gains (in terms of yield and profit) to build soil, rather than chasing yield and then fixing any damage it causes to soil later on. McAlpine farms a broad acreage at Buntine, in Western Australia's northern grain belt. I visited his farm for a field walk on a sunny winter day.

'If you build the foundation in your soil first, the yield will come,' McAlpine says. 'Agriculture has focused on the physical and chemical aspects of farming and has probably ignored the biological. Soil biology ties the chemical and physical properties together. All soil functions are mainly carried out by soil biota.' McAlpine talks of connections in the way an ecologist might. 'It now seems that the interrelationship and transference of the microbiome is the key component of the health of soils, rivers, oceans, plants and animals and the restoration of biodiversity,' he says. 'Food and fibre production should be about recognising what is now being promoted as the bioeconomy and the major role it can play in planetary health. Ultimately, we are the beneficiary and to achieve this we will need to scale this so it becomes the norm.' It really does make sense.

Eckard reiterates the importance of livestock for subsistence farmers in developing countries. 'Ironically, to be vegetarian in a Sub-Saharan

African village, you would need animals,' he says, and talks me through his reasoning. The livestock are corralled at night. The manure is collected and used as fertiliser. The animals are used to plough the paddocks. 'If you didn't have livestock, you would need to buy in fertiliser and get a tractor and run it on diesel. The greenhouse gas emissions for that system are higher without livestock than they are with livestock.' He says it's also important to think more broadly about how emissions from livestock in those systems are apportioned, and that our thinking needs to move beyond cows emit methane therefore they are evil. 'If you take the greenhouse gas emissions and you say some of it is dowry, some of it is instead of synthetic fertiliser, some of it is power instead of diesel, some of it is to milk production for family nutrition and so on. Once you have apportioned it out like that, then the greenhouse gas per unit milk production is actually better than a high-producing, highly efficient Gippsland dairy farm. It depends on how you apportion the emissions. But you could argue that those are among the most efficient systems there are.'

Eckard remarks that today in Australia, dairying and beef are completely different industries; the average dairy farm is only dairy and the average beef farm only beef. He suggests that we have to look back at history, back to the times when Australian farms were more mixed than many are these days. It takes me straight back to thinking of my grandparents' farm – milking cows, selling cream, feeding skim milk to pigs, selling steers for beef. Or the wheat and sheep farmers I grew up among, who grew crops and grazed sheep on the stubbles. Diverse farming systems with inbuilt synergies and resilience. But the push for efficiencies is a push to specialisation and uniformity, as we see time and time again. The epitome of that may well be the humble chicken.

CHAPTER 8

Chickens

AFTER DRIVING FOR an hour and a half from our suburban Perth home, I pulled up at a farmhouse and a woman bustled out to greet me. 'The young pullets are over this way,' she said and I followed her to a pen behind the house. I selected four birds, paid the woman and drove off, delighted to once again be the proud owner of a small flock of Australorps. I have kept a lot of different breeds of chooks over the years, but Australorps are my firm favourite.

Australorps are, as the first half of the name suggests, an Australian-bred bird. They are big fluffy chooks, usually black but sometimes blue-grey and occasionally white. The breed was developed in the early 1900s to be a dual-purpose bird: that is, suitable for producing eggs and the occasional bird to grace the table for a Sunday roast. The old way was to fatten any roosters from a clutch of chicks and chop their heads off when they were a decent size while keeping the hens as layers. With Australorps, as with other dual-purpose, heritage breeds, it would take up to six months for a rooster to reach table-bird size. Roast chicken was a rare treat. Australorps are quite good layers and a hen can be expected to lay 200 or more eggs in a season. Yes, eggs are seasonal. Chooks 'go off the lay' in winter, mainly driven by daylength. When days start getting longer again as spring approaches, they come back on. But none of that works in today's production-focused systems. Artificial lighting is used to trick the birds' natural diurnal rhythm into thinking it's always laying season.

Australorps may have once been the prized bird of the Australian poultry industry but you won't find them in commercial production these days. Dual purpose birds are out. Specialists are in. And the specialists found in commercial egg production (layers) and those found in chicken meat production (broilers) are completely different breeds. The industries are also totally separate. Farmers who raise chickens either raise broilers or layers, much like cattle farmers are generally either beef farmers or dairy farmers.

People have been keeping chickens for a very long time. There is some contention over exactly how long, but it's in the order of thousands of years, certainly at least 4000 and possibly as much as 8000. Our modern domesticated chickens are descended from the Red Jungle Fowl of South-East Asia. Why this and not some other avian species became our close companions is not really known. But they have become ubiquitous with human settlement across the world. Romans probably spread them throughout Europe, but exactly how the Romans got them is a moot point as is their spread elsewhere over the globe. They may have gone to South America around the time of Columbus, but some scholars suggest they were there long before Columbus set off on his voyage. It's hard to disentangle myth and fact. It does, however, seem likely that early domestication was more for sport and religion than eggs and meat. Cockfighting was an obsession across many nations and the not-so-humble chook also featured, and continues to feature, in religious ceremonies in some places.

Today, the chook is a bird of global domination. As Andrew Lawler puts it in his book *How the Chicken Crossed the World*, 'Add up the world's cats, dogs, pigs, and cows and there would still be more chickens. Toss in every rat on earth and the bird still dominates. The domestic fowl is the world's most pervasive bird and most common barnyard animal. More than 20 billion chickens live on our planet at every given moment, three for every human.' Lawler was writing in 2015. By 2018, the global chicken population had risen to over 25 billion, keeping in sync with human population growth and maintaining the three-birds-to-every-human ratio. They are the most important agricultural animal on the planet.

Australia does its part in upholding the global chickens-to-people ratio. Like elsewhere in the world, at any one time there are about three chooks in Australia for every person. But even that doesn't give a true indication of how many of these birds there are because most of them are meat chickens and meat chickens have very short lives. The phrase 'at any one time' is the giveaway. The actual number of chickens hatched and raised in Australia each year is much, much higher than the 75 million you may have roughly calculated from the three-for-every-person statistic. The Australian chicken meat industry slaughters 590 million chickens a year to provide the 46.4 kilograms of chicken meat consumed by each Australian each year, on average. Chicken is Australia's favourite meat and makes up 46 per cent of the meat eaten in the country.

It hasn't always been this way. It hasn't even been this way for long. The worldwide surge in chicken meat consumption began in the late 1940s in America with a competition sponsored by a leading poultry retailer. The competition sought to find the 'Chicken of Tomorrow', which would be a 'broad-breasted bird with bigger drumsticks, plumper thighs and layers of white meat.' Up until that time, the emphasis in chicken farming had been on egg production and meat had been more or less a by-product – basically the excess roosters and old hens past their laying days. The competition successfully found the meat bird it sought and the era of the broiler chicken had arrived. From those original Chicken of Tomorrow competition winners, the Arbor Acres breed was developed. It remains one of the dominant breeds in the chicken meat industry. The Arbor Acres breed is now owned by Aviagen, which also owns the Indian River and Ross chicken breeds. The other big name in chicken meat breeds is Cobb-Vantress. Between them, Aviagen and Cobb-Vantress completely dominate the global chicken meat industry. They own the genetics that powers the production. Most chicken we eat in Australia is either Cobb or Ross.

In Australia, fertile eggs are imported to begin local breeding operations with the international genetics. These are the great-grandparents of the meat chickens. According to the Australian Chicken Meat Federation (ACMF), there are two or three importations of each major breed each year. 'These fertile eggs are hatched out in quarantine stations in Australia before being released to breeder farms,' ACMF says. The next generation is then created by crossing different breeding lines, carefully controlling the genetics to get the desired results. And the number of birds increases dramatically with each generation, until we get to the third generation. They're the ones that get eaten. In *Tamed*, University of Birmingham anthropologist Alice Roberts writes that 'a single great-grandmother hen, back in the pedigree flock, can have an astonishing 3 million broiler-chicken descendants.'

While those numbers are mind-boggling at one end of the scale, the concentration of ownership of the industry is surprising at the other end. In Australia, the two largest chicken meat companies, the privately owned Baiada Poultry and the publicly listed Inghams

Enterprises, supply about 75 per cent of Australia's chicken meat. These companies control 'all aspects of production from breeder operations, chick hatching, feed milling, nutrition and health advisory services, quarantine facilities, laboratories and meat processing,' the government agency AgriFutures Australia reports. 'The majority of chickens produced (80 per cent) are grown on farms owned and operated by approximately 700 contract chicken growers. The remaining 20 per cent of broiler chickens are produced on farms owned by the integrated companies or by smaller independent operators.'

Australian broilers never live in cages and pretty much all of them have white feathers. The images we all see of brown chooks in cages are not meat chickens; they are hens kept for egg production and we'll get to those a little later in this chapter. For now, let's stick with their fatter cousins.

All meat chickens arrive at the barn as fluffy yellow day-old chicks. For the first three weeks of their lives, they remain in the sheds. During that time they lose their fluffy yellowness and grow their white adult feathers. Until they are fully feathered, they cannot maintain their body heat very well and need to be kept warm, so the temperature of the barns is carefully regulated. This is why all meat chickens stay inside for those first three weeks. (As do all layer hens.) Once they are feathered, broilers being raised in a free-range system will be let outside by means of doors opening on the sides of the barns. (Birds that aren't free range stay inside their entire lives.) It can take the free-range chooks a few days to venture out, but once they do, the chickens will generally go out each morning when the hatches are opened, return inside as the day heats up, then go out again when it cools off. At night, they go back in and the hatches are closed to keep them safe from predators.

Along with the access to the outside world, free-range chickens are kept at slightly lower densities than conventionally raised broilers. Regulations stipulate conventional birds can be kept at densities of up to 40 kilograms per square metre. That figure is a little hard to picture, but it means up to around twelve birds per square metre when they are fully grown. The question is, is that enough space? The RSPCA says no, and to get their accreditation the birds need to be given a bit more space (a maximum stocking density of 28–34 kilograms per square metre, depending on the ventilation). Free-range chickens have the same stocking density as the RSPCA's and certified organic birds generally get a bit more space again. Currently, about 78 per cent of Australian chicken comes from farms accredited as either free range or RSPCA approved, or both.

The four Australorps in my backyard have a coop that is about 4 square metres and each of them weighs about 3 kilos, so that neatly works out at about 3 kilograms per square metre. Plus they get let out from time to time to nibble on the lawn and *not* scratch the garden beds to pieces. It's hard to imagine how crowded they would be if there were ten times as many. But when I look at videos of chooks in broiler barns, they don't appear overcrowded. They each seem to have enough space to move around, but they are certainly in a big crowd. There are a *lot* of birds in a broiler barn. As many as 60,000 birds per shed. Granted, they are very, very big sheds with tunnel ventilation and, in free-range systems, doors that open to the outside range during the day, but that's a big crowd to be in. I wonder if that's stressful for a chicken. Maybe it's a bit like being in a city – you don't know all the individuals and they're certainly not all friends, but their presence in your vicinity is not generally a great hardship and may confer some benefits. But maybe I'm anthropomorphising way too much and should stick to the science.

I asked animal welfare experts Dr Lauren Hemsworth and Maxine Rice what the evidence says. Hemsworth and Rice, and the Animal Welfare Science Centre at The University of Melbourne where they are both based, have spent a lot of time looking at animal welfare, including the welfare of chickens. Rice says hens can recognise between twenty and thirty other chickens. 'More than that and it's about judging friend or foe,' she says, but adds that this may not necessarily be stressful, provided other needs are met. Rice says there is still a lot of research being conducted to investigate this. Both researchers agree that my analogy of what it's like to be in a big crowd is probably reasonably accurate. 'Space allowance and the provision of resources appear to be more important in determining the type of interaction between hens than actual group size,' Hemsworth says. I take that to mean that the huge numbers in a shed are okay as long as there are enough food and water points and other things that chooks like, such as areas in which to dust bath and scratch and perch. So maybe the big crowd doesn't matter.

When the broiler industry took off in the 1960s, the entire emphasis of the breeding programs was on rapid growth. It came with problems. A lot of the breeding focus was on increasing breast muscle, which meant the birds were unbalanced. Their skeletons didn't grow rapidly or strongly enough to support their body weights. Breeding has changed. There is more consideration of traits other than rapid growth (although given that in the beginning rapid growth was 100 per cent of the focus, any consideration of other traits would be an increased emphasis). Aviagen now says its breeding objectives are around 30 per cent focused on animal welfare (by reducing aggression and feather-pecking, for example), 15 per cent on feed conversion and sustainability, 35 per cent on reproduction and fitness, and only 20 per cent on growth and yield. This isn't to say broilers don't grow incredibly quickly. When they are slaughtered at around six weeks of age, they can weigh 3 or more kilograms. Incidentally, they are slaughtered at six to eight weeks of age because that is when they reach the desired slaughter weight. The industry is at pains to point out that it's not because they can't live longer because they are too big for their skeletons; it's simply that they are the desired size.

Amazingly, they have eaten less than 2 kilograms – 1.6 kilograms to be precise – of feed for every kilogram of weight they have gained. In a life cycle assessment of the Australian chicken meat industry, sustainability consultants Dr Stephen Wiedemann, Eugene McGahan and Glenn Poad reported, 'As a food product, chicken meat is highly efficient. As an example, the total greenhouse gas emissions for the production phase (i.e. not including retail and cooking) for a barbeque chicken are similar to the emissions generated by driving a car to collect the chicken.' It also uses very little water. Again, Weidemann and colleagues say, 'the average roast chicken (1.7 kilograms) requires less water to produce throughout the whole supply chain than an average four-minute shower.'

The rapid growth of meat chickens is one of the things that has made chicken meat so much cheaper in recent decades. It means less feed is needed for the chickens to grow to their desired weight. It means they occupy the sheds for less time and one batch of chickens can be moved out, the shed cleaned and disinfected, and the next lot moved in quickly. The extraordinary growth of broilers is down to genetics and feed. It's not due to added hormones. Australian chickens have not been fed growth hormones for over sixty years. They're not on steroids. They're not fed antibiotics unless they are sick. All these things are myths, probably perpetuated because the growth seems so ... abnormal. It might be time the chicken meat retailers stopped putting 'no added hormones' and 'no antibiotics' on their packaging, because it makes it look like there usually are.

These aren't the only aspects of chicken meat production that are poorly understood by consumers. Meat chickens do not have their beaks or toes trimmed and males and females are used. All fresh chicken sold in Australia is grown and processed here. And, as we saw earlier, meat chickens are not raised in cages. It sounds like meat chickens have reasonably good, albeit very short, lives. But what about their deaths? Because, let's face it, even if we wrap it up in the euphemistic 'processed' favoured by the chicken meat industry rather than the more telling 'slaughtered' I tend to use, somewhere between the sawdust-strewn barn floor and the chicken curry on my plate, a chook died.

When the broilers are ready (in the chicken farmer's view, not the chicken's) for slaughter, birds are caught and put into crates and taken to the abattoir. There they are slaughtered, plucked, cleaned, cooled, graded, and dressed or cut up. Easy. Right? The RSPCA describes it thus: 'Once at the abattoir, chickens are rested in their transport crates or modules for up to two hours to allow them to settle from being transported. Chickens are stunned (rendered unconscious) before slaughter. In Australia, stunning occurs either by electrical waterbath stunning or controlled atmosphere (gas) stunning. Chickens have to be removed from their crates and be consciously shackled for the electrical stunning process. For gas stunning, birds are not consciously shackled but either remain in their crates or are transferred to a conveyer system that takes them through the gas. Once unconscious, the bird's throat is cut allowing the bird to bleed out and die.'

None of this sounds particularly pretty but opportunities for consumers to see it for themselves are scarce. The idea touted by many that abattoirs should have glass-walled viewing decks, or webcams, so people can see what goes on and make their own minds up about it, seems laudable. American animal welfare researcher Dr Temple Grandin is one advocate of this. As she puts it, 'Transparency has a wonderful psychological effect because people and animals behave differently when they know someone is watching.' So not only would glass walls have the potential to show people how their chicken meat (or any meat, for that matter) is produced, it could also help alleviate any mishandling that may occur.

Death is easy to shy away from. It's easier to not think about the chicken that died to put the flesh in the plastic-wrapped package on the supermarket shelf. But if we choose to eat meat, surely it's better to be informed about the processes involved in getting it there.

Then there's that whole other chicken-based industry. Eggs. In Australia, over 20 million layers produce 6.3 billion eggs annually, providing the 249 eggs we each eat on average in a year. Forty per cent of Australian layers live in cages. ('Cage' is the word the egg industry uses for what is often called 'battery' in public discussions.) The rest live either cage free in barns or free range (much like their broiler cousins). Laying hens were moved inside to cages so chook farmers could have more control over their environment, protect them from the weather and predators, and also from pathogens. While they sound like sensible reasons, the move has been a subject of great public anguish. The amount of space each bird gets in a caged system is small. Very small. It can be smaller than an A4- sized piece of paper. Granted, laying hens are not very big (much smaller than my Australorps) but, still, that's not much space.

Australian Eggs, a member-owned organisation that provides services to egg farmers, lists more benefits than disadvantages of caged eggs, in comparison with free-range eggs. The positives listed are mainly to do with chicken health, while the disadvantages are to do with welfare associated with behaviours, like reduced social interaction and inability to roam, perch, dustbathe or explore. Australian Eggs also states that caged eggs are cleaner (because there's less dirt), cheaper to produce and buy, and have a lower environmental footprint. As they put it, 'Every egg production system in Australia, whether cage, free-range, or barn-laid, has its advantages and disadvantages and there are trade-offs between different and sometimes conflicting measures of animal welfare.' It makes sense when they put it like that and, despite thinking it's a bit of a PR spin, I'm almost sold. But I can't get past the lack of space and inability to perform the normal behaviours that occupy most of a non-caged chook's time. For me, I've always thought of that as a deal-breaker and I've opted for free range whenever I need to buy eggs. And then I met Ian Wilson.

Wilson is a third-generation egg farmer and the president of the Commercial Egg Producers Association of Western Australia (CEPA). The Wilson family runs a small egg farm on the southern edge of Perth; they have a shopfront that sells eggs, poultry feed, pullets, manure and some other local produce. Most people only go as far as the shop. I get special treatment. I get to go behind the scenes and meet the chooks. First, I have to put covers over my boots as a biosecurity precaution. Once I've done this, Wilson leads me to the packing shed. We watch as two young women pick eggs off a conveyor belt and pack them into cartons. 'We're only a small operation,' Wilson says. 'So we pack by hand. In larger operations, it's done by machines and they can pack thousands of eggs an hour. Here, we pack about 10,000 a day in full production.'

We leave the women to their egg packing and walk to a large shed. Wilson talks as we go. He speaks in a steady voice with quiet conviction. Outside a shed a conveyor belt is spilling small eggs onto a rubber-lined tray. Wilson tells me the shed currently has young chooks who are just starting to lay, which is why the eggs are small. Wilson knocks on a door. I expect someone to open it from the inside, but no one does. Wilson pauses for a moment, then opens the door from the outside and we stand in the doorway and look in. There are about 4000 pullets looking at us. They are slightly built, brown birds, with a few white feathers here and there. Some are on perches. They watch us for a few minutes then go back to their business, sitting on perches, drinking from drippers or pecking at the feed. I am pleasantly surprised that the shed doesn't smell. At all. I mention this to Wilson. He says ammonia levels in the sheds are monitored and he points to the huge ventilation fans at the end of the shed and the flooring under the chooks. It is made of rubber and is gridlike, so the droppings can fall through to the ground below. Wilson tells me that when we go into the next shed, I will see the level of droppings is higher; over the life of the chooks, it will build up almost to the level of the floor. (The hens stay in the same shed for their commercial lives.) Once the birds' productive life is over and they are moved out, the flooring is lifted and the shed cleaned out and disinfected, ready for the next lot of birds. At Wilson's farm, the manure is bagged and sold.

I ask if the chooks move around the shed much, because somewhere in my research I've read that hens tend to occupy the same part of the shed for most of their lives. 'Well, see that bird there with the lighter feathers?' Wilson says, pointing to a perching bird that looks slightly different from the others. I nod. 'Every time I open this door, she's sitting there.' He leaves me to make up my own mind about whether that means anything or not.

Wilson's operation is free range but these young pullets are kept confined for the time being while they learn to lay their eggs in the nest boxes. 'Wherever a hen lays her first six eggs, that's where she'll keep laying for the rest of her life,' Wilson says. 'So we train them to lay in the boxes.' He goes on to explain how they are 'trained' by the area around the nest boxes being made darker than the other areas of the shed. Chooks will instinctively seek a darker place in which to lay, so this training is taking advantage of a natural tendency. Laying in the nest boxes makes it easier to collect the eggs and prevents breakages. After a few weeks, the mesh curtains surrounding the raised rubber grid flooring are lifted to give the birds access to the surrounding litter area. Once they get used to that, the hatches to the outside are opened and the birds are free to range, at least during the day.

Wilson closes the door and we walk over to another shed. Again, he knocks, pauses and then opens the door. Suddenly, it dawns on me: 'You're knocking to let the chooks know you are here, aren't you?' He smiles and nods. 'Yes. Smothering is a real problem in sheds. If the birds get a fright, they can bunch up in a corner and after a few minutes the first ones that got to the corner are dead from smothering. We knock to warn them that the door is about to open.' He points to electric fence wire on the ground just inside the shed and explains that is to train the birds to stay away from the door and away from the corners where they could get smothered. When chooks are confined to cages, smothering is not a problem as they can't bunch en masse.

This second shed houses older birds. As Wilson had previously said, the manure level is higher but, again, the shed doesn't smell. I notice that quite a lot of the birds are missing feathers. I ask if it is caused by feather pecking, which is where birds peck each other's feathers. It can be a problem in chicken flocks. 'This lot just seem to have had trouble holding on to their feathers,' Wilson says. 'Every lot of birds we get is slightly different. The breeders are always working towards breeding birds that produce more eggs with less feed. I think these ones have swung a bit too far. They're putting everything they have into eggs, not much into feathers. I've told the breeders that.'

There is a dead chook lying on the ground just outside the shed. I ask about mortality rates. Wilson lifts a clipboard file from a hook near the shed door. It's a record of daily deaths inside the shed. Most days there are four or five, often only one or two. I don't see any zeroes, but nor are there any numbers above seven. And there has been a spell of very hot weather in the past week or so and there are thousands of birds in the shed. I can't help but be impressed. These hens aren't yet at the end of their productive lives – they will keep laying for several more months. Their mortality rate so far is about 6 per cent and is tracking about as would be expected for a free-range egg system, perhaps slightly better than expected. CSIRO has reported mortality rates of up to 10 per cent in free-range layer flocks in Australia over their productive lives.

Wilson looks at his watch. It's ten o'clock. Time to open the hatches and let the girls out because they will have laid their eggs for the day. Wilson winds a lever and we walk around the side of the shed to watch the chooks racing outside. One climbs up into a tree. A few others slip through a small gate and into a larger paddock of grass. Most scratch around and peck at the ground. They look happy enough. But they didn't look unhappy when they were in the shed either, which is where they would have stayed if they were barn birds. I ask Wilson if he thinks it makes much difference to the chooks. He says he doesn't know, but that consumers think free range is better. 'We'll produce what the market wants us to produce,' he says and then he reiterates the thing he said to me on the phone when we first spoke. 'Caged hens are a lot easier to manage than free range. In the

1960s, when we first introduced cages, diseases and other problems just disappeared. Now, consumer pressure is seeing more free-range birds and all the old diseases are coming back, and more besides. In cages we never need to use antibiotics. In free range, we do. You never get internal parasites in cages but you do in free range.'

I tell Wilson he's messing with my head. I've always seen this as a clear-cut issue – battery cages bad, free range good. Now here's someone whose whole life is about chooks and their care and he's throwing doubt on my assumptions, because surely, mortality rates and disease levels, and the use of anthelmintics (dewormers) and antibiotics, count for something? Count for a lot. Surely being free of disease is high on the list of freedoms that constitute good animal welfare?

Poultry veterinarian Dr Rod Jenner thinks it does. Jenner is pragmatic but kind in a way that befits his profession. He tells me it's important to be careful not to get too emotive when talking about free-range and caged hens. 'A lot of the debate has been about public perceptions and community expectations, and I think community expectations bring into play a lot of emotive value judgements,' Jenner says. 'The emotional judgements that the community is making about birds and their good life is very different to my perceptions as a veterinarian.' As a vet, who is in among the birds on a regular basis, Jenner has insight into what the birds are experiencing and perceiving, and whether or not their lives are good. 'I've seen many, many birds in cages that are quite content, quite happy,' he says.

Jenner also confirms exactly what Wilson said to me when I visited his poultry farm: there are a range of diseases seen in free-range birds that aren't seen in caged birds. And they are very hard to control. He uses the term 'historical diseases' and tells me they were effectively managed out of the industry when chooks were moved inside – in both egg-laying and meat-producing systems.

'Those diseases are returning,' he says. 'We're still coming to grips with free-range systems and how birds should be managed to reduce disease. Avian flu is a real problem. In 2020 we lost almost 500,000 layers in Australia because of avian influenza. The risk is low but the consequences are horrendous.' Jenner predicts another outbreak of avian flu in Australia within the next two years, due to the link between wet weather and avian flu spread in wild ducks. In the UK, a widespread avian flu outbreak over the northern summer of 2021–22 meant that all poultry had to be kept indoors to prevent interaction with wild birds. After some months of indoor confinement, no eggs or chicken meat produced in the UK was able to be sold as free range. The restriction was lifted in May 2022 but the episode serves as a salient reminder of the risks.

Jenner says backyard birds are also a potential biosecurity risk for the chicken industries, and one over which there is very little control. I confess to him that I keep chooks. He admits he would too if he didn't work in the industry. 'Just keep them separate from ducks and wild birds,' he says. I don't tell him that I used to keep ducks and for a while they mixed with my chooks. I make a silent resolution that if I ever get ducks again, I will keep them well away from my chooks and also to be more vigilant with biosecurity around my chook pen. Avian flu is spread bird to bird, and occasionally bird to person, but person-to-person transmission has never been reported. So far. The world has learned that sometimes these species barriers are breached. I make another mental note to make sure any suspicious deaths in my chooks are investigated.

Jenner says another consideration is the limited range of anti-biotics available for use in poultry disease control and the associated issue of antimicrobial resistance. Before Covid, antimicrobial resistance was considered by the World Health Organization to be the biggest single threat to human health around the world. 'We've got to take that into context,' Jenner says. 'That's one of those sleepers that people don't take into account and don't get emotive about. The veterinary industry, and ag industry in general, is working very, very hard to be more judicious in antibiotic use. We use very few antimicrobials now. In fact, in the caged bird industry I'd say we use none. Because there's no infectious diseases in those flocks. The only time we use antimicrobials is in ranging birds and because the incidence of free-range farming is going up, so is the use of antimicrobials. So, we're actually pushing the tide uphill here, trying to improve our antimicrobial stewardship and, at the same time, battling these diseases.'

The RSPCA is actively campaigning to end the use of cages in egg production. They argue that their use is inhumane and that considering animal welfare to only be an absence of disease is outdated. The RSPCA says, 'Positive affective states in layer hens require not only the absence of disease, hunger, and thirst, but also the opportunity for hens to perform behaviours which they are motivated to perform. These behaviours include nesting, foraging, ground-scratching, perching, and dustbathing.' The relative importance of those different behaviours is actually not well understood; it's one of the areas animal welfare researchers are working on, but public opinion is very much along the lines that all these behaviours are crucial. Caged egg production has been banned in some overseas jurisdictions, most notably the European Union and Canada. There was talk of Australia introducing a ban to be effective from 2036, but that now appears unlikely.

Furnished cages are sometimes put forward as an alternative housing system for laying hens. These are cages that have more space and 'furniture' – a perch, a nest box, somewhere to dustbathe, that sort of thing. They are suggested by some as a way of balancing the hens' innate behavioural needs with the management structures that make it easier for health to be managed on a large scale. Wilson doesn't think Australian egg producers are likely to want to invest in furnished cages, even if they have the basic set up to enable a relatively easy transformation. 'They might be preferred today,' he says, 'but the public will likely still see them as cages. No producer wants to invest all that time and money in infrastructure that won't be able to be used in five years or so. It's too big a risk.'

I ask Jenner what sort of eggs he buys. 'Cage free or barn laid,' he says. 'From my clients. I wouldn't buy from a farmers' market because there's not the control on the egg handling and food safety. I dislike organic because we can't treat organic chicken flocks with antibiotics and they won't allow chickens to be fed meat meal. Chickens are not herbivores; they are omnivores.' I knew chooks were omnivorous – they love worms and bugs and need high-protein diets to be able to lay eggs – but by this stage my head is reeling. Nothing else in the research I have done for this book has confronted me quite like the things I have found out about chickens. I thought I knew about chooks. I thought my opinions were informed and intelligent. But time and again, I came across things that turned me upside down and inside out.

The egg industry, like the chicken meat industry, is dominated by a couple of breeds, most notably ISA and Hy-Line. As in the chicken meat industry, these too are international genetics – ISA stands for

Institut de Sélection Animale, a French organisation that bred ISA poultry. A click or two on the ISA website shows that the breed is now owned by Hendrix Genetics, an American company that also owns half a dozen or so other laying chicken breeds. ISA Browns are the most well known in Australia, but the company produces other breeds as well, notably ISA Whites. Hy-Line is owned by another American company. In Australia, Hy-Line Browns (and another laying breed called Lohmann Brown – I'm seeing a theme with the naming of these breeds) are hatched and distributed by Specialist Breeders Australia, the largest supplier of day-old chicks and point-of-lay pullets to the Australian layer industry. In layer breeds, the genetics are imported at the grandparent stage – so two generations later we get to the birds that lay the eggs that are sold.

Layer hens are quick-moving birds with bright eyes and personality, even though they all look pretty much identical. They eat voraciously but churn it all out as eggs. Wilson tells me his birds get 900 grams of feed a week and you can pretty much guarantee they'll lay six eggs a week, so they're producing roughly 300 grams of egg for their 900 grams of feed. They start laying around four months old, and continue to lay an egg every twenty-four or twenty-six hours or so for the next year. After this, productivity will drop off and the eggs will become fewer and the shells thinner, meaning a larger portion of the eggs will crack and break. When she's about eighteen months old, maybe two years old, a layer's commercially productive life is over. Spent layers are a bit of a problem for the egg production business because they're not worth much. A portion of old laying hens are sold off to be backyard hens, but most aren't. Most are euthanased. A lot end up in pet food.

And, of course, it's only the hens that lay eggs. Like many of us, hens have brothers. These male chicks are of no use whatsoever to the egg industry. They don't have the genetics to be quickly fed up to become table birds. They simply won't put on the weight like their broiler cousins. The male chicks are culled after hatching. It's an ethical issue and a significant production cost for the egg industry. CSIRO has done some clever genetic research and come up with a potential solution.

The CSIRO team developed a way of adding a fluorescent marker that is only passed on to the male offspring. This marker can be identified in the fertilised egg so they can be removed from production early in the process, before incubation. The way chicken sex determination works means that the marker cannot be passed on to the female chicks, so although the technique is a genetic modification, the female chicks don't have it. It is impossible for them to carry it. I spoke to Dr Mark Tizard, one of the CSIRO researchers involved in developing the technique. Tizard says male chicks are not something the public thinks about a lot. 'With poultry, the simple thing is that roosters don't lay eggs,' he says.

There are two methods currently used in the hatcheries to deal with the male chicks – instant maceration and asphyxiation. As Tizard puts it, instant maceration sounds dreadful and may look shocking, but it is actually remarkably humane. As an indicator of this, the RSPCA has approved instant maceration. 'If done appropriately, it is the most speedy and humane way to deal with the male chicks,' Tizard says. 'The trouble is we anthropomorphise. But the chick has just hatched. They don't know what is happening. They may get a feeling of falling but then they are gone. In an instant they are dead. There is no sense of fear.'

Whatever way it's done, the male layer chick is hatched to die immediately, which sounds unethical and wasteful. Tizard is convinced the CSIRO team has a workable solution, not just for the Australian egg industry but for the global egg industry. It hasn't been rolled out to the layer hatcheries, partly because of the GM technique involved in the process. Tizard says that, ultimately, the public will decide whether this is a great way out or not. He says the hatchery companies are also hesitant. But in mid-2022, Hendrix Genetics – the company that owns a lot of international layer chicken genetics – stepped forward and began working in partnership to test whether CSIRO's solution would really work and fit with how chicken growing operates in the real world. It will be an interesting space to watch in coming years.

Tizard says male chick culling is a multi-layered issue. 'As scientists we don't come in to make any moral judgements, other than if there is an issue, what can we as scientists bring to the issue to help to solve it,' he says. 'We also check along the way that it is completely safe; after all, if this goes into practice, our friends, our families, our children will encounter eggs coming from this, and of course we will be eating them ourselves.'

I asked Damien Kelly from Specialist Breeders Australia (SBA) about male chicks. SBA is the largest supplier of layer hens to the Australian industry (but they don't use Hendrix Genetics). Basic maths and basic genetics suggest they hatch as many male chicks as female chicks, so they have a lot of male chicks to deal with. 'We've been pushing to sell the males,' Kelly says. He tells me they have found a, so-far small, market for day-old cockerels supplying the domestic Asian market. 'They are sold to growers as day-olds and take sixteen to eighteen weeks to grow out. It's still only a small percentage at this stage, but there is a market there.'

He's not sure if they will adopt the CSIRO technology or not if it becomes commercially available. 'There is currently technology being used in Europe to determine the sex of the bird in ovo [in the egg] within the first few days but it is not commercially viable here in Australia just yet,' Kelly says. 'We work very closely with the RSPCA and we are constantly looking at new technologies coming to market.'

The European solution differs from the CSIRO approach in that it requires all eggs, including those with male chicks, to be incubated for a short time, whereas CSIRO's technology identifies the male eggs without any incubation. If the CSIRO solution is used to identify male chicks before incubating, it should reduce the cost of producing layer hens and solve one of the ethical issues in the egg industry. It won't solve them all and it will require community acceptance of GM technology in the production process. Tizard understands public perceptions will need to be handled carefully, even though the hens that are bred from any program that uses the male gene marker will have absolutely no trace of the marker in them. (Incidentally, even if they somehow could carry it, their eggs would still be fine to eat, the sorting marker is a protein that would not cause any harm; and as Tizard points out, the parent chickens live very happily with it.)

Public perception is important in all aspects of the chicken industry. We see that with free range versus other systems. But when we dig down, the issues are complicated to tease apart. Eggs and chicken meat are efficient ways of producing good-quality protein. Yes, there are ethical and welfare issues. During my chat with The University of Melbourne animal welfare experts, I ask them if the issues with the chicken industries are about scale. Dr Lauren Hemsworth says it's a complicated issue. 'To produce enough food to meet current demand, you need scale,' she says. 'There is a price point at which people will pay for welfare-friendly products. However, increased scale is going to still be needed to meet current demand. There are challenges in some large-scale systems, but it is complex.' She says we need to use science to inform our discussions and ensure high welfare in all systems regardless of scale. 'So often, it comes back to the human who is managing the animals, rather than the system itself and its scale,' Hemsworth says.

Poultry farming is like any other form of animal husbandry, or anything for that matter. There are some people who do it really well and others who don't do it so well. Somewhere along the line, I heard someone say that good animal husbandry in the chicken industries means caring for the birds, but they're not pets, they're livestock. Perhaps that's where I go wrong in thinking about the egg and chicken meat industries. My chooks are pets, with names (Parsley, Sage, Basil and Rosemary). Having a few backyard chooks is nothing like having a 100-metre-long barn filled with 30,000 layers or broilers, or even a smaller shed with 4000 birds like I saw at Wilson's farm. Between them, my four chooks will lay about 800 eggs a year for about five years or so. They'll cackle loudly each time they do so and look at me quizzically when I open the back door. They'll give me something to do with the kitchen scraps and contribute to the compost I put on my garden. When they die, I'll bury them under the fruit trees. It's incomparable to what has to happen to put 6.3 billion eggs into Australian stomachs each year.

I'm not sure what the answer is, but if I have to buy eggs, I'll look for ones that come from a small producer with a limited number of hens that get to run around outside – someone like Wilson, even though he doesn't necessarily agree with me that free range is the best option and even though the science tells me that scale isn't really the problem. I'm more comfortable now with barn-laid eggs, and less judgemental about caged layers, but I'm still part of that community push demanding free-range birds. It just feels better to me that chooks have the opportunity to live outside. But I know that doesn't produce cheap eggs to feed the multitudes and I honestly can't reconcile the biosecurity and disease issues. I hope free-range chickens will have somewhere to hide when hawks fly overhead, because that stresses chooks a lot. I liked it better when I had a more black-and-white view of chicken industries. For now, I'll keep a few chooks of my own to supply the eggs I want, but I know that isn't an option for everyone. As for meat, well, I'm not ready to give up chicken curry just yet (although I admit it has taken a lower priority in my meal planning since I started really investigating this). I continue to opt for free range, despite what I know about the issues such as exposure to predators and soil-borne diseases. But I also decided to check out another chicken-raising system a little more. Sitting outside the mainstream, pasture-raised chicken may offer some answers.

Southampton Homestead nestles in a valley surrounded by hundred-metre-high forested hills south of Balingup, Western Australia. In this idyllic setting, Jeff Pow and Michelle McManus produce pasture-raised chicken, duck and beef. The chicken is the mainstay of their business. Duck and beef are sidelines.

There is a micro-abattoir at Southampton Homestead. It's an unassuming building, reminiscent of something you might find at a mining camp. I stand just outside it where dozens of crates are lined up, each containing seven chickens; hundreds of chickens in all. It is a harvest day, as Pow calls it. He grabs a chicken from a crate and holds it against the white plastic apron he is wearing. A quick squirt of water to the back of the bird's head to soak the feathers. Pow then holds the bird by the body and places its head between two electrodes. One hundred and twenty volts jolt through the wet feathers and instantly render the bird unconscious. Pow puts the limp body into a cone, head down. He picks up a very sharp knife and makes an incision behind the trachea, severing the jugular. Blood pours into a bucket as the bird's legs twitch. Within minutes it is dead, having never regained consciousness from its electric shock.

Pow takes the dead bird from the cone and puts it to one side. When he has a few lined up, they go into a water bath – 63 degrees centigrade for forty-five seconds. Out of the water bath and into the plucker. The bodies rotate around and rubber nipples rub the feathers from their bodies. In less than a minute, they are perfectly plucked. Pow takes them out and, opening the door beside him, places the bodies into the small refrigerated room where the processors are at work. Heads and feet are cut off then the chickens are eviscerated. The internal organs come out in one piece. The liver and heart are put aside for separate packaging. The birds now look just like chickens you see for sale in the shops. In another section of the small abattoir, other workers weigh and package the birds before putting them into the blast chiller. From there, they will go to the distributor and from there they will be sold and they will end up on someone's dinner plate.

I expected to feel confronted by watching the process. I expected to feel queasy or unsettled. I didn't. The only moments the chickens looked uncomfortable were as they were held and squirted with water. Even then, there was no squawking and very little flapping. There was no struggle. I watched the birds in the crates on death row. They preened and rested. If they were at all stressed by any notion of their imminent deaths, they didn't show it.

Pow kills all his own birds, about 12,000 a year. He would like it to be otherwise but hasn't yet found anyone he completely trusts to do it. He doesn't use the word 'kill'. He says 'harvest'. 'This is our harvest,' he says. 'We see the slaughtering as just one part of the harvest. I am grateful to every one of these birds. Grateful for the food they provide and for the work they do in regenerating the pastures while they live here.' Pow and McManus raise their birds in chicken tractors, mobile pens that are moved across the paddocks daily. Some animal welfare researchers are critical of this approach, due to lack of temperature control for the birds and exposure to predators. Pow and McManus deal with these issues by waiting until the birds are fully feathered at three weeks of age before putting them out into the mobile pens; up until then they are kept in a heated indoor pen. They don't raise birds through the hottest part of summer. Maremma guard dogs live with the chooks and keep the predators at bay.

As well as the pasture and associated bugs, the Southampton chickens are fed a fermented grain mix, grown and harvested from a nearby farm. It takes about 7 kilograms of the grain mix to raise the chickens to slaughter weight at around ten to twelve weeks of age, which is more feed and slower growth than conventional barn or free-range systems. But for Pow and McManus, it's not just about the chicken meat.

'Food and farmers, that's what we produce here,' Pow says, referring to the residency program he and McManus run for people who want to come and learn about their approach to farming, so that they can go off and build their own enterprises. 'Thirty years ago, there were fifty-four small abattoirs across the south-west of Western Australia,' he says. 'Fifty-four. Do you know how many there were when we set up here in 2014? Zero. None. They'd all gone. We're the only one.'

Pow is proud of what they do at Southampton and the way they do it. He would like to see more of the same and has contagious enthusiasm about land management and growing food in a sustainable and regenerative way. 'Anyone can visit and stand where you are standing and watch what we do,' Pow tells me as the 'harvest' continues. 'One of our fellow farmers, Tammi Jonas, calls it radical transparency.'

When I visit at the end of summer, there is a tinge of green on the paddock behind the chicken tractors. Pow says this is from the nutrients (from the chook poo) and activity of the chickens being on the ground, scratching around. 'One day, once a year,' he says, referring to how often the chicken tractor sits on a patch of ground. The small herd of beef cattle benefit from the nutrient-enriched pastures. This looks to me like good chicken rearing, good meat rearing. But it comes at a price. The Southampton pasture-raised chicken retails at a little over double the price of conventional free-range chicken, which is already more expensive than conventional barn-raised chicken. I ask Pow and McManus if it is possible to feed the world in this way. 'I think we have to stop talking about "feeding the world" and using that as an argument against small-scale agriculture,' McManus says. 'We have to focus on local and regional food systems, and how food is produced – and industrial agriculture doesn't seem to be "feeding the world" anyway.'

McManus, who is a sustainability consultant as well as a farmer, says she doesn't think she and Pow do everything right. 'There are things we can improve,' she says. 'There are always things to improve. It doesn't all have to be done in one day. No one has to be perfect.' Pow and McManus buy their chickens in as day-olds. They are of the same international genetics used by the huge chicken corporations. 'Nothing else grows quickly enough to be economical,' Pow says. 'Heritage chickens are also much harder to process – harder to pluck and harder to eviscerate. It would take much longer.'

I sit at the dining table at Southampton with McManus and Pow and their current residents. We eat pasture-raised chicken slaughtered just across the way in the micro-abattoir. It is poached in white wine and butter, and served with roasted potatoes and broccoli. It is divine. We talk about chicken genetics and dream that maybe one day there will be locally produced chicken raised from local genetics here in the South West, something that adds to local food security and helps reduce the stranglehold of the huge international corporations.

'It would have to be able to reach slaughter weight by fourteen weeks,' Pow says. I guess we're talking about a new 'Chicken of Tomorrow'. We talk generally about farming and the environment and the importance of connection and good, wholesome, nourishing food. And, for a moment at least, I see the answers clearly. I realise I still haven't let go of hankering for the simple farming systems of my childhood, even though they obviously didn't hold all the answers.

CHAPTER 9

Pigs

'THAT OLD sow has farrowed,' Dad said. 'She's down the corner of the paddock and the boar is hanging around.' I was only seven years old but I knew this was serious. The boar would kill the piglets; they're not known for paternal love. The sow should have been moved into one of the farrowing pens before she had her piglets, to keep them safe, but she hadn't been moved in time and so had birthed her piglets – farrowed – out in the paddock.

'We'll have to move her and the piglets,' Mum said. She and Dad came up with a plan and told us our roles.

There were a couple of small shrubs in the corner of the paddock where the distraught sow was trying to protect her piglets from the boar. Dad went down along one fence with a bucket of slops – boiled wheat, oats and barley. Staying safely outside the paddock, he dropped a small feed trough over the fence. The boar looked across at the noise. Dad leaned over the fence and poured slops into the trough. 'C'mon!' Dad called. 'C'mon. Come here and eat, leave her alone.' The boar, tusks protruding out the sides of his mouth, grunted as he shoved his nose into the slops. The mother pig lifted her nose in the direction of the food but didn't move far from where her babies squirmed on the ground. As the sow was looking towards where Dad was dropping more slops over the fence into the trough, Mum ducked through the fence and grabbed a couple of piglets, small and pink and squealing the second she picked them up. Mum put the piglets into a bucket and handed it over the fence to my brother.

'Run!' she yelled at him, as she hid behind a shrub. Rick didn't need telling twice. He raced off, as the sow came charging across towards the fence where Rick was running, the piglets now squealing blue murder in the bucket. With the sow distracted, Mum grabbed more piglets and put them in another bucket, which she handed over the fence to me.

'She's coming back Mum!' I screamed, feeling tears in my eyes. 'You have to get out of there!'

'No, she'll follow you and the piglets. You stay on your side of the fence and run after Rick. The sow can't get through the fence. Go! Run!'

I picked up the bucket, heavy with piglets, and ran, trying hard not to bump the bucket on the ground. My arm ached. 'Keep going,' Mum said, coming up behind me, a bucket of piglets in each hand. The mother pig was at my shoulder, the other side of the fence, her great bulk snorting and shuffling along.

We followed the fence around and to the back of an empty farrowing pen, the piglets squealing all the way and the mother pig right beside us, with just the wire fence keeping us safe. We emptied the piglets into the pen. Mum leaned over and opened the gate and the sow rushed into the pen. The piglets clamoured towards her. She sniffed at the piglets then flopped onto her side, lying down, her belly round. The piglets stumbled around, finding teats. Sweet hairless things, tiny pink button noses and curly tails, squinty eyes not yet open. There were eleven of them, falling over each other in their confusion.

'They're so cute!' I said, delighted. But even then, I knew the reality. In six months or so, as soon as they were big enough, these piglets would be sent to market. That was just the way it was. We raised pigs for pork, bacon and ham. We lived in town but there was enough wannabe farmer in Dad that he had decided to become a part-time pig farmer, renting a few paddocks and pig pens a short distance out of town. Our pigs were free range, but we didn't call it that in the 1970s. It was just the way most pigs were raised. Pigs lived in paddocks. The sows were – all going to plan – put into smaller individual pens to give birth and raise their piglets, mainly to prevent the other pigs killing and eating the piglets. For most of the time, the pigs were in larger paddocks, with a big muddy waterhole to slosh and wallow in. They would coat themselves in mud to keep the flies off their delicate skins.

Like chooks, pigs are omnivorous. Their domestication was probably aided by their willingness to eat almost anything – leftover food scraps, meat, grain, grubs, vegetables and fruit – and their ability to turn it into meat. Wild pigs are indigenous across Europe, Asia and North Africa and were first domesticated around West Asia about 8000 years ago. Once domesticated, they were spread by farmers across Asia and Europe, sometimes being bred, intentionally or not, with local wild pigs.

But not everyone took to pork. Eating swine is taboo among millions of religious people from several different faiths, including Jews, Muslims and some Christian denominations such as Seventh Day Adventists. Yet in other cultures, such as some in the New Guinea Highlands, pigs are revered and must be sacrificed and eaten at every significant festival and rite of passage.

———

When Dad kept pigs, it was common for pig farmers to get off-cuts and meat scraps from butchers and feed these to their animals. This practice is now illegal in Australia; no pigs here (including pet pigs) are allowed to be fed 'swill', which is classified as foods, scraps or food waste that contains or has come into contact with meat or meat products. This is due to the associated risk of serious disease. They can, however, be fed processed meat meal and also fish meal. (The processing removes the risk of bacterial contamination.) Unlike ruminants, pigs have monogastric digestive systems – that is, one stomach – and they don't do well on pasture alone. They need other things as well, such as grains, fruits and vegetables, and a good source of protein. When Dad had pigs, he envied the supply of skim milk that fattened the pigs on my grandparents' farm so quickly. He also admired the intensive piggeries being built on some farms at the time, with special stalls for the sows to farrow, where their piglets were not in danger of being crushed by their mother's bulk as she lay down to feed them.

The move to indoor piggeries that Dad was watching in the 1970s had begun a decade or so earlier, around the same time so many segments of agriculture were being revolutionised and intensified. It's the trend that has continued to give us the intensive agricultural industries we see today. Dad never got a new piggery; his pig farming venture lasted only a few years before he gave it up and sold all his pigs. But the broader changes in pig farming marched on.

At any given time, there are around 2.4 million domestic pigs in Australia, spread across 4300 'pig production sites', as the pork industry calls piggeries. I stress domestic in that sentence because there are about ten times that many feral pigs roaming the country.

Pigs were brought to Australia with the First Fleet in 1788. Soon after that, some escaped. They are one of a multitude of introduced species that have survived very well in the wild and are an ongoing problem. They are one of the most damaging feral species running amok in the Australian landscape. I'll leave the feral pigs alone and concentrate on their farmed relatives, but maybe creating some sort of industry out of harvesting feral pigs could be a good idea for reducing their numbers.

As with other livestock, pig numbers have increased dramatically since the mid-20th century. Between 1961 and 2014, global pork production increased by a factor of 4.5, from 24.8 to 112.3 million tonnes. And again, as with other livestock, the diversity of breeds once found across farms has been greatly reduced. There are eight purebred pig breeds in Australia, of which three – Landrace, Large White and Duroc – dominate the intensive commercial industry. Ninety per cent of Australian domestic pigs now spend their lives indoors. The remainder spend some or all of their lives outside. Only the ones that live outside all of the time are classified as free range. This is only about 5 per cent of pigs in Australia. Free range sounds like it would be best for animal welfare, but the industry body Australian Pork cautions that free-range pigs are more exposed to predators, disease and the weather, which sounds just like the reasons the chicken industries give for moving chooks indoors. Except pigs also get sunburned, especially the white-haired, pink-skinned ones that dominate pig farming today. It's worth noting that being kept indoors does not necessarily mean being kept in small confines. 'Loose housing', as it is called, means the pigs live in small groups in indoor pens. But it does mean they don't go outside to wallow in mud and root around in the dirt. And some are kept in very close confines for at least some of the time.

A pig pregnancy lasts just under four months (three months, three weeks and three days is the measure often given). An average litter is around seven piglets, but it can be much, much more. Up to seventeen is fairly common and a team of Dutch researchers thinks twenty-two is not unreasonable. Amazingly, as sows have been bred to produce more piglets per litter, the number of teats they have has increased to enable them to suckle a larger number. Most sows have two litters a year. Compare this with the single calf a cow produces in a year or the one or two lambs a ewe produces annually and it becomes obvious that pigs are capable of tremendous production, which is likely one of the reasons they have come to be used in intensive systems. Moving pigs indoors to intensive systems solved some of the problems pig farmers like my dad faced, but brought with it others.

Pigs poo. And wee. They don't sweat so regulate their temperature by drinking water and urinating. They eat a lot (like pigs, you could say) and what their relatively inefficient digestive systems don't use comes out the other end. If a small farmer has a few pigs, the excrement is a bonus – it's great fertiliser. But when you put hundreds or even thousands of pigs inside, it quickly becomes a waste disposal problem akin to that of a town or small city.

Pigs are actually very clean animals with highly developed noses. They tend to toilet in the same area but it still needs to be disposed of once it's deposited. Dealing with piggery waste can be a problem. It is high in nitrogen and phosphorus and it can contain pathogens. Manure releases greenhouse gases – the pork industry is responsible for 9 per cent of the livestock sector's greenhouse gas emissions (ahead of chicken but behind cattle). In some modern piggeries, waste digesters turn the problem into an asset by converting waste into biogas to run the piggery. Others compost it or spread it on paddocks. In others, it remains a problem.

Overall, the environmental performance of pork production in Australia has improved in the past four decades. This is because efficiency and productivity have increased through breeding and new management approaches, including better manure management.

But what's it been like for the pigs?

Pigs get bored. They have a strong 'seeking' behaviour; they want things to explore. With nothing else around, they often turn to other pigs' tails. Tail biting, where pigs chew the tails off other pigs, can be an issue. It is most often solved in intensive systems by docking the tails and sometimes by giving the pigs something else to play with.

Confining sows individually in sow stalls, or gestation stalls as they are sometimes called, solves the problems of sows fighting and individual sows can be more easily monitored. The industry body Australian Pork says they were introduced 'to protect individual pregnant sows from fighting, which can cause both injuries and abortions. Sow stalls also allow sows to be protected while they are individually fed, so they will not be pushed away from their feed by a "bully" sow.' Sow stalls are about the length and width of a fully grown sow and do not allow the sow to turn around or leave. Australian Pork describes sow stalls as a 'highly confining type of housing that pregnant pigs on some farms are kept in'. The American animal welfare researcher Dr Temple Grandin has likened pigs being in sow stalls to a person living in an economy plane seat. Now it might be all well and good to spend some time in an economy plane seat, especially when there's an attractive destination at the end of the journey, but to live in one full time sounds torturous. To the pork industry's credit, they have reduced the use of sow stalls and now limit the amount of time a sow may spend in one. Australian Pork says, 'Today, we aim to ensure sows are kept in loose housing from five days after mating, until one week before they are ready to give birth. This period is about 105 days.'

That's 105 days that they previously spent in close confinement, and still do so in some countries. Much of the animal welfare research I looked into for this book singled out the pork industry in Australia as being especially proactive in addressing welfare concerns.

In part, these changes have come from consumer pressure, which has also seen an increase in the amount of free-range pork available. It's tempting to think that all pigs should just be let outdoors but this is a simplistic view. Grandin suggests that because modern pigs are bred to grow quickly and efficiently (as in, by eating less food), they do not necessarily have the traits they need to live outside. They often have sensitive, light-coloured skin with very little hair. They may be too aggressive to live with other pigs. We get a bit caught in a loop with this: we move pigs inside to protect them from the elements, then we selectively breed them to do well in confined conditions, then we decide they should be given some freedom, but we have bred out the traits they need to do well in free-range systems. When consumers develop strong attitudes to something like sow stalls, it's not as simple as opening up all the cages and letting the pigs go free. That would not necessarily result in good animal welfare. And there are other subtleties that get lost in the public debates.

I wanted to see inside an intensive piggery for myself but for months I was thwarted by biosecurity concerns. First it was Covid, with lockdowns and border closures, then Japanese encephalitis put the pork industry into a spin. Just when that seemed to be settling down, there was an outbreak of foot-and-mouth disease in Indonesia and all Australian livestock industries went on high alert. Biosecurity is a real issue in livestock industries. It can be tempting for non-farmers to look at biosecurity notices on farm gates and read into them a desire for secrecy that simply isn't accurate. Disease outbreaks can and do occur as a result of spores tracked in on shoes or clothing; the threat is real, the consequences potentially disastrous. Animals can also be alarmed when unfamiliar people venture into their spaces at unfamiliar times. I had all but given up on getting inside a piggery but then Stephen Hoffrichter told me I could visit his pigs.

Hoffrichter raises pigs in the two-storey piggery his father built forty years ago on the family farm at Esperance, on the stunning southern coast of Western Australia. (The piggery has spectacular ocean views.) He sells about 300 baconers a week, which he says used to make him a big producer but no longer does; piggeries, like so much in agriculture, have become larger in recent decades and many now produce more than this. 'We wean close to twelve piglets per sow per litter,' Hoffrichter tells me. He says if he didn't use farrowing crates, half the piglets wouldn't survive; they'd be crushed. That would raise serious welfare concerns and would also drastically reduce productivity. Australian Pork has investigated alternatives to the farrowing crate but have not found anything that maintains comparable piglet survival (by protecting piglets from death by being crushed by their mother).

It's important to realise that sow stalls and farrowing crates are different. Farrowing crates are the enclosures a sow is put into to birth her piglets, and she remains there until the piglets are weaned, which is generally around four weeks later. Farrowing crates allow the sow to stand up, lie down and stretch out. The piglets are kept safe in a separate section but can still nurse from their mother, and they have a warm place to sleep.

When Hoffrichter expanded his piggery a few years ago, he built the new farrowing crates a little larger than regulations stipulate. As I follow him along the alley between the pens, a sow is farrowing. A newborn piglet, still wet from birth and trailing its umbilical cord, is crawling around looking for a teat. Her older brother, born minutes before, has already dried off and latched on. The swollen belly of the sow indicates there are many more piglets yet to come. In the next pen, a dozen or more piglets clamber over their mother and suckle. Hoffrichter points out a tiny dead piglet. 'There's one that got crushed,' he says. 'It still happens sometimes with the crates, but nowhere near as much as it would without them. Where's the animal welfare in that? If you let piglets get crushed?' We walk on. Hoffrichter looks back over his shoulder at me as we go down ramps and along corridors. 'Don't slip,' he keeps saying to me. It's true that the footing is a bit slippery in parts. I am wearing a pair of borrowed wellington boots and disposable overalls supplied by Hoffrichter (biosecurity takes precedence over appearances). But I'm pleasantly surprised by how clean the shed is. It does smell, but it's not a terrible stench; there's no nostril-burning ammonia scent. It simply smells piggy.

'We don't hose out the pens,' Hoffrichter says. 'Some piggeries do, but we don't. We have that open drain and that gets flushed out. That's all.' He points out the drain as he explains the system. The floors of most of the pens are concrete and the open drain runs along one end of the pens. The water flushes down through and out to a dam, and from there is put out on the surrounding paddocks. We walk through the entire piggery. Hoffrichter hides nothing. He shows me the sows in loose housing waiting to be moved into the farrowing pens when they get nearer to the ends of their pregnancies. And he shows me the sows lying in sow stalls. They are tight for space, there's no denying that. They can stand and lie down on either side. They can't turn around. They have feed and drink. A lot of them are lying down dozing. Some are standing, pushing at their feed troughs. They look remarkably healthy. They are shiny and well proportioned, with good straight legs and sound feet.

As we walk along, Hoffrichter stops and looks at a small amount of a creamy coloured, pus-like substance on the floor near one of the sows. 'That's not good,' he says and goes on to explain that it's possibly a burst ovarian cyst or something similar. The sow will be checked and probably culled. There are no second chances here. 'If she wasn't in a stall, we couldn't pick up things like that,' he says. These sows have just been artificially inseminated. They stay in the stalls for about a month in total and are then moved to the loose housing once it is confirmed that the pregnancy has 'stuck', and then into the farrowing crates later. I'm not horrified by the sight of the sows in the stalls. Other than the one sow with the discharge and two dead piglets, there is absolutely no sign of any illness or morbidity of any kind anywhere in the piggery.

We stand watching the weaner piglets play in straw – Hoffrichter weans the piglets at four and a half weeks of age. He says it gives them a better start and that, by that age, the litter of piglets will weigh as much as the mother. 'Our sows produce as much milk as a Friesian cow,' he says. 'They're good mothers.' There are 150 piglets playing in the straw. They are ridiculously cute. 'The animal welfare people like seeing that,' Hoffrichter says. 'They like them being on straw and rooting around in it.' I have to admit that I do too. But then again, none of the pigs I have seen seems bored or distressed.

It takes almost two hours for us to complete the tour and during that time I have seen about 6500 pigs. The piggery is not a bucolic storybook scene, but neither is it a shop of horrors. The pigs are remarkably healthy and calm. Hoffrichter proudly tells me that his piggery is disease free. And also that he won a national award for best pork chop a few years ago. 'I must be doing something right,' he says with a laugh.

Hoffrichter has been farming pigs all his life. He speaks about it with passion and knowledge, but as we talk there's an undercurrent of frustration that keeps bubbling to the surface. 'Forty years ago, my Dad took me to my first pig farmers' meeting,' he says. 'In those days, there'd be 180 or 200 farmers at a meeting. The other day I took my son to his first meeting. These days, there's only around five or six there, and half of them are in suits. But the issues are still the same. The conversation is around the need for branding and quality assurance and traceability.' Hoffrichter is concerned about consumers' lack of understanding of what it takes to produce food, and dreams of making a film that goes right through the pork production cycle, sparing no details along the way – mating, pregnancy, birth, raising piglets, abattoirs and butchering. He thinks people need to know the realities of food production. He reckons we'd probably be better off if everyone still had a bit of land and raised their own food, but the pragmatist in him knows that is not the world we now live in.

'The thing is, we've got to feed people,' he says. 'We raise pigs for food. Some people might look at the label, at the quality assurance and welfare standards, but most people will just buy the cheapest.' Hoffrichter says the problem is that the price is determined by supermarkets and cheap imports. He says Australian pork is produced with about the best quality controls and animal welfare in the world. 'There's no control over those things with the imported product, but Australian producers have to compete with those prices,' he says. 'It's made it very hard.' He says he likes pigs and pig farming is a good way of life, with money coming in every week, but he's sick of the paperwork involved now and the pressures that come with being a price taker. He has no bargaining power when it comes to the price he receives for his pigs; it's dictated by the market. If farrowing crates are banned, Hoffrichter won't upgrade his piggery; he'll go out of pigs and leave it to the bigger piggeries that have greater economies of scale to play with. 'I'm a big small producer. I'll be the next to go.' That would be a personal loss for Hoffrichter and his family, but also another step in the ongoing changes in our food production systems that can be seen as a loss for us all. When we are thinking about animal welfare and making assertions from the comfort of our well-fed lives, we need to remember the wellbeing of farmers.

Associate Professor David Beggs, The University of Melbourne veterinarian and animal welfare researcher I introduced back in the Cattle chapter, says it is important to make a distinction between animal welfare and animal ethics. He speaks eloquently on the topic in podcasts and a TED Talk, and over the phone when we finally catch up. 'There's an official definition of animal welfare, which is how the animal is coping with the conditions in which it lives,' Beggs says. 'The reason we care about it is because it's how the animal feels.

'That's different to animal ethics – which is about how humans feel about animals.' Beggs gives an example of a dog raised for meat in Vietnam and a lap dog living in Australia. He says that from an animal welfare viewpoint, each dog is entitled to the same things, regardless of the human perspective on what its life is about. 'Regardless of what humans feel about it, the animal still has the right to a good life and a humane death. It's how we look after animals during their life and how their life ends that's important from an animal welfare point of view.'

Beggs says animal welfare arguments often centre around the extent to which we should avoid animals suffering. 'Most of the cruelty rules in most Australian states are about exactly that, prevention of unnecessary suffering,' he says. 'There's an important word there – *unnecessary*. In any life, some suffering is necessary. A good life, a life worth living, will likely include some terrible moments.' He uses his own experience as an example, pointing out that he, like most people, has had times of pain, sadness, anguish and suffering, but that overall, he considers his life definitely worth living. I can relate to that.

Beggs says that while animal welfare is a science that enables us to look at how the animals are doing, animal ethics is important because it gives agricultural industries social licence to do what they do. Social licence is a term first used in the mining industry around the turn of the millennium. It refers to community acceptance, beyond legal and regulatory requirements, of the way in which a business or industry goes about its work. It is something that is increasingly discussed in agriculture, at all levels and across all products.

'Social licence is really important,' Beggs says. 'When we raise animals and we kill them on other people's behalf, so that they can eat them, it just removes the death one step away from the people who are consuming it, and they become a bit shocked by the whole thing because they are not usually confronted by the deaths of other things.' Beggs says the risk for livestock industries is not so much that people will stop eating meat and other livestock products but rather the pressure put on producers as a result of animal activist campaigns. 'They do things that make them feel good but actually involve no personal sacrifice of their own,' he says, in particular referring to people signing petitions and making comments on social media. 'My worry is that the supermarkets are continuing to respond to these things for their own publicity purposes in the name of animal welfare when often it's got very little or nothing to do with improving animal welfare outcomes.'

Beggs is talking, again, about the distinction between animal welfare and animal ethics. Many of the campaigns about livestock farming are about ethics, not welfare. I've come to realise it's an important distinction. I don't say that to belittle ethics in any way – ethics and morality are obviously crucial to the human condition – but views on animal ethics vary greatly depending on cultural and societal norms, whereas animal welfare is measurable and definable. I also think that Beggs' comment about any life containing some degree of suffering is an important thing to remember. He points out that in the human world we applaud people who make sacrifices to achieve goals (think of sportspeople training for years for a few minutes on a podium), but in the animal world this is not the case. We tend to think farm animals should not make any sacrifices, without remembering that farm animals can have much higher welfare than wild animals. In this sense, farm animals could be seen as being rewarded with better health and welfare for putting up with not having the freedoms wild animals enjoy. 'Animals in nature die of starvation, predation, disease, injury or some horrible combination of these things. And if they were in our care, we would not consider it to be humane,' Beggs says.

University of Western Australia philosopher Dr Nin Kirkham says there are many schools of thought on the ethics of the way we treat animals in agriculture. 'There are significant differences between humans and animals, and these differences are relevant in working out what kind of treatment is owed to each species,' she says. Kirkham says this means that a pig has the right to be treated like a pig and to live a good life for a pig, but it does not have the right, nor the need, to be treated like a human.

'Some may argue that it is species chauvinism or speciesism to think that membership of one species rather than another should, by itself, confer moral standing on a being,' Kirkham says, as we chat over coffee. 'However, using the notion of speciesism to make claims that animals have the same kinds of rights or moral status as humans is problematic.' She points out that humans are the only moral creatures; we are the only ones that concern ourselves about what is and isn't 'right'. 'Unlike many moral philosophers, I think being a human being grants you a moral status,' she says. 'That you are not just a member of the species *Homo sapiens*, but a human being, has moral relevance. It is relevant to the kinds of things that it is okay to do to another human being, and the kinds of things that can be allowed to be done to you and not be done to you. And that is different from what is okay to do to other species. We should not mix that up.'

I ask how this view fits with something like the argument that a pig is probably as intelligent as a dog, and if that is relevant. (I say probably because inter-species intelligence comparisons are fraught with difficulty.) Kirkham quietly collects her thoughts before she speaks. 'I don't think the principal reason that we give something moral standing is because of its possession of particular kinds of capacities,' she says. 'Capacities are morally relevant but they're not the full story.' She gives the example of a chimpanzee having about the same sort of cognitive capacities as a toddler. 'If a human toddler stayed at that level due to some accident or misfortune we would consider it a tragedy,' Kirkham says. 'But if a chimp stays at that level, it's the natural development of a chimp. Right? So the cognitive capacities play different roles in our understanding of the life cycle and what is good for those entities. The way its life naturally unfolds should help us determine what is good for it.'

I ask Kirkham about what this means for the idea of raising animals to kill them for food. She tells me she's perfectly comfortable with animals dying so that she can eat meat. 'You have to remember,' she says, 'that if the vegans have their way, it won't be a question of whether pigs and cows die. It will be a question of whether they live at all. If we don't eat beef, there will be no cows, because vegans won't want the milk either. There won't be chickens and there won't be cows and there won't be sheep and there won't be pigs. They just won't exist. I would rather a cow lived a good cow life and I got to eat it as well rather than they didn't exist at all.'

Of course, not everyone agrees.

Australian philosopher Professor Peter Singer argues that 'of all the ways in which we affect animals, the one most in need of justification today is raising them for food.' Singer, author of the 1975 book *Animal Liberation*, which is accurately subtitled 'The definitive classic of the animal movement', hasn't eaten meat since the early 1970s. The book is a call to vegetarianism. He writes, 'The people who profit by exploiting large numbers of animals do not need our approval. They need our money.' And further, 'Hence the need for each of us to stop buying the products of modern farming – even if we are not convinced that it would be wrong to eat animals who have lived pleasantly and died painlessly.' It's pretty strong stuff. Singer calls for an end to all livestock farming and also to the use of animals in scientific experiments. In a more recent book, *Ethics in the Real World*, Singer writes that his 'own view is that being a vegetarian or vegan is not an end in itself, but a means toward reducing both human and animal suffering, and leaving a habitable planet to future generations.' He writes that '*if* there is no serious ethical objection to killing animals, as long as they have had good lives, then being selective about the animal products you eat could provide an ethically defensible diet.' That's his emphasis on the *if* and, on this point, Singer concludes, 'Going vegan is a simpler choice that sets a clear-cut example for others to follow.'

In *Animal Liberation*, Singer writes that animals are 'treated like machines that convert low-priced fodder into high-priced flesh', leading to the use of methods that will reduce production costs. He also writes that 'killing animals for food (except when necessary for sheer survival) makes us think of them as objects we can use casually for our own nonessential purposes.' Singer goes on: 'Given what we know about human nature, as long as we continue to think of animals in this way we will not succeed in changing the attitudes that, when put into practice by ordinary human beings, lead to disrespect – and hence mistreatment – for the animals.' I take issue with this. I think I must have a rosier view of humanity than Singer does, certainly of farmers. I also don't think that valuing an animal's utility necessarily means it won't be cared for. Often, the contrary will apply.

Beggs disagrees with people who think we should not farm animals but says he respects their right to hold their views. In particular, he disagrees with 'those that hold the view that, because we have to kill them, we should not have had them in the first place.' He says, 'I worry that this philosophy is misguided because death and suffering still happen with food crops and with plant-based fibre, but they're just one step further out of sight. I think the world would be a better place if we all spent our time trying to maximise happiness and minimise suffering and we didn't try simply to avoid death.' Beggs talks mostly about cattle, but his ideas are largely transferable across livestock industries.

'I think our farmers should celebrate the animal welfare outcomes and the biodiversity that can come from pasture-based farming,' he says. 'I love that our farms can coexist with birds and snakes and trees and all manner of wildlife, albeit at lower levels than if there were no farms. I'm content with the ethics of farming where cows can choose to walk or sit for most of the day, where they can be members of a herd and they can feel the satisfaction of social interaction. Where they can experience moments of pleasure, albeit that there may also be moments of suffering, and they can experience contentment, even if it's not 100 per cent of the time. Where they can have a life worth living.'

Beggs also says it is important that livestock industries continue to improve animal welfare. 'Farmers should be transparent about the way they manage animal welfare and animal welfare risks,' he says. 'Continuous improvement in time is a good thing to work on.' Scientists such as Beggs, and Rice and Hemsworth, whom I referred to earlier, work towards quantifying animals' welfare and establishing what different animals need to have good lives. That's the science of animal welfare. 'But science can only tell you facts,' Beggs says, 'It can't tell you whether they are good or not.'

To decide whether we should or should not do something, we need morals and ethics. Kirkham explains how we use relational categories to manage our moral interactions. She uses the distinction of how we treat family differently from friends, who are also treated differently from strangers. Those distinctions are important in how we navigate our way through life. Similarly, she says, we have different categories for pets and livestock and wild animals, and the individuals within those categories are treated differently depending on our understandings of what is appropriate treatment for those categories. (Like my chooks compared with those I saw at Wilson's farm; welfare is important in both situations, but the lives led are different.)

As Kirkham talks, I am reminded of something I observed during a visit to an outback sheep station. While walking around near the homestead, I noticed an interesting little pen with a swish cubby-house style shelter, which I was told had been used to house a pet sheep. The pet sheep had fallen into disrepute by eating the homestead vegetable garden and the station manager's wife wanted it gone. The station manager was fond of the pet sheep so he transported it hundreds of kilometres to his brother's farm where it could live a comfortable life as a pet, without eating the vegetable garden. Meanwhile, several thousand sheep lived out in the huge paddocks of the sheep station. They were primarily raised for wool, but some would be sold off for meat, and the station manager himself regularly slaughtered one or two to supply meat for the cookhouse. I asked him about the apparent contradiction between these things. He looked directly at me and said there was no contradiction. It was simple, he said: 'You don't eat pets.' I tell this story to Kirkham and she nods. 'Exactly,' she says. 'There is a difference.' She says this is at the heart of non-farmers' lack of understanding of how farmers treat livestock, because if you don't see a livestock category as being different from a pet category, then you expect all animals to be treated like pets. 'But they're different,' Kirkham says. 'And they're allowed to be different. There are philosophers who say that's irrational and you need to focus on the facts independent of any kind of pre-existing normative constraints or expectations. But that is not realistic. When we get to the heart of what it is to be a moral being, I believe we see that relationality is at the heart of morality.' Kirkham says that to try to relate to all living things as equal is a very difficult position to maintain, because it's not actually how we exist and behave in the world.

That is not to say that we don't have moral duties to other species. Just as we have moral duties to strangers. For Kirkham, this comes back to our moral obligation to enable animals to live appropriate lives. For a sheep to live out its 'sheepness' and a pig to live out its 'pigness'. I think this is crucial. I am still not entirely sure that a pig living inside a shed for its entire life gets to live out its pigness, although the ones I saw in Hoffrichter's piggery were certainly not distressed and did appear to live reasonably good lives. But I'm struggling to let go of the idea that pigs need to be able to root around in the ground, wallow in mud and build nests for their young (although not in the corner of the paddock where the other pigs and boar have access). I think a free-range pig has a better chance of doing these things, but I understand that brings with it higher production costs and higher prices for the consumer. I also recognise that keeping large numbers of pigs free range can bring with it a wide range of environmental concerns, such as nutrient runoff and land degradation. Free-range pigs are harder to manage in many ways, at least at scale. Yet, I'm still drawn towards livestock being kept outside for most of the time, even though I am well aware of the difficulties and the risks they may face out there.

CHAPTER 10

Sheep

Two friends dropped in at my house separately, a couple of days apart, in the middle of a cold wet winter. The first, a part-time farmer (I'll call him Steve, but that's not his name) was fresh back from checking his sheep. He lives and works in the city but has a small farm, an hour and a half away, where he raises sheep. He runs a few hundred ewes and sells the lambs as prime lamb. 'How's lambing going?' I asked as he came through the door. Steve groaned, ran a hand over an anguished face. 'It's terrible,' he said. 'This last deluge caught us unprepared. So many newborn lambs that we couldn't get to shelter. We lost so many.' He shook his head. 'I have to get things set up better. I need more shelter for the lambing ewes.' The lack of shelter in his lambing paddock is a sore point for him. I know the backstory.

The previous year my husband, our kids and I had helped Steve plant thousands of seedling shrubs in a sandy paddock. Our labour was free but the venture cost Steve thousands of dollars in ground preparation and seedlings. The native shrubs were carefully selected to provide forage and shelter. The plan was that once the shrubs were established, the paddock would provide a safe place in which ewes could lamb. The newborn lambs would be able to hunker down against the shrubs, protected from wind and rain. It would also provide summer feed when pastures were scant. And it would help stop the light sands of the paddock from blowing away, while also providing habitat for native wildlife. What a fabulous win-win-win-win situation. My family was excited to be involved in such a venture and happily spent the day in the dust and dirt as we placed the seedlings in the prepared furrows. Steve went back a couple of times over the coming weeks and watered the shrubs. (Quite a time-consuming and difficult exercise, considering the size of the area and the lack of irrigation.) The winter that year was very dry and, despite these efforts, hardly any of the thousands of planted shrubs survived. Steve's nursery paddock didn't eventuate so when the dry winter of that year was followed by a wet winter the next year his ewes had little shelter when they lambed. He walked the paddocks picking up dead lambs to prevent them from attracting predators that might come in for easy pickings and disturb the remaining ewes and lambs, exacerbating the carnage. He was distraught and could barely talk about the loss.

My second visitor dropped in a couple of days after Steve. I'll call her Suzie, but that's not her name either. Suzie too had just arrived back in Perth after a trip to the country, and she too had a sheep story to tell. 'I stopped on the side of the highway for a quick pee and right there in the paddock was a dead lamb,' she said. 'It was just left there to rot. Disgusting.' As she was about to drive away, Suzie noticed a farm ute entering a driveway a little way along. She flagged down the farmer and had a conversation with him about the dead lamb. It left her upset and convinced that the farmer didn't care about his sheep at all. 'There are laws, you know,' Suzie said to me. 'Farmers have to provide shelter for their animals. It's just not right they are left out in the paddocks with nothing. It was freezing out there.' Her tale stood in stark contrast to my observations of Steve's experience and concern.

I'm confident that most, if not all, farmers seeing a struggling animal that could not be saved would put it out of its misery – the humane death good welfare requires. But there will be unfortunate occasions when death occurs in a paddock before any intervention is possible. That death, while regrettable, will not be met with the same level of anguish as the death of a beloved pet. That's the reality. And it may be at the heart of why some people oppose livestock farming, the inability or unwillingness to define or accept a difference between the lives of livestock and pets. I've come to think this distinction, and the distinction between animal ethics and animal welfare, are at the heart of conflict over how animals should and shouldn't be treated in farming. Too often, things that are paired off to be argued and debated don't really belong on the same page. Same animal, different situation, different concept. Same welfare considerations; different ethics. I know I see the categories separately, and that I draw arbitrary lines within species, as well as between species. I eat chicken but not my pet chooks. I eat cows but not horses. I'm comfortable eating sheep but still not entirely comfortable eating pork. I wouldn't eat dog. I'm not saying it's logical. It's just the categories I operate within, and they are different from other people's. But I feel very strongly that all animals, regardless of the reason they are raised, should be kept healthy and free of disease and be able to express their innate behaviours. Those things, to me, are welfare considerations. And my ethics say welfare is important.

In the first days after birth, lambs are vulnerable. It's an uncomfortable topic to talk about, but research shows that around a fifth of lambs die between birth and weaning. Lamb loss is an issue that is recognised within the livestock industry and considerable research is directed towards addressing it, because of its welfare implications and also the financial cost it carries. And there are a lot of sheep farmers doing all they can to ensure as many lambs that are conceived actually make it through to gambolling around the paddock and, let's face it, to the saleyards and from there to abattoirs and finally onto our plates. Australian farmer and writer Anika Molesworth writes eloquently of the farmer's responsibility in this regard in her book *Our Sunburnt Country*: 'To create life with the intention of sacrificing it may seem to some a peculiar thing to do … There is a weight to that role that is hard to describe.' Later she writes, 'Food is life. And it's this understanding that carries the weight of a farmer's role and gives an importance to their work that cannot be overstated.'

Tim and Georgie Leeming farm over 1500 hectares in western Victoria. It's good sheep country, with rolling hills cut through by tree-lined creeks. It's into the sheltered area along the creeks that the Leemings put their ewes when they are about to have triplets. They use portable electric fences to cut the long creek-line paddocks up into small cells and put just ten to fifteen ewes into each cell. 'If you have a couple of ewes lambing under the same tree in the same hour and they're each having multiple lambs, it's potential chaos,' Tim Leeming says. 'The chances of mis-mothering are high. Around 90 per cent of lamb and ewe mortality occurs between late pregnancy and the first two days of lactation. Since we started using tight joinings and tight lambing times with small mobs, we've significantly reduced our ewe and lamb mortality.'

Joining is the somewhat euphemistic term livestock farmers use to describe mating. It's the period of time in which the male animal is put in the paddock with the females – in this case, the rams in with the ewes. With sheep, farmers will generally run one ram for every fifty ewes in the mob and generally they run in mobs of a few hundred or more ewes. Still, Murdoch University research has shown that most of the lambs in a mob will come from a small number of rams – most of the rams out there aren't doing much while a few are 'working' very, very hard. So to speak. The same research also showed that most pairs of lamb twins actually have two fathers. Interesting!

When Leeming says they run 'tight joinings' he means the rams go in with the ewes for a very short time – in his case, as little as two weeks. It's more common for farmers to 'put the rams in' for five or six weeks, or even longer, to make sure each ewe has a chance to ovulate while within cooee of a ram, because if she doesn't ovulate she won't accept any ram's advances. And he won't be particularly interested in her anyway. The Leemings get around this problem by running 'teaser' rams with the ewes. Teasers are vasectomised rams; they look and behave like fertile rams but they shoot blanks. Their presence in the ewe flock gets the ewes in the mood and stimulates them to ovulate. The teasers are then taken out of the flock and the 'real' rams put in. Being on good feed also helps bring ewes into ovulation, as it does with many animals. The Leemings put the rams in with the ewes for a second joining a few weeks after the first, but around three quarters of their ewes conceive in the first joining.

After joining, almost all Australian ewes stay out on pasture, with some extra feed if required. A lot of sheep produce twins, or even triplets, and very occasionally quads. It's good for farmers to know just how many lambs a ewe is carrying and best practice these days involves ewes being scanned. Dust-proof ultrasound scanners are used by specialist operators to check the ewes' pregnancy status. Ewes are then drafted in separate mobs depending on whether they are carrying singles, twins, triplets or haven't managed to get pregnant. The non-pregnant ewes are called 'dries' and what happens to them depends on the farmer's approach to such things. Often they are culled, another euphemism. This usually means they are sent to slaughter, but they may also be sold to a farmer who will give them another try at getting pregnant. Most ewes will produce a lamb (or two or three) each year for somewhere between five and eight years before being culled from the flock. Their gestation period is a little under five months and lambs are usually weaned around three months of age. The ewes spend the other four months of the year recovering from pregnancy and lactation and getting in condition for the next joining period. (If they are a wool-producing breed, they will be shorn sometime during the year as well.)

Knowing how many lambs a ewe is carrying helps a farmer provide her with the right amount of food. She needs enough to make sure the lambs grow well and that she can produce a good quantity of milk after giving birth. But not so much that she gets overly fat or produces too big a lamb, or lambs, because that leads to no end of difficulties with birth.

The idea behind a tight joining and scanning for pregnancy status is to make sure as many lambs are born within a short period of time as possible. By doing this, all the lambs are close to the same age and size, which makes them easier to handle. The first big event this helps with is lamb marking. This is where lambs are given various vaccinations, ram lambs castrated, tails docked and lambs 'marked', as in given an ear tag to identify them. The ear tag gives an individual identification to the lamb and, in some cases is electronic. The animal can then be followed throughout its life – paddock to plate, as is said. At this stage, electronic identification (eID to those in the game) is mandatory in Victoria but not elsewhere in Australia, although some form of identification is compulsory across the nation. In theory, this means that sheep can easily be traced, which can be very important in the event of disease outbreaks or other biosecurity challenges. Similar systems are in place for all Australian livestock.

Australia is a fairly clean place as far as sheep diseases go and is free of some of the devastating pathogens that are endemic elsewhere, such as those that cause foot-and-mouth disease (although at the time of writing the Indonesian FMD outbreak was potentially threatening that). If you are a sheep, Australia is a pretty good place to live.

Except for blowflies.

If you're a sheep, or a sheep farmer for that matter, the sound of blowflies is more than an annoying buzz. Flystrike – where blowflies lay eggs that hatch into maggots that feed on the sheep's flesh – is a major problem for Australian sheep and sheep farmers. It's as disgusting and painful as it sounds. Flystrike is estimated to cost the Australian sheep industry more than $200 million annually in lost productivity, control and management, not to mention the associated animal welfare issue. While all sheep can be affected by flystrike, the problem is most prevalent in Merinos, which are the sheep most commonly raised in Australia. About 30 million of the 40 million breeding ewes in Australia are Merinos. Australian Merinos are noted for doing well in harsh conditions and producing a lot of exceptional wool. They also tend to have wrinkly skin, especially around the breech area: that is, around their backsides. This can get very mucky, despite annual crutching and vigilant control of internal parasites (having worms makes sheep poo runnier, so it makes the wool dirtier – I'm sure you appreciated that detail!). When it all gets mucky, flies find it particularly attractive.

The standard approach to preventing flystrike in Australian Merinos has long been a procedure called mulesing, developed by a South Australian Merino breeder named JHW Mules in 1936. It involves cutting the wrinkly skin from around the breech area leaving a smooth (scarred) area that is less likely to get dirty and attract flies. It's performed on young lambs, most often at the same time as lamb marking. I've never heard a sheep farmer say they like mulesing, but I have heard a lot say they prefer it to dealing with flystruck sheep.

I've also heard a lot of farmers say mulesing is unnecessary, and that other management options – breeding for less breech wrinkle, crutching more often, applying long-acting chemicals – can be used. (Crutching is simply cutting the wool from around the backside. It's like shearing, but only done on a small part of the sheep and is expressly to clean up the sheep. Most sheep get crutched at least once a year, sometimes twice.) Flystrike is easier to manage in some climates and seasons than others – warm damp weather at the start of summer is particularly problematic. Merino sheep would be a lot easier to manage in Australia without the Australian sheep blowfly. Sheep flystrike is an issue the rest of the world doesn't have to deal with to the same extent.

Australian Wool Innovation (AWI), the peak industry body for woolgrowers, says breech flystrike is a complex and challenging issue. The organisation has invested heavily in research to find alternatives to mulesing. They state flystrike management must be based on best practice, evidence-based science and enable stepwise, sustainable animal welfare improvements. In other words, there's no point in everyone instantly stopping mulesing because that could lead to a disastrous increase in sheep morbidity and mortality due to flystrike. (Just like we can't suddenly let all the confined pigs go free.) But the public has a fairly low opinion of the practice.

It's worth noting that mulesing is classified as a surgical procedure and in the majority of cases these days is carried out with pain relief. It's one of those practices that seemed like a good idea at the time it was developed (and probably was – it has undoubtedly saved many thousands of sheep from painful deaths due to flystrike). But public opinion has moved on (aided by some very high-profile anti-mulesing campaigns) and the industry is still playing catch-up. It's a difficult problem. And I think it plays on the minds of people who work with Merinos far more than the general public realise, both in terms of its impact on animal welfare (positive and negative) and its public perception.

Of course, mulesing is really only an issue for the wool industry, not the sheep meat industry, right? So it doesn't really affect sheep meat production, right? Well, yes, but not really. As in the figures given earlier, about three quarters of the Australian ewe flock is Merino. Most of the lambs from those ewes end up packaged in meat trays in supermarkets and butcher shops. Raising sheep has generally been about producing two products: meat and wool. This has been one of the attractions of sheep – two products from the one animal provides two income streams, and diversified income reduces farmers' risk and market exposure. If wool prices are down, perhaps meat prices will be up. And vice versa. In a dry year, sheep may not put on much weight, but they will always grow wool (and serendipitously, Merinos grow finer wool in drier conditions). In these ways, sheep meat and wool are complementary in many farming enterprises. (Some farmers do concentrate exclusively on meat by raising sheep from breeds, such as Dorpers, that shed their wool. Others, even if they don't have Merinos, will have a wool clip to supplement their income. It just won't be the same quality of wool as from Merinos. The Merino breed has been favoured in Australia because of its adaptability to our dry and variable climate.)

Sheep have usually been run alongside other farming enterprises. The classic combination in Australia is wheat and sheep, which is how most of the farmers around my childhood hometown farmed. Wheat crops only grow during the winter months. The rest of the year, sheep can graze on the stubble left in the cropping paddocks.

Remember earlier on when I was talking about rotations in cropping paddocks? Including a pasture rotation in a cropping cycle – that is a year when the paddock is sown to a mixture of pasture species, such as clover and rye – will do no end of good in terms of raising soil carbon and breaking disease cycles, not to mention providing an opportunity to grow a legume to add nitrogen to the soil. And a pasture phase only works if you have animals to graze it. As much as there's a popular view (as discussed in the Cattle chapter) that we need to stop farming ruminants because they eat crops that could feed people directly and they belch methane, the reality is far more complicated. For me, it always comes back to the reality that a resilient natural system always involves plants and animals and, at their best, farms should be resilient natural systems. I see an ongoing place for livestock on farms. I think the vast majority of livestock farmers care about their animals, even when things don't go to plan. They choose to work with animals because they like them. I don't think animals are always farmed perfectly, but I think farmers are well aware of their need for transparency and ongoing trust to maintain social licence.

Abattoirs with glass-walled viewing areas are something I have heard veterinarian Dr Holly Ludeman talk about on many occasions (and something I have mentioned before). Ludeman is committed to transparency in livestock industries, which led her to founding the non-profit organisation The Livestock Collective. The organisation has lofty aims, but Ludeman is no shirker when it comes to big tasks. She is the veterinarian who took on cleaning up the reality and reputation of live sheep export after shocking footage aired on television in April 2018. (You may remember it; if you don't, I say lucky you, because it was beyond awful.) As Ludeman says, the video was distressing for everyone, including sheep producers and all those who work along the supply chain – shearers, truck drivers, stock-people, the feed suppliers and everyone in between. 'The footage highlighted the significant void of information the industry had allowed to occur, there was no "normal" to refute the images being shown by activist organisations,' Ludeman says. 'If there is a void in information, it will be filled.' She is working hard to make sure the livestock industries tell consumers their own stories, including how and why they do things and what they can do better.

I've spoken to Ludeman on many occasions and have toured a live sheep export quarantine facility with her. She is clearly frustrated with the negative focus on live export and, like many others who work in livestock industries, sees it as a crucial part of the livestock supply chain in Australia and for many of our trading partners. I admit that I used to drive a vehicle with a bumper sticker calling for an end to live export. I no longer do. I've met too many people, good people doing good work (Ludeman among them), who support the industry and for whom it is an important part of their overall farming business. I have also come to understand that the horrific footage from 2018, inexcusable as it was, is not the norm. Not by a long way. There's a lot more to the story than those pictures portray.

The Australian newspaper reported in May 2022 that the whistle-blower responsible for the distressing footage was paid by Animals Australia. Lyn White from Animals Australia is reported in the article as saying the payments were not publicly revealed by the organisa-tion because it was 'not relevant to the evidence gathered and that it would cause the live export industry to undermine evidence that exposed cruelty in their industry'. The article quotes White as saying her work in the field of live animal export investigations led to the suspension of live export on several occasions. (White was appointed a Member of the Order of Australia on the 2014 Queen's Birthday

Honours List for her animal advocacy and animal cruelty investigations. She is quoted on the Animals Australia website as saying, 'I truly believe that the greatest ethical test that we will ever face is how we treat those who are at human mercy.')

Ludeman cites community attitude research conducted for the livestock export industry that showed people are concerned about the oceanic transport part of the journey but says the voyage is often disproportionately focused on. 'A typical voyage of sheep to the Middle East will take twelve to fifteen days to get to the first port, depending on the speed of the vessel,' Ludeman says. 'The animals are well cared for during the journey.' She says mortality and morbidity have been greatly reduced. Post-mortems are conducted on any animals that die, to help improve future practices.

There are strict standards and regulations around livestock transport within and from Australia, including a need for animals to be 'fit to load', densities at which they can be loaded and the length of time they can travel. Ludeman says that during an ocean voyage, a veterinary report is provided to the department of agriculture every day and this includes data from temperature-monitoring equipment on deck. She notes the improvements in live sheep exports have been significant. 'They have more room to move, can all lie down at once, have access to food and water, and are checked daily by crew, stockpeople and the veterinarian,' she says.

We all hear the terrible stories on the news when these guidelines aren't adhered to, but it's worth remembering that these stories make the news because they are awful and unusual; the vast majority of livestock are transported humanely and safely and we hear nothing about it. Ludeman says that, when talking about live export, before and after the journey are also important. She says that although infrastructure varies from country to country, it has generally been greatly improved under the Export Supply Chain Assurance System.

'Kuwait is currently the largest sheep importer,' Ludeman says. 'They have a large, purpose-built facility, with the capacity to hold 100,000 sheep, and a state-of-the-art abattoir. The abattoir, like many in the region, has a public viewing gallery of the slaughter process, which is a cultural requirement for customers. Importing markets have significantly matured and the days of sheep in boots of cars are gone for Australian livestock.'

I have often heard people say we should slaughter and process all the animals here rather than export them live. There is sense in that idea, but currently we do not have the processing facilities or cold chain (the refrigerated storage and transport infrastructure required to store and distribute perishable food products) set up to meet the entire demand. The cold chain in destination countries is often also lacking. There will likely always be a demand for live animals imported into countries that cannot raise enough animals themselves to meet their demand for fresh meat. There is an argument that if Australia ends up not supplying these animals, they will simply be sourced elsewhere. As Ludeman says, 'Australia can continue to fill part of the demand and set world animal welfare standards or move away, lose market share and not be part of further global changes in animal welfare.' Ludeman wants us to be setting the benchmark.

At the time of writing, stopping live export from Australia is once again on the table. Let's hope that if it is stopped, it is done in a timely and orderly manner, rather than by a quick ban. History shows quick bans don't work well for farmers, livestock or importers. Let's also hope that the void created is not filled with a worse option. It's also worth noting that we do already slaughter and export a lot of meat, including into Islamic countries with requirements for halal slaughtering.

The sheep was stunned, rendered unconscious, then its back feet placed in shackles so the animal hung head down. The Muslim slaughterman, invoking the phrase 'Bismillah' (in the name of Allah), drew the sharp steel blade across the sheep's throat, severing the trachea, oesophagus, jugular, and other main arteries and veins of the neck region. Blood gushed and splashed onto the concrete floor and down the drain. The sheep's body barely twitched. It was quickly dead. After the initial rush, blood trickled before diminishing to drips.

I was at a halal-certified abattoir. I hadn't specifically gone to see halal slaughtering; I had wanted to visit an abattoir to see this critical part of the meat supply chain for myself. It just so happened that Cam Ferris, general manager of Hillside Abattoir, agreed to me visiting and that Hillside is halal certified. All their meat, regardless of whether it is intended for Muslim consumers or not, is halal. Ferris says it's easier than trying to run two different processing lines.

Regardless of the cultural and ritual aspects of the process, all animals in Australia must be rendered unconscious before slaughter. In halal and kosher slaughter, death must be caused by loss of blood. The result of these requirements is that in halal and kosher slaughter in Australia, the animal is stunned, then bled out. Other than in halal or kosher abattoirs, Australian animals may be killed by stunning prior to being bled out. The difference is in what actually causes the death – the stunning or the bleeding. The Australian Veterinary Association would like to see CCTV installed in abattoirs 'to assist in meeting animal welfare requirements. CCTV would allow establishments to observe and verify handling, stunning and slaughter operations, and inform training requirements.' This is an idea similar to the glass-walled viewing decks discussed earlier. As far as I'm aware, it hasn't yet happened in Australia but I'd like to be told I am wrong on that.

Ferris talks me through the process as we walk around the kill floor, following the line of sheep carcases as it wends its way along. He shouts so I can hear him above the noise; it's very noisy. There are dozens of workers, all wearing ear protection, each performing a small task – this one making precise cuts to sever the hide from the back legs, this one lining up the hide so machinery can pull it from the body, this one cutting off the feet, this one opening the abdominal cavity, this one eviscerating, and so on. I'm impressed by the skill, by the precision with which they work. Despite the noise, the place is calm. Workers smile as we pass, nod a silent hello. The work is methodical. Knives are cleaned and sterilised in between every cut. Meat inspectors check every carcase, looking at vital organs for signs of disease, assessing the carcases accordingly. In another part of the building, we watch someone separating livers and hearts from the viscera, and others taking the intestines and using a machine to clean and roll them. Once boxed, the intestines (runners, they are called at this stage of the process) will be shipped to China.

Every time we enter or leave a room, there is a washdown station where we sanitise our hands and wash our white rubber boots. (Ferris lent me a pair, along with a disposable white coverall and hairnet, before we embarked on our tour. I'm glad there weren't any mirrors.)

Outside the building, Ferris shows me the blood and viscera vats, and where the hides are salted and sorted. Nothing is wasted. The hides are sold to be made into leather and sheepskin products. Blood, bone and leftover viscera go to be processed into meat meal and fertiliser. Where there is a market for organs, they are separated, packaged and sold, as I saw happening with the intestines, hearts and livers. 'We were separating and selling tripe up until recently,' Ferris tells me, but they were no longer doing this when I visited. He was looking for a new option. 'We have a responsibility to maximise recovery,' he says. 'But we have to look at what it takes to recover it.

We do look at the financial aspect, the economics of it. We have to look at the footprint of it – the utility inputs, such as water and energy, versus the products we can recover.'

Back inside the building, we visit the chiller. It's definitely chilly. 'About minus 2 at present,' Ferris says. Hundreds of sheep carcases are hanging, carefully being brought down to below 7 degrees Celsius. Ferris explains to me that the heat extracted from carcases as they cool can be used to heat water used inside processing rooms. He says there are many initiatives like this in meat processing and the Australian Meat Processor Corporation is very good at supporting innovation.

We go into the boning room, but no one is working in there at the time. Staff shortages, largely due to Covid and associated problems with worker availability, meant that when I visited, the abattoir was operating way below capacity. The kill floor was running for the morning, then in the afternoon, the staff moved on to the boning room. This is where the carcases are broken down into the cuts of meat we see in the shops. Ferris opens the door to another coolroom. Inside, boxes and boxes of meat are piled up, waiting to be trucked to shops and for export. Not all of Hillside's meat is processed this way; a lot is sold as full carcases.

Back at Ferris' office, we take off our white boots, hair nets and coats and I thank him for letting me see behind the scenes; for his openness. He tells me he has nothing to hide so I ask him what he thinks of the idea of abattoirs having glass walls or viewing decks. 'I don't have a problem with that idea,' he says. 'I've just been on an industry tour overseas and you see a lot of viewing decks in abattoirs in some countries. It's good for people to see what's involved.'

As I drive away, I am surprised by a realisation that death seemed like such a small part of the abattoir's work. I guess I had thought that a slaughterhouse was all about death. There's no denying that it is a place of death, but it was much more than that. It was also a place of food preparation, and food safety is critical to the way things are done. It's a place of work, of camaraderie. I'm touched by what I have seen. Affected in some way. Neither disgusted nor alarmed. More informed, more thankful. Friends had warned me that I wouldn't want to eat meat once I had seen inside an abattoir but it didn't have that effect on me. It wasn't a ghoulish shop of horrors. Death was quick and humane. There was care and skill. It was not without reverence. I drove home along country roads with sheep grazing paddocks by the roadside, lambs dozing in the sunshine. I still had questions about farms and food, but I could look at that bucolic scene and at the same time own the reality of the slaughterhouse.

Abundance –
Four of the rest

CHAPTER 11

Canola

KOJONUP IS AN unassuming town in the southern wheatbelt of Western Australia. Lace curtains still hang in the window of an abandoned roadhouse on the northern edge of town. But down the hill and into the town centre, there is a suitable amount of bustle for a small regional centre. A couple of good cafes do a busy trade serving coffee and lunches to the passing tourists and locals. None of this gives any indication of the stoush that put the town in the spotlight a few years back and made international news. The argument, which turned into a court battle, was between two neighbouring farmers who, the media liked to point out, had been to school together and came from families that had long been friends. The dispute was about canola. Genetically modified canola, to be precise.

Before we get into what happened in Kojonup, let's get clear on what genetically modified actually means. As we saw in the Potatoes chapter, genetically modified – GM – organisms are developed using biotechnology rather than traditional breeding methods. An organism created using gene technology is called a GMO – a genetically modified organism. If a gene is inserted from another species, it is called transgenic. So transgenic is a subset of

GMOs; not all GMOs are transgenic. It's fair to say that transgenic organisms were one of the things that raised the ire of activists when GMOs were first in the news. The idea of moving genes from one species to another didn't seem 'right' to some people, even though viruses have been doing that forever. From the start, genetic modification attracted controversy.

Back to Kojonup. Steve Marsh farmed his land organically and attracted a premium for his certified organic oats, barley, wheat and livestock. Across the road, Michael Baxter farmed his land conventionally. When the Western Australian government lifted its moratorium on GM crops, Baxter planted a GM variety of canola called Roundup Ready. At harvest, he swathed and windrowed his canola. This is a common harvesting technique often used for canola. It involves cutting the plants just before they are ripe, raking them into rows (called windrows) and leaving them to dry, before coming back and harvesting the grain from the dried seed pods at a later date. It gives farmers options as far as timing harvest of their various crops and helps prevent the canola seed pods 'shattering'. This is when the seed pods burst open and the seed falls to the ground. Shattering of seed heads is common in many plants as it is a good way for the plant to disperse the seeds; it's not so great for people wanting to harvest the seeds. Reducing shattering has been a goal of plant breeding for millennia.

While Baxter's canola was drying in its windrows, some blew across the road and onto Marsh's property. Marsh's organic certification with The National Association for Sustainable Agriculture Australia (NASAA) came with a zero tolerance for GM 'contamination' and he duly lost organic status across 70 per cent of his farm.

Marsh sued Baxter for negligence and nuisance, claiming damages for the loss suffered because he had to sell his crops and livestock as conventional produce, at lower prices than the same products would have achieved if they had been organically certified. The case was tried in the Western Australian Supreme Court and Marsh lost. He appealed to the High Court and again lost.

The case has been held up as everything from a disagreement between two neighbours who should have sorted it out over a couple of beers, to a David and Goliath battle between the small organic farmer and the international agribusiness giant Monsanto. The latter because Monsanto, the patent owner of Roundup Ready canola, paid Baxter's legal bills. Legal experts have suggested Marsh would have done better to sue his organic certifier rather than his neighbour, because NASAA's zero tolerance for GM contamination is not in line with the tolerance levels of many international organic bodies, such as those in Europe and the United States. These jurisdictions don't allow GM plants to be grown in organically certified enterprises, but do allow for a tiny amount of 'contamination'.

In the Marsh v Baxter case, the Supreme Court ruling said the organic certifier's response in the circumstances was 'unjustifiable' and that the certifier had misunderstood its own rules. Monash University Associate Professor of Law Karinne Ludlow says it is impossible to set a zero level on a product when the certification scheme refers to the means of production. So it could be argued that Marsh should not have lost his organic certification because some GM canola plants blew onto his property. He was not actually growing them. He was not employing a non-organic production method. Curiously, Marsh didn't even have canola growing on his property. But the presence of GM material on his farm meant he lost the certification. Had he not lost his certification, there would probably never have been an argument, let alone a legal battle.

At the heart of the court case is a broader argument over the use of GM technology in agriculture. It's more a chasm than an argument. It's a difference in philosophy. It's a topic that has somehow skipped sensible discussion and jumped right into emotional argument, with cries of misinformation from both sides.

Let's begin with canola. The name was coined in Canada in the 1970s to refer to varieties of rapeseed that were low in erucic acid and thus much more palatable. It's a contraction of 'Canada' and 'oil, low acid'. Originally canola was a trademarked name but is now used across North America and Australia to refer to edible rapeseed oils. Canola, like its parent rapeseed, is a brassica, the same family that contains cabbage, cauliflower, mustard and radish. Also like its parent rapeseed, canola is primarily grown for its seeds, which are high in oil. It's used as cooking oil, in salad dressings and to make margarine; the usual sorts of uses for any edible oil. It also gets used as biofuel.

After the seeds are crushed to extract the oil, the leftover meal is used as animal feed. This is an interesting aspect of the 'grain' that goes to feed animals; some of it is leftovers after the good bits have been extracted and some is lower grade that is considered not fit for human consumption. It's hard to get a handle on just how much animal feed comes from these sorts of 'upcycled' uses and how much is good stuff that could have been eaten by people. (But from the sheer volume of grain that goes into animal feed, I think it's fair to assume that a lot of it would be fit for human consumption.)

Canola was first grown in Australia in 1969 but it didn't really take off as a crop here until the 1990s, when researchers developed blackleg resistant varieties suitable for Australian conditions. Up until that point, blackleg, which is a devastating fungal disease that makes the canola stems go black and wither, had limited the success of Australian canola growing. Since the 1990s, canola production has rapidly expanded across southern Australia. It's the crop that turns paddocks a stunning shade of yellow when it flowers in winter and spring. Canola is now grown on almost 3 million Australian hectares, making it the third most important broadacre crop in the country after wheat and barley. Over 4 million tonnes were harvested in Australia in 2021.

Most Australian canola is exported to Asia for human consumption or to Europe for biofuel, the latter being the most lucrative. The EU market pays a premium for non-GM canola because it gives more options. Tight restrictions on GM food in Europe mean GM canola can only be used there as biofuel, whereas non-GM canola can also go into the food supply.

Canola can be highly profitable – although the words farmers often use are 'reliably profitable', and reliability in farming profits is not a small thing. Probably the main reason it has been so widely adopted is its usefulness as a 'break crop': that is, as a rotation between cereal crops. As it is from a completely different family to the cereal crops like wheat, oats and barley, it provides a good break for the soil, preventing the build-up of pests and breaking the disease cycle of many pathogens. It also gives farmers an opportunity to control weeds that are difficult to manage in cereals. Because cereals are grasses, controlling grass weeds growing among them can be difficult. Canola broadens the options. Which brings us nicely to Roundup Ready canola.

Roundup is the Monsanto brand name for the herbicide glyphosate, which is the most widely used herbicide in the world. (Monsanto was acquired by Bayer in 2018, but the Monsanto brand name is still used.) The amount of it used is staggering. From when it was released in 1974 up until 2016, over 8.6 billion kilograms of glyphosate (the active ingredient, not formulations) have been applied across the world. It's not without controversy. It hit the headlines in a notable way in 2015 when the International Agency for Research on Cancer (IARC) – an agency of the World Health Organization – released a report saying glyphosate was 'probably carcinogenic'. It's important to understand that this assessment was only about the potential hazard of glyphosate; it wasn't saying that exposure to glyphosate would automatically cause cancer. It's also worth noting that lots of other common everyday things, like sunlight, alcohol and coffee, fall into the same risk category. In other words, take note, but you probably don't need to be alarmed. Not yet at least.

Findings, such as that one from the IARC, form part of the information that regulatory bodies like the Australian Pesticides and Veterinary Medicines Authority (APVMA) use to determine how chemicals should be regulated and used. (I feel there should be a rule somewhere about the length of the names of these organisations and the many acronyms they cause writers to use!) Following the IARC finding, the APVMA conducted a review and concluded that the weight of scientific evidence pointed to glyphosate being safe. Dr Matthew O'Mullane from APVMA said numerous scientific studies and forty years of extensive use worldwide provided compelling evidence for its safety. This was in line with other regulatory agencies across the world.

Glyphosate kills most plants. Normally, it kills canola. But not Roundup Ready canola. Roundup Ready canola is resistant to glyphosate, so farmers can spray the growing crop with glyphosate to kill the weeds without harming the canola. Now, it's important to note that Roundup Ready canola is not the only herbicide-tolerant canola variety available to farmers and nor was it the first. That prize goes to TT canola. TT stands for 'triazine tolerant'. Triazine is a group of herbicides widely used in agriculture and horticulture. Triazine is highly toxic and can persist in the soil, which can cause problems for the crop grown the year after it is used. TT canola was originally bred in Canada in the 1980s. A maize crop was sprayed with triazine herbicides; the maize died but some nearby canola plants didn't, even though they were also sprayed. These surviving canola plants were used to breed triazine tolerant canola. To be clear, the herbicide tolerance in these plants is only to triazine; glyphosate would kill them. (Likewise, Roundup Ready canola is killed by triazine and other non-glyphosate herbicides.)

The idea of TT canola never took off in Canada, but researchers in Australia ran with it and by 2006, 70 per cent of canola grown here was TT varieties. It seems farmers liked the options it provided. By then, other similar options had been released that provided herbicide-resistant canola varieties. Like TT varieties, these were developed using traditional breeding methods. And like any herbicide-resistant crop, growing them tends to cause more herbicide to be sprayed. This can lead to herbicide-resistant weeds developing and the herbicide can persist in the soil. But herbicide resistant weeds can, and do, develop whenever herbicides are used. It's a massive problem. The point here is that having crop varieties that are resistant to herbicide is a useful tool that increases growers' options for herbicide use and weed control; whereas herbicide resistance in weeds is a difficult management issue that limits herbicide usage. Confusing, I know. But bear with me.

Monsanto's herbicide-resistant offering to canola growers was Roundup Ready and the point of difference with this, other than glyphosate being the herbicide it is resistant to, is that it is classified as GM. When it was approved by the Office of the Gene Technology

Regulator (often shortened to the OGTR, if you want yet another acronym) in December 2003, Roundup Ready canola became the first GM food crop approved to be grown commercially in Australia. It was not grown in Western Australia until 2010, because up until then a state government moratorium prevented it. In Australia, Federal *and* state governments play a role in regulating GM crops. Currently, GM moratoria still exist in Tasmania and South Australia. GM canola is now grown in all other states. It is not grown in the Northern Territory, simply because no canola is grown there. In Western Australia, which produces most of Australia's canola, 34 per cent of the canola grown in 2017 was GM.

There are two other GM crops now grown in Australia – safflower and cotton. Safflower is another oilseed, which is only grown in small amounts in Australia. It was approved for commercial production in 2018. And cotton is cotton. Almost all cotton grown here is now GM, engineered to be resistant to a devastating insect pest (it contains the Bt gene I mentioned in relation to potatoes). We don't usually think about cotton as something we eat, so perhaps that makes people feel differently about it. But cottonseed oil is extensively used for frying fast food.

Long before GM crops were approved to be grown in Australia, GM foods were approved for sale. That happened in 1996. It was two years earlier in the US. Since then, uptake across the world has been considerable. By 2015, more than 18 million farmers in twenty-eight countries had grown GM crops on 180 million hectares. Canola is among the top four GM crops cultivated around the world; the other big players are maize, soybeans and cotton. These four crops between them account for 99 per cent of the land area sown to GM crops.

The Australian government's statutory authority on food standards, Food Standards Australia New Zealand (FSANZ), says 'gene technology has not been shown to introduce any new or altered hazards into the food supply, therefore the potential for long-term risks associated with GM foods is considered to be no different to that for conventional foods already in the food supply.' To date, the products of nine GM food crops are approved for sale in Australia: canola, corn, cotton, lucerne, potato, rice, soybean, sugar beet and safflower. Scientists and regulators often state that in the decades since people started consuming GM food there has *never* been a known case of an adverse response. There's not a lot of logic in fears about GM food.

But logic doesn't always hold sway, especially when fears and feelings get involved. From the moment GM crops were planted in paddocks, they attracted controversy. Activists raided farms known to be growing GM crops and the crops were ripped from the ground. British writer Mark Lynas was among the early activists. He says he saw GM as humankind acquiring too much technological power. 'Something was bound to go horribly wrong,' he says. 'These genes would spread like some sort of living pollution. It was the stuff of nightmares.'

That was what he thought.

Until he changed his mind.

Lynas's epiphany came when he was researching a book on climate change. He says the reason he changed his mind so totally and dramatically was fairly simple. 'I discovered science.' Lynas describes the anti-GM campaign as the most successful he has ever been involved with. And as being wrong and explicitly anti-science. 'For me, this anti-science environmentalism became increasingly inconsistent with my pro-science environmentalism with regards to climate change,' he says. 'This contradiction was untenable in the long-term.'

He says that when he began investigating the scientific literature on GM, his 'cherished beliefs' about GM turned out to be little more than 'green urban myths'.

It is healthy to question new practices and new varieties of plants and animals brought into agriculture. I'd go so far as to say it is essential. But why the outcry over GM? Why single GM out as being inherently bad? As one friend told me, 'It's not so much that it fails the pub test, more that it fails the is-it-safe-for-the-grandkids test.' But does it? Lynas writes that the 'general level of public fear about GMOs is not very high, but people generally think that GMOs are possibly bad and they ought to go for the non-GMO product. So, it is a big challenge to improve people's understanding.'

Ghent University, Belgium, philosopher Stefaan Blancke writes, 'negative representations of GMOs are widespread and compelling because they are intuitively appealing'. Basically, something new can be seen as a threat and it makes sense to oppose a threat. Lynas describes opposition to GM as being aesthetic, as being the privilege of the well-fed people in wealthy countries who are 'blinded by romantic nostalgia for the traditional farming methods of the past'. Lynas sees particular danger in this when the overfed developed world exports anti-GM ideas to poverty-stricken places; he calls it a form of neo-colonialism.

I remember being fearful of GM foods when I first heard about them, worrying what their introduction might mean. Some disastrous genie that once let out of the bottle would never be contained. I don't know where these thoughts came from. Perhaps it was simply a fear of the unknown. Perhaps I was reading too many sensationalised news reports. Logically speaking, it seems to me now the whole issue of GM contamination, so called, is a house of cards. It has no scientific basis. It's built on feelings and lack of understanding. Science has consistently and convincingly demonstrated the safety of GM food and GM crops.

But despite all I have said on the topic, a niggle of doubt remains in my mind.

GM is hard to understand. It's hardcore science. I have a degree in biological sciences but it doesn't equip me to truly understand the techniques used today. Molecular biology is a field that has rapidly advanced in recent decades. By rapidly, I mean meteorically. Anything I remember from my 1980s university genetics lectures just doesn't cut it; a certain level of trust in the science and the scientists is required. Science may well be completely convinced of the safety of GM, but there are few decisions we make, as individuals or as a society, based purely on science. I can't actually think of any.

As individuals, many of the biggest and most far-reaching decisions we make in our lives are based on feelings and intuition, the very things that science criticises anti-GM campaigners for employing. In general our choices about where we live and with whom, the work we do, how we spend our time, are largely based on feelings. We can add what we eat to that list. Unless we are hungry. Eating based on feelings is a privilege reserved for the world's well fed.

Somehow, we need to rationalise that with the reality that science doesn't always get it right. It's science's ability to reassess and shift and change that gives it great strength. But it also takes a toll on public trust. It seems to me that science is the best tool we've managed to develop for understanding how things work and how to fix things. So far at least. But, as we saw when we investigated the difference between animal welfare and animal ethics, science doesn't give us the tools to answer all our questions. It doesn't – can't – shouldn't – answer moral questions of right and wrong.

Still, there are other things that science gives us that we accept, almost blindly and certainly willingly. Flat screen televisions, solar power, cars, quick-dry fabrics, smart phones. The list is endless. I think the difference is that we easily see personal benefits to these things. A GM canola crop is a little different. We see no personal benefit. Unless we are farmers trying to control a wild radish or ryegrass problem in a prized cropping paddock. Then it gets very personal.

The science says it is highly unlikely that problems will be caused by crops and foods *because* they are GM. Its products are not necessarily any different to those produced by conventional breeding methods. DNA swirls and mixes and creates new life forms. That has been going on since the first strands of DNA formed way back in distant time.

That's not the same as saying a GM crop will always be good, or that problems won't arise from them. But the GM techniques themselves will not be the cause. Rather, the issues would be due to the specific organism. And a problematic organism could well be created using non-GM techniques. Hopefully, any such things will be discovered and rectified before they are released and become full blown disasters.

Agricultural species can and do lead to unintended consequences, regardless of the pathway used to bring them to farming. Think of just about any weed or feral animal running amok in the landscape. No one planned to have 24 million feral pigs out in the bush. Cane toads sounded like such a great way to control cane beetles in sugar crops. Until it became obvious that they were an environmental disaster. As Blancke suggests, the risks and benefits of anything should be assessed on a case-by-case basis, regardless of the process used to develop it. A lot of the complaints about GMOs, such as the use of pesticides and the involvement of multinational corporations, are equally associated with many non-GM crops. This is certainly the case with the non-GM herbicide-resistant canola varieties. In this respect, they are no different from GM Roundup Ready canola. (It's worth noting that GM cotton, engineered to fight its own battles, actually requires less pesticide to be sprayed on the crop.)

The additional cost and slowness to market imposed on GM varieties by the regulatory environment makes developing new ones prohibitively expensive for all but the large agribusiness companies. There is some irony in this; we tend not to like big companies holding too much power, but we set things up so only the big companies have the resources to play the game. In a further irony, the tools we use to assess the costs and benefits in all these cases are scientific. Just like the tools used to develop GM, and non-GM, crops.

GM is a technique, not an end product. It might be time we got over a blanket fear of it. And surely all those paddocks full of yellow canola flowers are good for bees.

CHAPTER 12

Bees

I T's A MYTH that bee suits prevent you from being stung. They don't. Bees can easily sting through the fabric. Heck, they can sting through the leather gloves – I can attest to that. Bee suits are usually a loose-fitting, white cotton fabric overall – long arms, long legs. White is a colour said to calm bees, hence suits and most hives are white. A mesh-fronted hood zips onto the suit. Long gloves, with leather on the fingers and palms, come over the sleeves. Boots are usually worn, up under the trouser legs, with the elastic at the bottom of the trousers fitting tightly to the boots. The idea is that no skin is exposed and there are no gaps where a bee could crawl inside the suit. But, like I said, bees can, and do, sting through the suit. They also, on occasion, find a hole or a gap they can crawl through. It's rather disconcerting, to say the least, when you realise the bee buzzing around your face is on the same side of the veil as your skin.

Of course, there are experienced beekeepers who don't wear gloves or veils or even bee suits. I am not an experienced beekeeper. I bought a bee suit a few years ago and became the sporadic, casual 'apprentice' to two friends, Helen and Kirsten, who keep beehives as a hobby. It's always an adventure to go 'into the hives' with them.

First, a puff of smoke from the smoker; beekeepers use smoke to calm bees. It masks the pheromones bees release when alarmed so prevents the alarm signal from warning the hive that there is an intruder. With the bees somewhat calmed, we lift the lid to expose the inner workings of the hive.

Helen, Kirsten and I lift and check the frames, smoking the bees when they become too buzzy. The change in their demeanour is easy to pick – they buzz louder as they become agitated by our presence. When really annoyed, they 'ping' at us, divebombing us. Some hives are more aggressive than others; each has a personality, determined by the queen and her pheromones. Unfortunately, there is something of a correlation between aggressiveness and productivity; more aggressive bees tend to be more productive. We work quickly, to limit the disturbance to the hive. The bees don't like being robbed. They aren't really storing honey for people to take. They are storing it to feed the colony. Honey is bee food. But even when they have plenty of honey stored in the hive, they keep making it for as long as nectar is available. (Beekeepers leave enough honey in the hive for the bees to consume.)

Helen and Kirsten use hives of the same basic design used by thousands of beekeepers around the world. It's a design invented by an American preacher called Lorenzo Langstroth in 1851 that has stood the test of time. Four-sided boxes – no top or bottom – sit on top of each other. The frames, on which the bees build their honeycomb and fill it with honey, sit inside these boxes, hanging from the top. The space in between the frames is referred to as 'bee space'. It's a space that is wide enough for the bees to crawl through, not so wide that they fill it with wax, and not so narrow they fill it with propolis. (Propolis is basically bee glue used to fill crevices in the hive; it also has health giving properties.) Discovering bee space was the great gift Langstroth gave the world. Bee space is between 6 and 9 millimetres wide. If the space between the hanging frames was wider, the bees would build out into it and cement the frames together, making it hard for the beekeeper to lift the frames out to check the bees and harvest the honey.

The frames Helen and Kirsten use hold about a kilogram of honey each when full. Some beekeepers use deeper frames and bigger boxes, but the basic design and bee space between the frames remain the same. They're just heavier to lift when full of honey.

When the native marri trees are laden with creamy white blossoms, the frames are heavy with delicious, dark honey. We lift and check as the bees fly and buzz. We put aside any frames that are fully capped; that is, full of ripe honey and sealed with a wax cap. Bees only cap honey when it has reached the correct density. They make honey by collecting nectar, mixing it with saliva, and fanning it with their wings to evaporate excess moisture as it ripens. If it's not capped, it's not ripe. Beekeepers can test the density of honey to make sure it is ripe, but the bees just know. Honey taken too soon will be watery and will not keep. Honey that is ripe pretty much lasts forever, and people have been robbing bees to get honey pretty much forever as well. Perfectly good honey has been found in ancient Egyptian tombs.

Bee stings have always been a deterrent to robbing hives. It is only the female worker bees that sting. They're also the ones that do all the work inside the hive and make up most of the population. Each worker bee lives for about six weeks, during which time she does a range of jobs in the hive, culminating in being a forager in her final couple of weeks. These are the bees seen out buzzing from flower to flower, collecting nectar and filling the pollen baskets on their back legs with sticky yellow pollen to carry back to the hive.

The queen is the other female in the hive. She's larger than the worker bees and is the only egg layer. She also lives longer, up to a few years, all of which is spent in the lower chamber of the hive, laying eggs in honey cells. (In domestic hives, a 'queen excluder' is used to make sure the queen only lays in the egg chamber and not in the frames from which honey will be collected. It's easy to 'exclude' the queen because of her larger size. A queen excluder is simply a sheet of plastic laid across the top of the brood box. It has holes in it big enough for the workers to get through, but too small for the queen to do so.)

Only once in her life does the queen fly from the hive – her nuptial flight, when she is followed by male bees, called drones. This is the one time she mates. She will mate with several drones, and then the queen carries the sperm from that nuptial flight for her entire life. In commercial beekeeping, and for most hobbyists like Helen and Kirsten, new queens are bought from specialist breeders. These queens are artificially inseminated, so miss out on the nuptial flight.

The queen's job is to lay eggs to produce the replacement bees for the hive. She lays unfertilised eggs to produce drones and fertilised eggs to produce workers. The workers will occasionally choose to raise a new queen. They do this by creating a queen cell in which they feed a female (worker) larva on 'royal jelly', a highly nutritious substance they make for just this purpose. When a new queen emerges, she will kill any un-emerged sister queens and fight the old queen to the death. A hive can only have one queen. After the new queen's nuptial flight, she will return to the hive and begin her egg-laying life. (When beekeepers put a new queen in a hive, they kill the old queen first. The new queen is put in a small box with a wax seal. By the time the workers chew through the wax and the queen emerges, her pheromones will have infiltrated the hive and the workers will accept her.)

The drones are the only males in the hive. They don't do much. They don't make honey or clean the hive or defend it (they don't have stings). They hang around and eat and wait for a queen to emerge from a hive somewhere nearby. When this happens, they fly off in the hope of being one of the drones that will mate with her. If honey supplies are low, the worker bees will throw the drones out of the hive, but the rest of the time they tolerate them. Overall, the hive operates as a super organism, composed of different parts that each know their role innately; one queen, a couple of thousand drones, and tens of thousands of workers.

The bees commonly used for honey production are European honey bees. They inhabit hives the world over, having, like so many things, (you guessed it) spread across the globe with colonisation. But nowhere in the world are honey bees healthier than they are in Australia. Elsewhere in the world, varroa mite is a scourge.

As American writer Hannah Nordhaus describes in her book *The Beekeeper's Lament*, 'The varroa mite is a bloodred-to-brown, tick-shaped creature, about 1.8 millimeters long and 2 millimeters wide. It has eight legs, a hairy, shiny dark shell, and a sharp, two pronged tongue designed to pierce a bee's exoskeleton'. Having pierced the exoskeleton, the mite proceeds to suck its haemolymph, which is bee blood. Nordhaus writes that since 1987, varroa has been *the* major cause of honey bee mortality across the US. She also writes that no one knows exactly how it first arrived in the US. Varroa mite and other bee diseases are the reason why people aren't allowed to bring honey into Australia.

For years beekeepers and researchers have been saying it is only a matter of time before varroa mite infiltrates Australia, but in the interim significant effort is being expended in keeping it out. The National Bee Pest Surveillance Program administered by Plant Health Australia conducts surveillance at seaports and airports across Australia, as these are considered the most likely places disease could enter. It could be a stowaway hive in a ship's cargo or a more maleficent smuggling operation. The value of the surveillance system became apparent when varroa mite was detected in New South Wales in June 2022. An immediate eradication plan was enforced; moving beehives was prohibited in New South Wales and 1693 hives had been euthanased by early July in a bid to eliminate the mites. At the time of writing, the success or otherwise of this venture was unknown. I hope that, as you read this, Australia is once again varroa free.

It's not just honey supplies that are threatened by varroa and the loss of bees. One of the immediate concerns in the wake of the New South Wales varroa incursion was the pollination of Victorian almond trees. With movement of beehives banned in New South Wales, the normal movement of hives down to Victorian almond orchards could not occur. It's easy to forget just how interconnected life is when sitting in a city cafe drinking an almond milk latte. AgriFutures Australia estimates a third of the food that ends up on our plates does so thanks to honey bees. A third! 'From almonds to avocados to the meat we eat, honey bees are vital for the pollination and production of many of our favourite foods,' AgriFutures writes. The meat we eat? Yes, even meat needs honey bees to pollinate pasture plants to enable them to seed and regrow. AgriFutures estimates honey bees contribute $14.2 billion annually to the Australian economy in honey and pollination services. All that from one small insect. Well, thousands and thousands of individuals from one insect species.

While honey bees are the poster child of the insect world, as far as human food goes, they aren't the only contributor. There are myriad other insect pollinators, including native bees, that contribute to our food supply. And around the world, two billion people in

130 countries regularly eat insects. We're not talking about the odd grub mixed in with the salad leaves. These are insects deliberately eaten as part of people's diets and the selection available is immense. More than 2100 different insect species are eaten. Australia has around 62,000 native insect species. Of these, sixty have been documented as being part of Indigenous Australians' diets. This includes witjuti (also called witchetty) grubs, bogong moths and honey-pot ants.

Ancient Greeks and Romans ate insects, but somewhere along the line they fell out of favour in the Western diet. Except cochineal. Also called carmine, Natural Red 4 or E120, this red food colouring is made from crushed scale insects. In the future, insects may be doing more than colouring the icing on our cakes and pollinating our almonds. They could be in for a resurgence on our dinner plates.

Insects are high in protein, omega-3 fatty acids, iron, zinc, folic acid and vitamins B12, C and E. So why aren't we all eating them? Apparently, it's not aversion, or the 'yuck' factor as this gets called; it's lack of opportunity. At least that's what Royal Melbourne Institute of Technology (RMIT) researchers discovered when they surveyed Australian consumers. The RMIT crew found that about a third of their survey respondents had previously eaten insects. Of those that hadn't, the most common reason for not having done so was lack of opportunity, rather than aversion. More than half said that increased availability and greater awareness of nutritional information would be most likely to make them try insects in the future. That's good news for the handful of commercial insect growers in Australia.

Commercial insect farming uses minimal water, energy and land, so is considered to have a low environmental footprint. CSIRO sees it as the fastest-growing of a number of opportunities to grow protein for the world's burgeoning population. It expects Australia's insect protein industry to grow to an annual production of $10 million by

2026. That's from a 2021 base of just fourteen businesses. CSIRO is keen for us to get over any stereotype of insects being pests or dirty or dangerous or only eaten in times of desperation. They'd like us to replace those views with 'a narrative that embraces ... untold stories of cultures where entomophagy is considered mainstream'. Entomophagy. What a word! The eating of insects. Worldwide, the insect market is expected to reach $1.4 billion by 2023. That's a lot of insects. Actually, it's a lot of crickets. Despite the thousands upon thousands of insect species in the world, only about five are regularly farmed in commercial enterprises. Crickets are the most popular.

Food Standards Australia New Zealand (FSANZ) assessed three insect species – super mealworm (*Zophobas morio*), house crickets (*Achaeta domestica*) and mealworm beetle (*Tenebrio molitor*) – and found there were no safety concerns regarding people consuming them. They did say foods containing them must be labelled as such. No one can sneak cricket powder into your burger patty without telling you.

But an SBS article on entomophagy (I just had to use that word) reported that we may inadvertently eat thousands of insects each year. They reported that common foods, such as flour, chocolate and fruit juice (or pretty much anything that is mixed and ground up), may unintentionally contain portions of or even whole insects. These could include beetles, thrips and aphids. And apparently plant-based diets are more likely to be higher in insects and bits of insects.

I went looking in my local supermarket for insects to eat. I didn't find any. Well, none packaged ready for sale. I found some online instead. In the interests of book research, and increasing curiosity, I ordered crunchy granola with crickets, cricket corn chips, ant candy, spicy mealworms and crunchy crickets. I passed on the cricket flour, even though the RMIT researchers found insect-based flour was the insect-based food people were most likely to try. But I decided that if I was going to eat insects, I wanted to have the complete experience.

As I waited for my parcel to arrive, I grew increasingly nervous about trying insects. It wasn't so much the yuck factor as a hesitancy due to the allergy warning. Insects contain similar proteins to crustaceans – they're closely related – so people with shellfish allergies should avoid insects. I don't have a diagnosed shellfish allergy, but I have been known to get a bit tingly around the lips from eating prawns; it's the main reason I avoid crustaceans (other than not liking them or the idea of them). Anyway, I had a book to write, and my package of insects duly arrived at my doorstep.

I decided to wait until everyone was home to open the packets, so one night when my son and his girlfriend were over for dinner, and my daughter was also home, I announced to everyone that we were having an insect entree. The idea met with immediate resistance. There was debate about whether the insects would be eaten before or after dinner, or perhaps not at all. But in the end we all partook of the insect taste test.

I opened the crunchy crickets first and passed them around. The cricket I pulled out of the packet was unmistakably a cricket. I put it into my mouth and chewed. It crunched. The dominant flavour was of the salty, spicy coating. It was a bit greasy. Not much else.

We opened the mealworms. We all found them much harder to eat than the crickets because they looked too much like maggots. We tried the corn chips. Then we got some 'normal' corn chips out of the pantry and tried them for comparison. The 'normal' ones were better but it's hard to say why; perhaps it was perception rather than reality. I didn't really get the point of the ant candy – high protein or not, it was still a lolly. But maybe it's an entry-level product to get people used to the idea of eating insects, to sweeten any potential revulsion. None of us was enthusiastic about tucking into any of the insect products and no one asked for seconds. It seems unlikely that my household will be one of those that contributes to the burgeoning insect protein market. Not on our dinner plates, at least. Maybe I'll feed them to the chooks.

I'm only half joking. One of the opportunities for insect farming is in waste management and animal feed production – grow insects on municipal organic waste and feed them to pigs and chickens. Fight Food Waste Cooperative Research Centre is working with a company called Goterra on an innovative system that uses black soldier fly larvae (yes, maggots) to convert food waste to high protein feed for aquaculture and intensive poultry, pork and beef farming. (It could potentially replace the protein in these feeds currently derived from soy.) But one of the hurdles is the regulatory environment, which has some way to go to catch up with the idea of using maggots to get rid of food waste. The actual concept makes a lot of sense. As Goterra puts it on their website, they're using 'waste as a resource to feed our insects instead of throwing it away, adding nutrients back into the food chain.' The end product is 'high-value protein ingredients' produced from 'food and organic waste in just twelve days'. There's a lot to like about that.

Doing something sensible with food waste is a pressing issue. Fight Food Waste Cooperative Research Centre CEO Dr Steven Lapidge says global food waste is a $1.6 trillion per year problem. Yes, *trillion*! He says that food is wasted during production and consumption phases. In poorer countries, loss tends to be during production and distribution, due to difficulties in supply chains and storage. In richer countries, it tends to be at the consumer end – that soggy cucumber in the bottom of the vegetable crisper and the milk that goes off before we drink it. Or the leftovers from the too-big serve on our plates, at home and at restaurants. It's hard to imagine all these little things adding up to over a trillion dollars' worth, but that's what the figures say. Australians throw out 20 per cent of the food we buy. Twenty per cent. A fifth. It doesn't matter how you say it, it's an awful lot.

I asked Lapidge if a stat I had heard was correct: that if food waste was a country, it would be the third-highest greenhouse gas emitter in the world. 'Yes,' he says, 'that is correct.' That's emissions made up from resources used to produce the food that is then wasted, and also emissions from the food as it rots.

A lot of the emissions from rotting food is methane. Lapidge says 8 per cent of global greenhouse gases come from food that is 'lost' or wasted. That's almost as much as the road transport sector. But the environmental damage of food waste doesn't stop there. Lapidge runs through the figures. 'A land area the size of China is used to grow food that is lost or wasted,' he says. 'A quarter of the fresh water used in agriculture and 23 per cent of the fertiliser is used to grow food that is lost or wasted.' This is food that could have been eaten. Which is criminal, given there is more and more pressure on our food production systems from the world's growing population. Lapidge says that to feed everyone in the world in 2050, the world will need 7400 trillion calories more than it produced in 2010. Figures from the World Resources Institute show that halving world food waste could close this gap by 20 per cent. In other words, if we stop wasting so much food, we won't need to produce so much more. Which is pretty obvious, but the figures are nonetheless compelling.

Australia, along with a lot of other countries, has signed up to be part of the global effort to halve food waste by 2050. The Fight Food

Waste Cooperative Research Centre is working towards helping to make that happen. They are looking at ways to turn food waste into useful stuff and also at ways to improve processing and packaging to reduce food waste. The black soldier fly larvae project is one aspect of this. The research centre is also investigating consumer behaviour to reduce the amount of food we buy and then throw out, because a lot of it comes back to us as individuals. For example, it is estimated that 3.5 per cent of total meat production (that's 155,000 tonnes with a value of $670 million) is wasted each year. Ouch. It doesn't matter how sustainable the production of food is if it gets thrown out instead of being eaten. Which makes me feel rather guilty about those insects I bought (and the soggy cucumber in the fridge). I am glad I can feed them to chooks rather than putting them in the bin. They'll love them. I can see great value in using insects as feed for a range of farmed animals. In a world hungry for protein, that's becoming very important.

CHAPTER 13

Salmon

I HAD NEVER THOUGHT about people who produce salmon as being farmers until a few years ago when I interviewed someone involved in the industry. She talked about livestock, feed, pens, animal welfare, genetics, environment, sustainability, staff, markets, processing, producing food; in short, she talked about all the things that farmers who farm the land talk about. During the interview, I realised aquaculture was farming in the same way agriculture is; it's just the medium is different. It's also a much newer industry – people have grown fish, molluscs and crustaceans in farm dams and ponds for a very, very long time, but doing so at huge scale is relatively new.

Tasmania is the home of the Australian salmon industry. It has grown from virtually nothing three decades ago to be a big deal. Like anything that grows rapidly, especially when it uses natural resources to do so, it is not without controversy.

There are three players in Tasmanian salmon. The biggest is Tassal, which produces around 70 per cent of Australia's salmon and employs about 1200 people. Petuna, with a workforce of around 300, is considerably smaller than the other two. It began as a husband-and-wife team, Peter and Una Rockliff, but they have since sold the enterprise.

The Rockliffs didn't begin as farmers; they began as fishermen. The other player is Huon Aquaculture, which is bigger than Petuna but nowhere near as big as Tassal. Huon Aquaculture was started by the Bender family, who initially farmed sheep and cattle and then, from 1986, also produced salmon. In 1994, Frances and Peter Bender bought the salmon farming operations from the broader Bender family and focused solely on that. From small beginnings they built Huon Aquaculture into a multi-million dollar business. In 2021, they sold it to JBS Australia, the Australian subsidiary of the international conglomerate JBS Foods.

JBS Australia claims to be the 'largest multi-species processor, exporter and feedlotter in Australia'. They don't just do aquaculture, they're also into sheep, cattle, pigs and plant-based protein. They do the whole deal: 'finishing' the animal, slaughter, processing, packaging and distributing. They have kept the Huon Aquaculture brand, as they have kept a lot of the brands they own. Many of them sound like small-time family farms; everyone seems to want to cash in on that idea. There's something about it that appeals to consumers, including me. Research from US organisation The Center for Food Integrity shows consumers believe the bigger a farm or food company is, the more likely it will be to put profit ahead of public interest. I know I've been guilty of this thinking. Whether or not there is validity in this belief is hard to discern. There is something to be said for the innovation that scale and profit enables, but there's also something to be said for the care that tends to be associated with smaller, more intimate, enterprises. In her enlightening book *Farm (and Other F Words)*, American journalist Sarah K Mock writes 'the current paradigm, which separates "small family farms" from "big corporate farms," doesn't actually help us find the farms that work well'. Mock argues that 'it's not the scale or the practice of farming that's broken, it's the whole idea we have of farms itself'. (She later cites three essential functions that a truly good farm should fulfil – 'produce healthy, affordable food or fibre, create livable, stable jobs, and not contribute to the degradation of soil, water, or other public resources.') Mock quotes an interviewee as saying that 'the folks who are small farmers and great businesspeople end up being big farmers and great businesspeople.' Which could help explain what has happened in the Tasmanian salmon industry.

An interesting thing about Tasmanian salmon is that they're not actually Tasmanian. Yes, they are grown in Tasmania but, just like almost all the animals and plants that feed us in Australia, they are an introduced species. They are Atlantic salmon, the species that has come to dominate the salmon aquaculture industries around the world. Ironically, and sadly, at the same time as Atlantic salmon has become one of the most abundant fish species in the world, its numbers in the wild have plummeted to the point where it is now one of the rarest ocean animals. As Dan Saladino writes in *Eating to Extinction*, 'It could be that 10,000 years after we began to tame cattle, pigs and sheep, we are taking a fish species along the same path, a domestication process in which the animals disappear from the wild but flourish in captivity, in this case occupying the ocean inside underwater cages.'

Salmon are grown in enclosures in natural waterways. They are fed pellets. The poop and waste falls to the ocean or estuary floor. That's been one of the contentious points. The waste has been reported as causing dead zones under the pens; basically, too many nutrients swamp the existing aquatic life. Salmon pens are a monoculture, with food brought in from outside. They are pretty much a feedlot for fish, with the attendant problems of high nutrient loads and highly confined animals.

There's something about salmon farming that reminds me of chicken farming. Take one species that people like and build a huge industry out of it. Reduce diversity. Focus on breeding and feeding to increase productivity. It produces a lot of food quickly, but I'm not sure it's necessarily the right path. Of course, salmon isn't chicken and salmon farming is nothing like the scale of chicken farming. Not so far at least. It has had colossal growth in the past couple of decades. It's also a few decades behind in terms of industry maturity.

Tasmanian writer Richard Flanagan has also drawn a link between salmon and chickens, calling Tasmanian Atlantic salmon 'the battery hen of the sea' in the book he wrote about his state's aquaculture industry. He's not a fan. Scathing is a word that comes to mind. The book's title gives it away: *Toxic: The Rotting Underbelly of the Tasmanian Salmon Industry*. Flanagan takes issue with the environmental, ethical, health and economic aspects of the industry. He writes, 'Justified as a solution to feeding the world into the future, the truth of salmon farming in Tasmania is the exact opposite: the theft of food from the poor, the commons from the people, and the future from the young, to feed affluent consumers and profit big business.'

Like many who find fault, Flanagan has attracted his own critics. A piece by veterinarian Dr Steve Percival published in Tasmanian newspaper *The Mercury* concluded, 'Mr Flanagan's book may well be his view of the salmon industry, but the truth is another story.' Percival has worked for Huon Aquaculture for over thirty years, so could be seen to have a biased viewpoint, although one person's biased viewpoint could be seen as another person's informed viewpoint. One of the things Percival took aim at was Flanagan's assertions about the misuse of antibiotics in the salmon industry. To be fair, Flanagan does say that Huon Aquaculture hasn't used antibiotics in its pens for some years and most of his assertions about antibiotic use are directed at Tassal. Flanagan writes: 'In 2019 Tassal used 62.28 grams of antibiotics per tonne of salmon – an extraordinary total of more than two tonnes of antibiotics being used in that year alone.' Flanagan says the high antibiotic use is due to disease burdens from overstocking. It does sound like a lot of antibiotics to be using at a time when the international One Health program, which recognises the link between the health of people, animals and the environment, is calling for judicious use. Overuse of antibiotics is one of the main driving forces of antibiotic resistance.

The NGO Environment Tasmania rates all three Tasmanian salmon producers as 'red' in their sustainability guide. They write that 'all score poorly on major sustainability and animal welfare indicators'. It all makes me glad that I don't like salmon. (Too fatty.)

But eating fish, especially fatty fish such as salmon, which are high in good fats like omega-3 fatty acids, is good for our hearts, eyes, blood, brains and joints. Fish don't actually produce omega-3 fatty acids; plants do. In the marine food web, omega-3 fatty acids come from microalgae, which are microscopic marine plants. Fish accumulate and concentrate the fatty acids, which makes them good dietary sources. Other animals that eat plants high in essential fatty acids can also be high in these fatty acids. For example, cattle and sheep that graze pasture are higher in fatty acids than those that eat concentrates. There are also a range of plants and plant products that are especially high in essential fatty acids – flax seeds, walnuts, chia seeds and soybeans are the big hitters. Eggs from chooks that have access to green feed are also high. But salmon is right up on the top of the list, along with that other very oily fish, mackerel. Sardines and herring also rank highly. It's not just about fatty acids though. Seafood is also high in other nutrients. Basically, fish is good for us.

There is some debate about whether eating farmed salmon has the same health benefits as eating their wild-caught relatives. Flanagan cites research that shows farmed salmon may contain only half the omega-3 fatty acids as wild salmon, and higher levels of omega-6 fatty acids, making the ratio of the two less healthy. But a Belgian study found most consumers perceived no differences between farmed versus wild fish. On average, though, the Belgian consumers slightly favoured wild fish for their taste, health and nutritional value. This was found to be especially the case among consumers over fifty-five years of age. But consumers thought farmed fish was more available and they saw no difference in the safety of farmed or wild-caught fish. The researchers say, 'Consumers' opinions and beliefs about farmed fish are mainly based on emotion and image transfer from intensive terrestrial livestock production rather than on awareness and factual knowledge of aquaculture.'

On the other hand, a UK study found some evidence to support the idea that as the percentage of fish in farmed salmon's diet decreases, so too do the levels of omega-3 fatty acids in the salmon's flesh. (That's because the omega-3 fatty acids are concentrated up the marine food chain; the little fish eat the microalgae that make the omega-3s, the big fish eat the little fish, and so on.) The UK study found that a 130-gram serving could supply as little as 26 per cent of desirable fatty acids or as much as 67 per cent, depending on what the salmon ate. While it's almost certainly better environmentally that farmed salmon don't eat wild-caught fish, eating them might be better for our health if they do. It appears the jury is still out on this point. It probably depends on what the wild-caught fish is replaced with in the farmed fish's diets.

Dietary guidelines, including Australian ones, consistently tell us we should eat more fish. But that is rarely investigated concurrently with environmental credentials of aquaculture and fishing. Noting this, a group of researchers looked at dietary guidelines and sustainability practices together, to give a broader view on where the best choices lay if Australian consumers wanted to choose fish that is good for them and good for the planet. They report that while average global seafood consumption has doubled over the past fifty years (from 9.9 kilograms per person in the 1960s to over 20 kilograms in 2016), Australians would, on average, have to increase their consumption by 40 per cent to eat the recommended 140–280 grams per week.

When the health of eaters and the planet are considered together, the researchers give the biggest tick to small pelagic fish. These are the ones that live in the middle of the ocean, neither on the surface nor on the bottom – in the water called the pelagic zone. (Lakes and rivers can also have pelagic zones and pelagic fish.) Think sardines and mackerel. But most Australians don't eat these fish – the researchers found only 1 per cent of people surveyed ate small pelagic fish. Most of these small fish caught in Australia (and elsewhere) are ground into fish meal to feed aquaculture fish (and pigs and chickens – cue the idea of replacing this protein source with insects grown on waste).

Tassal says they use 0.7 kilograms of wild fish to grow 1 kilogram of farmed salmon. Just a few years ago, it was over a kilo of wild caught fish to make a kilo of farmed salmon, so there has been a significant reduction. The rest of the salmon feed is made up of wheat, soya, corn, gluten, vegetable oils, meat and chicken meal, blood meal, poultry oil, vitamins, minerals and astaxanthin, which is a red pigment that gives salmon its pink colour. Wild salmon get astaxanthin from eating shrimp and such things, but farmed salmon don't eat shrimp so the pigment is added to their feed. If it wasn't, farmed salmon wouldn't be pink. (Astaxanthin is an antioxidant and can be bought in capsule form from health food shops. I'm neither advocating for nor denouncing this, just noting it.)

The Australian study that looked concurrently at the environmental impacts and health benefits of eating different types of seafood also scored molluscs, such as mussels and oysters, highly on sustainability and moderately highly on nutrition. The least sustainable and least nutritious seafood group was found to be crustaceans and low-omega-3 aquaculture fish. A category the researchers called 'popular table fish', which meant they were not large predators nor small pelagics, and were regularly eaten due to 'taste, texture, smell, and colour', ranked in the middle for sustainability and nutrition. The large predators, such as tuna, swordfish and shark came in below the 'popular table fish' for sustainability and about equal for nutrition.

Even though Australians don't eat as much fish, on average, as dietary guidelines recommend, between us we do eat a considerable amount and most of us eat it at least sometimes. A 2018 survey found 78 per cent of Australians had eaten either fresh, frozen or tinned fish in the previous twelve months; only 7 per cent of Australians don't eat fish at all and a third eat fish at least weekly. We also, as a nation, catch fish in a very large area of ocean. The Australian Fishing Zone covers more than 8 million square kilometres. To put that into perspective, it's an area larger than mainland Australia. Most of the fisheries within this area are managed by the Federal Government but those within 3 nautical miles of the coast fall under state control; this is where most aquaculture is based.

Australian waters are considered to have relatively low productivity, so the catch is not huge on an international scale. According to industry reports, the catch is also limited by strict regulations to ensure the industry's sustainability. In 2021, the *Fisheries Status Reports* (which is produced by ABARES, the Australian Bureau of Agricultural and Resource Economics and Sciences) gave the Australian fishing industry a sustainability tick for the eighth consecutive year. The reports investigated the status of 100 species across twenty-two fisheries, and looked at the fisheries' performance in terms of legal and policy requirements. That sounds like we can all happily buy wild-caught Australian fish and consume it with a clear conscience. But not so fast.

CSIRO researchers Dr Aysha Fleming and Dr Ingrid van Putten spent a year investigating the problem of bycatch in the Great Australian Bight. Bycatch is the stuff that is inadvertently caught during fishing. Basically, it gets thrown back into the ocean. Fleming and van Putten say 8 per cent of the global fish catch is discarded as bycatch. WWF-Australia says, globally, bycatch is thought to be the leading cause of death for whales and dolphins. WWF-Australia advises looking for the Marine Stewardship Council (MSC) certification when shopping for seafood. The MSC aims to ensure fishing does not harm the integrity of ocean ecosystems. Products that have been certified by them carry a blue tick on their packaging.

Fleming and van Putten suggest consumers should be a little more adventurous in their seafood choices. They write: 'In Australia, most people tend to dislike "fishy" flavours like sardines and cook fish in a way – flinging it on the bbq – that may not work for more delicate, unusual species like clams. We prefer boneless fish that flakes but isn't too soft or too oily (for example we love flathead, not eel).' Which makes me feel like they might have read my mind! They add that we have also become very used to eating the same things at any time of year, with little thought to seasonality. The result of all of this is that: 'molluscs may be too irregular, leatherjacket might have too many bones, and dogfish might just have the wrong name'. Fortunately, they offer a solution, suggesting that we need to branch out a little when eating seafood, opting to try new ways of cooking and to talk to fish sellers about what is fresh, seasonal and local. They write: 'Increased demand for a wider range of locally caught species would also reduce imported fish (Australia imports more seafood than it exports). This would help take the pressure off overseas fisheries that may be less sustainably managed than our own (which are subject to strict environmental regulations).' Finally, they conclude: 'Don't throw another shrimp on the barbie; make it ocean jacket or whatever has just come in fresh instead.'

With a resource harvested directly from the wild, there is little that can be done to increase yield. There are natural limits to what can be taken sustainably. Yet the human population continues to rise, so if most people are going to eat some fish, we will come to a crunch point where the amount taken from sustainable fisheries simply cannot meet demand. If we are going to eat seafood, then perhaps we should be farming it. But maybe we need to look beyond salmon. Would using a native species help alleviate the issues?

Barramundi is also farmed in Australia; most of the barramundi eaten in Australia is from farmed stock. Unlike salmon, barramundi is an Australian species. Like salmon, a large portion of the feed for farmed barramundi comes from wild-caught fish. According to the GoodFish Guide, there is about the same amount of wild fish caught to feed farmed barramundi as there is barramundi harvested, so while farming barramundi doesn't deplete ocean fish, it does rely heavily on them. The barramundi is probably better eating in almost everyone's opinion but if we increase demand for farmed barramundi, by default we increase pressure on wild fish stock. Farming barramundi is not a free ride out of the dilemma, unless a different way of feeding them is found. And as we saw with salmon, that's not necessarily a straightforward answer either.

Canadian Bren Smith, who describes himself as a fisherman turned ocean farmer, says the problem with aquaculture generally is that it tends to take ocean fish that want to swim away and confine them in pens. In his book *Eat Like a Fish*, Smith details how he came to see the North Atlantic fisheries in which he worked as being unsustainable, yet he was still drawn to the oceans and boats. He now 'farms 20 acres of saltwater, growing a mix of sea greens and shellfish'. Smith argues that aquaculture begins with species that have traditionally been wild caught and that people have a taste for – cod, tuna, salmon – and builds an industry around the existing markets. His ocean farm works differently. He writes, 'I needed a different starting point, based on the fundamental belief that our tastes must bend to the ocean's will. Regardless of existing market demand, what makes the most sense to grow in the ocean?' He came up with a layered system with clams at the bottom, then worked up the water column with scallops, oysters, mussels and kelp; a system he describes as a multi-layered polyculture. Smith quotes research from Dr Ronald Osinga at Wageningen University in the Netherlands. Osinga calculated that 500 20-acre ocean farms would produce 120 million pounds of shellfish and 11 to 40 million pounds of seaweeds. As Smith puts it, that's a lot of food. Crucially, they produce it all without requiring any inputs. Plus the system absorbs carbon and nutrients from the water, which, along with the employment it provides, is a huge benefit of the approach.

Where does that leave dinner? I still don't like fish much, so I'm unlikely to meet the Australian dietary guidelines as far as fish goes. I'll probably need to look elsewhere for my omega-3 fatty acids. On the rare occasions when I do buy fish, I tend to opt for popular table fish but perhaps I'll try to get more adventurous with small pelagic fish. Sardines for lunch, perhaps. I'm unlikely to start eating molluscs, but maybe I need to overcome my aversion and eat shelled things. And maybe I need to branch out to kelp.

It can be challenging to introduce new foods to our personal diets. It's easier to reach for the foods we know than to try the ones we don't. Although, once we try something a few times it can become a regular feature of our meals. Multiculturalism has expanded the culinary horizons of all Australians. But still, the arbitrary lines we all draw around what we will and won't eat, what we do and don't eat, are intriguing from personal, historical and cultural perspectives.

CHAPTER 14

Macadamia

I WENT HIKING. THE 13-kilogram pack on my back held everything I needed, or might need, for three nights, four days – a change of clothes, a raincoat, basic first aid supplies, including a snake bite kit, a sleeping bag and mat, utensils and food. The food was divided into meals and neatly packaged in zip-lock plastic bags. My evening meals were dehydrated and vacuum sealed – chilli beef and veg, bolognaise sauce and pasta, curry beef and veg. Just add boiling water to rehydrate it and then eat and enjoy.

I arrived, tired and hungry, at the shelter the first night. Dumped my pack. Filled my water bottles from the rainwater tank. Made a cup of tea. Soaked and heated my dehydrated meal. The forest around me was beautiful. Tall straight jarrah trees reached for the late afternoon blue sky. The understorey was a riot of spring colour. Orange and yellow petals of flame peas sat side by side like flamboyant old ladies at bingo. Purple-flowering hardenbergia wound its way over logs and tangled with the white-flowering clematis. The bright yellow wattles and red kennedia vied for the brightest-flower prize. A troop of splendid wrens, the male brilliant cobalt blue, danced through the undergrowth. Carnaby's black cockatoos and twenty-eight parrots screeched overhead.

It was stunning. Beautiful. Full of life. And with sudden, sharp, head-spinning clarity, I realised I would have no chance of survival in this environment I love so much were it not for the contents of my backpack. Thirteen kilograms of life-giving stuff and sustenance. Without it, and the assured water at the shelters at the end of each day's hike, I had no chance. I would be without food, shelter, warmth, direction and water. I had no real idea of what to eat in the bush – I knew the tender shoots of grass trees and the gum of marri trees are edible, but that wouldn't keep me going for long. I knew that possums and kangaroos are edible, but I had no means to catch, trap or kill one, let alone prepare and cook it. My connection to the bush – despite how much I love and value it – is intellectual and emotional. It is not physical, not visceral. Everything I eat comes from introduced plants and animals.

Our modern Australian food chain is a European farming and food system imposed on the landscape. The plant and animal species that dominate it, and that dominate the world's dinner plates, are from Middle Eastern, Asian, European and American roots. It is not an agriculture of this landscape. It has had to bend and coax and change the Australian land to bring forth the food to feed us. It, and the farmers who have made those changes, has been remarkably success-ful in many ways. The food now produced annually in Australia is enough to feed over 60 million people, far more than our population. Each Australian farmer feeds, on average, about 600 people each year; 150 in Australia and 450 overseas. It's an amazing achievement. We are a net food-producing nation. Over 90 per cent of the food consumed here is produced here.

But the cost has been high. Very high. Alienation of Indigenous Australians from their traditional country and associated social disruption and loss of knowledge. Erosion, salination, acidifica-tion, loss of biodiversity. Losses counted in hundreds of millions of dollars, but also intangible. Losses evident on balance sheets but also written across the landscape. When colonists arrived in Australia, they brought with them the agriculture of Europe and went about establishing it here, overwriting the land they found with one they knew. With determined ignorance of what they were removing, they established the foundations for the highly successful farming system we see today. Could it have been different?

There are over 6500 native foods in Australia. Through intimate and detailed knowledge, Indigenous Australians relied on that huge diversity to sustain their cultures for tens of thousands of years. Diets were local, seasonal and varied. Of the many foods native to Australia, only one has so far found a place in global agriculture – macadamia.

Endemic to Queensland and northern New South Wales, macadamia trees are now cultivated commercially in Australia, Hawaii, South Africa, Kenya, Malawi, Colombia, Costa Rica, Guatemala, and Brazil. They are an evergreen tree that favours semi-tropical environments and can grow up to 12 metres tall. The nuts are high in oil (76 per cent fat) and relatively low in protein (8 per cent) compared with other tree nuts, but they pack a punch with vitamins and minerals. They are encased in notoriously hard shells. Australia, fittingly, produces most of the world's macadamias but was not the first country to cultivate the nut commercially. That distinction goes to Hawaii, which is why the common name of Hawaiian nut is sometimes given to macadamias. Commercial cultivation began in the late 1800s and those original trees are still in production; they're a long-lived tree.

In Australia, the first commercial macadamia processing plant was established in 1954. Now there are more than 700 Australian growers producing about 50,000 tonnes a year, 70 per cent of which is exported to more than forty countries. According to the Australian Macadamia Society, macadamia is Australia's fourth largest horticultural export. (Almonds, table grapes and oranges are all higher.) The macadamia industry has a current annual turnover in excess of $100 million.

But why only macadamias? Why aren't there other Australian foods produced and sold in large quantities and grown in other countries? Why haven't other Australian foods followed in macadamia's footsteps? The Federal Government agency AgriFutures Australia says due to 'the accidents of geography and history, Australia was not endowed with high productivity plant and animal systems'. According to AgriFutures, some native plants and animals have been farmed but have failed to gain major traction despite considerable government support and valiant efforts from passionate promotors – in over twenty years wattleseed has not hit the million-dollar benchmark. Similarly, emus, which have been farmed for over thirty years, remain a $1–2 million sector. Put simply, 'most Australian flora and fauna are not (yet) well adapted to the needs of modern agriculture. Australia has a lot of native flora that is edible, but little that is compelling to modern consumers.'

There are only thirteen Australian native foods that are currently produced and marketed at any scale (albeit not huge) and certified through Food Standards Australia New Zealand (FSANZ). Some native foods are now hitting niche markets and, although the total forecast market value of all these foods in combination is only $5–7 million, it's a sector that stirs emotions. As AgriFutures puts it: 'The sector is high profile and "feel good" and generates discussion, attention, media and government investment disproportionate with its size for non-market reasons.'

One of the people passionate about native foods is Noongar woman Dale Tilbrook. It's a blustery autumn day when I pull up at Maalinup Aboriginal Gallery in the Swan Valley, on Perth's doorstep. Maalinup is owned and run by Tilbrook and her brother Lyall. They greet me at the door and laughingly welcome me to the chaos. Due to Covid and border restrictions, the gallery has been closed to the public for a while, and when I visit, the Tilbrooks are in the process of reorganising and getting things ready to reopen. Despite the disorder, the thing that strikes me most is the scent – a clean, fresh, deep citrus smell fills the room. I comment on it to Tilbrook. 'Lemon myrtle,' she says, pointing to a large pile of leaves drying on a tarpaulin spread on the ground. 'More lemony than lemon. It has higher citral levels than any of the citrus.' Then adds, with a nod to how much work there is to do before the forthcoming reopening, 'That all needs to be packaged up before we open.'

Lemon myrtle is one of the small-scale success stories of native foods. Tilbrook says it is one of those Australian herbs that has gained immediate acceptance because of its intense lemon-and-lime flavours and aromas. She says it's fabulous in both savoury and sweet dishes. When she says immediate acceptance, she means as soon as native foods began to capture the public's attention after decades upon decades of being ignored.

'It does go back to those first arrivals,' Tilbrook says. 'If we look at Western Australia, when the Europeans first came here, there were big yam gardens along *Derbal Yerragin*, the Swan River, which the Europeans took no note of really, other than that they were an inconvenience because they occupied the good alluvial soil along the river and they wanted that for themselves. They wanted the river access because that was the big transport artery and they wanted that good soil for their own crops.' The yams Tilbrook is talking about are *Warrine* (*Dioscorea hatifolia*), a long, thin, highly nutritious tuber.

Tilbrook says those yam gardens were cultivated by the 'old people' but the colonists, instead of trying to understand what a yam was and how it was grown and why, wiped them out. 'If you look at early settler maps from that time – around 1829 – you'll see the yam gardens marked on those maps as warren holes,' Tilbrook says. 'Warrine is our name for that yam. And holes, because it refers to the way in which it was harvested and left. Instead of digging individual yams, which is very hard work and no guarantee that you get a yam at the end of it, they would be collapsing the soil. Coming in from the side, collapsing the soil, gathering the tubers and not filling the holes. We were only tending those yam gardens twice a year, once in *Djeran*, autumn, this season now, and once in *Kambarang*, late spring. The rest of the time, you know, we were out doing other things across the land.' Tilbrook uses the Noongar names for the seasons. It's a calendar that recognises six seasons in a year, each dictated by the weather, what is flowering, how animals are moving, and what the Indigenous people did in response.

'*Birak*, first summer, for example, and *Bunuru*, second summer, we would be at the coast and coming up the estuaries,' Tilbrook says. 'And then in Djeran we'd be moving back up those rivers and back to our inland camps. So we left those holes open because that protected the yam gardens, because our local animals, like the Europeans on horseback, don't like uneven ground because it's too easy to break a leg. Those humps and hollows would also collect water and leaf litter, so they didn't need to be there the whole time. Mother Nature could take care of the yam gardens in the intervening period.' Tilbrook says roots and tubers, such as yams, were staple food for all Aboriginal people in the South West and more than 150 different tuberous plants provided food all year around. 'Don't ask me to name them all!' Tilbrook laughs, before continuing, 'But, you know, there'd be the yams; we'd also be harvesting the root masses of the *Yanget*, the bullrushes, along Derbarl Yerrigan. You might have heard of the Ravensthorpe radish? *Youlk* is our name for it. It's a juicy tuber from the carrot family.'

I had heard of Youlk but I didn't taste it until a few weeks later when I went to visit Mark Tucek. A horticulturalist by profession, Tucek is on a mission to make native food plants more accessible to Australians. 'We live in Australia,' Tucek says. 'Everyone has a lemon tree in their backyard. Why don't we have a finger lime? Modern Australians don't appreciate what's in their own backyard.' Tucek, who is a whitefella, regularly works with Aboriginal people including Tilbrook to educate others about edible native plants and to make the plants accessible. Through his business Tucker Bush, Tucek cultivates and distributes Australian 'bush tucker' plants for people to grow in their homes and gardens. (The term bush tucker is interchangeable with Australian native foods and native edibles – 'Call it whatever you like,' Tilbrook says. 'It all means the same thing. It's the plant food, and the meat food, we ate.')

As Tucek and I walk around his nursery, he pulls off a leaf here and there and hands them to me to taste, explaining the plants and their uses as we go. Then he upends a pot with a small scraggly shrub growing in it. He fossicks through the soil and extracts a round tuber and hands it to me. It's about the size of a large grape. I rub the dirt off and bite into it. It's crunchy and crisp. It tastes something like celery and something like carrot, but the texture is almost nut like. 'That's good,' I say. 'Not bad at all.'

'That's Youlk,' Tucek says. 'You bandicoot down around the roots to extract the tubers. It doesn't have to be dug up. It gives and gives.' He returns the plant to the pot. Youlk is one of the plants now available through Tucker Bush. I make a mental note to buy some and put it in my garden, to add as a crunchy addition to salads and a connection to place.

'Everyone should have an edible native plant in their backyard,' Tucek says. I ask him why we don't. He says that it's largely been a problem of lack of supply. They weren't readily available in nurseries. And that even if the plants were being grown and were available for sale, they weren't labelled as bush tucker so people didn't know they could eat them. People didn't know how to grow, harvest and use them. 'Everyone knows what a blueberry is but no one knows what a *Midyim* berry is,' Tucek says. For the record, a Midyim berry, according to Tucek, is among the most delicious of all the edible native plants, similar in taste and appearance to the blueberry and native to the area around Moreton Bay in Queensland. (I make another mental note to add Midyim berry plants to the native foods garden that is rapidly growing in my imagination.)

'If you want to grow broccoli, you get on the internet and there are a million bits of information about how to do that,' Tucek says. 'If you wanted to grow native lemongrass, there was nothing. You had to do it by trial and error.' Which is the void Tucek is attempting to fill. His original bush tucker range contained six different plant species, along with cultivation, harvesting and usage notes. 'When I put the range together, I picked plants that are easy to grow, rewarding and that enable people to pick things they are semi-familiar with,' he says. It took a lot of time and work to get the commercial nurseries on board and the plants into the right section in retail outlets. 'They were put in the native section,' Tucek says. 'Once they were moved to the edibles section, they sold. Then they started selling really well.' His label now adorns over ninety species, with growers in each state supplying slightly different ranges tailored to the local conditions.

Tucek says education is still a big factor. He worked with Noongar woman Marissa Verma to create the Tucker Bush Schools Program, where Verma would talk about the cultural aspects of bush tucker and Tucek would cover the horticultural aspects. 'I always get the kids to plant with bare hands,' Tucek says. 'No gloves, no trowels. Get the dirt under their nails.' He does this because of the beneficial feel-good bacteria, *Mycobacterium vaccae*, that has been shown to be one of the reasons why gardening often makes people happy. 'Getting your hands dirty is really important,' Tucek says. 'It really is good for you.' His enthusiasm is infectious and as we tour his nursery, the list of plants I want to grow gets longer and longer.

Tucek says it's crucial to include Aboriginal people when working with edible native plants, and he is also working with Tilbrook on some projects. He says it comes down to transparency and, with wild-harvested produce, traceability. 'You ask permission and you don't take,' Tucek says. Tilbrook is a fan of the way Tucek works and what he is doing, and vice versa. The respect is clear when I talk to each of them.

They also agree on their dislike of foraging and both mention people foraging for samphire, a small native plant that grows on brackish and saline, often waterlogged, ground. It's also called sea asparagus. 'Chefs were going down to the Swan River and foraging for samphire and doing damage,' Tucek says. 'I'm not a fan of foraging. It's okay for Aboriginal people but not for us whitefellas. I figured if it was available, they wouldn't go foraging.' Tilbrook says Aboriginal people can collect for cultural purposes but as soon as there is any commerciality involved, a licence is needed.

Tucek says demand from high-profile chefs is an important driver for the bush tucker industry. 'My website comes up if you google bush tucker plants, so I'd get chefs ringing me asking if they could buy produce, rather than plants,' Tucek says. 'I always said no, I don't do that. But you can buy a plant and grow it yourself. They didn't necessarily want to do that. One day, I decided that the next one that rang me, I'd say yes. So, I did. Then I had to figure out how I was going to package and sell it.' It seems this is the way the

Tucker Bush business is developing; jump in and then learn to swim. Tucek has now built a drying room and is slowly starting to supply dried herbs.

It's warm inside the drying room and it smells delicious. Tucek gives me a couple of samples to take and try – native thyme and native mint. His commentary runs on, bringing his central theme home time and again: 'I bet you have thyme and mint in your garden, but not native thyme and native mint.' He's right. I do. And I don't. (When I got home and tried the dried native thyme and native mint, they were terrific.) Tucek says he realised people wanted to use the plants but didn't really know how to do so. 'Then I needed to start putting recipes on my website, so now I have a recipe book,' he says. He's also written a book about bush tucker, *Bushfood for Beginners*. It seems there's no end to his enthusiasm and passion for making this work. But he says the best way to learn about bush tucker is to go on an Aboriginal tour. And then grow some in your garden. He's not letting go of his vision of a more Australian cuisine and an edible Australian plant in every garden.

I ask Tilbrook what she would like to see happen with bush tucker. She says there are things happening already, with plants being identified that can be made into crops. Some are being cultivated around Australia, such as quandongs in South Australia based on plantation trees, and wattleseed being grown in the Riverina and elsewhere. None of them is yet hitting AgriFutures' million-dollar benchmark, but maybe they don't need to; maybe the importance of bringing native plants into our national cuisine is about 'Australianising' our diets and providing on-country business opportunities for Indigenous people.

Tilbrook points out that there are many, perhaps up to a hundred, species of edible wattleseed in Australia, out of the thousand or more species that grow. 'It's the sort of plant you can put into quite degraded soil and still get a crop from it,' she says. 'The wattleseed, or the acacia trees, are actually great hosts for both quandong and sandalwood, so potentially you can have dual crops.' In talking about hosts, Tilbrook is referring to quandong and sandalwood being parasitic plants that need to attach to the roots of a host plant to thrive. Acacias make good hosts and have the advantage of being legumes, so they fix nitrogen into the soil. Some acacias have the added advantage of providing good fodder for livestock, so the benefits of adding these plants to farms have the potential to accrue. I ask Tilbrook if she sees it as more than a niche industry.

'It makes good sense because of the nutrient values,' she says. 'For example, wattleseed is 20 to 30 per cent protein, it's high in iron, it's high in zinc, it's high in magnesium, it's naturally low GI and it has dietary fibre. What's not to love?' I laugh; what's not to love, indeed. But Tilbrook hasn't finished. 'It's the kind of crop that you can put into sort of odd corners in a farm and it doesn't have to be planted in neat little rows. It can be doing its job here, there and everywhere. Although you can plant it in neat little rows if you want to.'

Tilbrook is pragmatic about how investment will flow into bush tucker industries. 'Most of the investment is going to follow on when we have more demand and more demand is going to come from export industry,' she says. 'Already, people are keen for us to have more wattleseed available, as a functional food to add to breads and cakes and other things.'

Tilbrook says the bush food industry was begun by non-Aboriginal people who saw opportunities with lemon myrtle, anise myrtle, riberry, the various native limes (such as finger lime), quandong and pepper berry. 'So these became the hero plants for bush foods, as it were, and until quite recently those hero plants were the only ones listed by FSANZ,' Tilbrook says. 'Considering there are 6500 edible plants in Australia, we've still got lots of opportunities and there is a big move afoot to increase Indigenous participation in the industry and to acknowledge Indigenous traditional knowledge. And more people willing to work with Indigenous growers or harvesters and ensure that the benefits are equally shared, or better shared than they have been in the past.'

I ask Tilbrook about the meats. 'We should all be eating kangaroo,' she says without hesitating. 'We should all be eating much more kangaroo because it's not only good for us, it's good for the environment as well. All our local animals have soft feet. They're not like the hard hooves or the cloven hooves that are digging up our fragile soil systems.' Tilbrook isn't so sure we should be eating other native animals though, because while they were traditional foods of Aboriginal peoples, the environment and their abundance have changed. 'Now you have to look at the destruction of habitat,' she says. 'What's left? There are a lot more kangaroos now than at the time of first European settlement because the landscape changed, all those grasses and crops and water. That has favoured kangaroos. Kangaroo is quality meat, lovely meat, which is full of protein, full of iron, low fat, low cholesterol.'

Tilbrook sees it as being up to consumers to say what they want and to drive the demand for native ingredients of all sorts. 'There's lots of opportunities to grow your own, especially with the soft-leaved plants and herbs, our beach herbs and some herbs that come from different parts of Australia,' Tilbrook says. 'You could potentially grow wattleseed yourself, but you have to be careful to get the right wattleseeds. Only about a hundred are edible. Some potentially could have high levels of toxins or antinutrients.'

Tilbrook says there is undoubtedly knowledge that was lost. 'Too many of the people who went before us passed away before they could pass on that knowledge,' she says. 'A lot of that knowledge would have been passed on when we were out harvesting. If you're not out there doing it, the need to talk about it disappears. Those things get lost in the mists of time if somebody's not standing next to somebody and knowing that's why you do it. There is still a lot of knowledge still intact and a lot of knowledge about plants that is being gleaned by scientists working on things, looking at the nutritional values of our plants, looking at potential toxins and antinutrients and saying this is good to eat, that is not good to eat.' Tilbrook says it started off as Aboriginal knowledge and now, some of it at least, can be knowledge for everyone. 'You can know that this plant is edible and perhaps you don't know what part of the plant to use or when to harvest it for best effect or how to use it. That's the local knowledge, that's the Aboriginal knowledge.' Tilbrook sometimes conducts tours that allow people to experience the taste of bushfood from the food she collects and also conducts cooking demonstrations using native ingredients. She stresses again the importance of not going out to harvest native plants in the wild and says growing your own is a much better option.

For most of us, and for most of what we eat, we rely on the effort and ingenuity of farmers and the agricultural systems they manage. But I think native Australian foods do have a role to play in our diets, and I'm with Tucek and Tilbrook in wanting to see them incorporated into our gardens and farms, and onto our plates.

Enough on your plate

THE SCALLOPED EDGES of the plates are gilt, a fine line of gold, worn thin now. Hand-painted nasturtiums, yellow and orange petals entwined with sage green leaves, decorate the bevel before the plates drop to their pale cream centres. The glaze is cracked in parts, dark scales of age spreading across the smooth surface. Mum packed the whole dinner set into an old wooden fruit box and gave it to me. 'Here, you should have this,' she said. 'Grandma would have wanted you to.' I attempted to protest but Mum wouldn't hear of it, brushed me aside, so I took the box. It felt like an act of thievery.

I had always liked the dinner set. It wasn't one that Grandma used often – she preferred plain white china. The nasturtium dinner set was a gift to her from my father's mother. Grandma One-Five-Six, as we called my paternal grandmother (her city house number was 156), had stayed with Grandma Karridale (my maternal grandmother, because of where she lived) for a while in the early 1950s. The dinner set was Grandma One-Five-Six's way of saying thank you. It was a generous gift; both when it was given by one grandmother to the other, and again when it was passed on to me fifty years later.

Part of me thinks the dinner set is too precious to use. I unpacked it carefully into a cupboard, stacked the plates neatly, closed the doors on it. But that didn't seem right. It's not what should happen to things made for use. So I try to use it, sometimes. I've dished up curry on the plates, then panicked that the turmeric stain would be permanent, a yellow tinge forever reflecting that I eat differently to my grandparents. But it washed off – handwashing of course; these plates were not made for the rigours of a dishwasher.

The thing I notice most when I serve onto the nasturtium plates is their size. They are small. Remarkably small. My modern dinner plates have a diameter almost 10 centimetres larger. The old entree plates are little bigger than side plates in my modern setting. In the seventy years since the nasturtiums were painted on the fine bone china, it's not just the food being cooked in Australian kitchens that has changed. The size of meals being dished up has increased as well. As have the waistlines the meals feed. A British study confirms my suspicion about plate and serving sizes. My old and new dinner sets reflect a trend; plates are now bigger. That study also found we tend to eat more when larger serving sizes are presented, and reducing serving sizes can dramatically reduce daily energy consumption (by up to 29 per cent among US adults).

It's not just how much we are putting on our larger plates that has changed in recent decades; the food we are serving is also different. I'm not the only one cooking different foods than my mother and grandmothers did. The 2016 *Trolley Trends* study, commissioned by Woolworths and completed by demographer Bernard Salt, found the meat-and-three-veg meal of the 1970s and 80s had 'fallen by the wayside' in Australia. The study reported that in the 1990s, Mediterranean produce, including zucchini, garlic, eggplant and red capsicum, reached critical mass in our supermarkets. In the 2010s, these Mediterranean products were joined by Middle Eastern counterparts such as Medjool dates, figs, almonds and pomegranates. More recently, the 'superfoods' kale, blueberries and sweet potato have become common on supermarket shelves. I can think of many other things that simply weren't on the shelves when I first became responsible for filling my own fridge and pantry back in the 1980s. Mangoes and avocadoes are newly abundant. Kiwifruit, persimmons, raspberries, honeydew melons, dragon fruit and lychees are all relative newcomers. Seedless watermelon and seedless grapes. Fresh chillies and ginger. Fresh turmeric and galangal are even more recent. Many of these things are thanks to migrants bringing familiar foods with them. Some are thanks to researchers developing new varieties. It makes it seem like our food is increasing in diversity.

But it's an illusion. While I have access to a much broader range of foods than my grandmothers did, the food supply across the world today is less varied than it was a couple of generations ago. As Dan Saladino writes in *Eating to Extinction*, 'What we're being offered appears at first to be diverse, until you realise it is the same kind of 'diversity' that is spreading around the globe in an identical fashion; what the world buys and eats is becoming more and more the same.' Think for a moment of the last time you travelled somewhere 'foreign'; the labels on the supermarket shelves may have been written in a different language with prices in a different currency but, unless you were in an impoverished country, there was probably still bread, noodles, rice, milk, chicken, tomatoes, potatoes, carrots, onions, apples and bananas. All regardless of the time of year; transport trumps seasonality all over the world. Saladino again: 'Whether you're in London, Los Angeles or Lima, you can eat sushi, curry, or McDonald's; bite into an avocado, banana or mango; sip a Coke, a Budweiser or a branded bottle of water – and all in a single day.'

If you eat chicken anywhere in the world, it will most likely be a Cobb or Ross chicken, regardless of how it was raised. If you consume dairy products, they will probably be made with milk from Friesian cows. If you buy a banana, it will almost certainly be of the Cavendish variety. Bananas are perhaps the epitome of uniformity in our food supply. Not only are almost all bananas sold in shops Cavendish, all Cavendish bananas are clones. Every single one is genetically identical, grown from suckers of parent plants, not from seeds. (When plants grow from seeds, the mixing of genes from ovules (plant eggs) and pollen (plant sperm), gives genetic variation in the offspring. But in vegetative reproduction – that is growing from suckers or cuttings – the new plant is genetically identical to its single parent.) This lack of genetic diversity means the world's banana crops are especially susceptible to disease. We've seen that before.

The other thing that has changed drastically in recent decades is abundance. The rationing and associated frugality of the post-war years has been relegated to history in modern wealthy countries. We talk now about the cost of living, but the amount we spend on food has fallen. The International Food Policy Research Institute reports that between 1974 and 2005, real food prices fell by about 75 per cent, but have become more volatile since then. But even with the instability of the past decade or so, the real cost of food remained relatively low until the Covid pandemic. In 2022, it rose above 1975 levels for the first time, according to the UN Food and Agriculture Organization's World Food Price Index. Despite the media frenzy about food prices, our food remains relatively cheap. However, there are some confusing statistics regarding how much our food costs us. The Australian Bureau of Statistics (ABS) reported the price of food and non-alcoholic beverages rose almost 6 per cent in the year to June 2022. But the ABS also reported a 2 per cent decline in household spending on food in the same period. If food is more expensive, why aren't we spending more on it? The ABS attributed part of the decline in household food spending to more meals being consumed outside of the home. And maybe many households are spending less because we are buying more cheap food, saving money to use on expensive housing. I'm not sure what exactly is going on, but there is evidence to suggest food costs us a smaller proportion of our income now than it did a generation or two ago. Modern agriculture and supermarkets have accustomed us to expecting cheap food. US figures indicate Americans spent less than 10 per cent of their income on food in 2021, compared with 17 per cent in 1961.

There are Australians who struggle to buy food to feed themselves and their families and I'm not diminishing their plight. According to University of Melbourne researchers, between 4 and 14 per cent of Australians experience some form of food insecurity. They report that a million Australians 'run out of food and can't afford to buy more, and many more skip meals or eat cheaper, less healthy foods to cope with not having enough money to buy food.' During the first year of the Covid pandemic, the problem was exacerbated, with requests for emergency food relief from charities jumping by 47 per cent. In the midst of our abundance, these figures should be seen as a source of national shame. Ironically, access to fresh, healthy food is often worst in rural areas, leading to an over-reliance on foods that have a long shelf life and, often, fewer nutrients. This dearth of good-quality food in rural and remote regions has been linked to higher obesity rates outside of metropolitan areas.

The *EAT-Lancet Report* named food production as one of the largest drivers of global environmental change, contributing to climate change, biodiversity loss, freshwater use, interference with the global nitrogen and phosphorus cycles, land-system change and chemical pollution. The crux of the problem is that there are so many people in the world and all of us need to eat, preferably three meals a day. The world population will continue to grow, at least until well into this century, so demand for food will continue to rise.

The hungry ask what is for dinner in the hope there is something, anything, to eat. On this front, there is cause for restrained optimism. Our ability to feed the world's people has improved dramatically. As Australian science journalist Julian Cribb writes in *The Coming Famine*, 'When the Green Revolution began, one in three of the world's people faced hunger or died from the diseases associated with it. By the early twenty-first century this had fallen to one in eight (or 850 million)...' As Cribb puts it, this is still an unacceptably high toll in human suffering. But it's worth remembering that, despite the many criticisms levelled at the Green Revolution and the industrialisation of agriculture, progress has been made in feeding the world's people.

But there are signs that progress may be slowing. In recent decades, the speed at which yields are increasing has slowed down; yields are still increasing, but not as quickly. If you look at it on a line graph you would see it has levelled off – we have flattened the curve. Cribb attributes this to lack of government research into agriculture. He writes that at the start of the 21st century, rich counties were only spending 1.8 cents in every science dollar on agriculture. Cribb adds, 'At the turn of the millennium, public investment by all governments worldwide in improving food production totalled just $23 billion.' He contrasts this with the $1.5 trillion spent on armaments. It behoves us to pressure governments and the private sector to invest in agricultural research. We need to continue to improve the way we produce our food.

———

I could look at more species in my exploration of food, farming and environment – the rest of the top seventeen species that feed us or more of the rest. The story would be the same. The species that feed us have been bent by our will and ingenuity to do so over millennia. We now rely on a dangerously narrow range of species for most of our food, and an even more dangerously narrow suite of varieties or breeds within those species. We hand more and more of the control over what we eat to larger and larger global corporations at the expense of local-scale farms and farmers. We rely on an ever-diminishing number of others to grow and provide our food and we generally understand very little of what they do. We are overfed and under connected.

The links between food, farming and environment are nuanced and complicated. It's a complex, messy system – or perhaps not really a system at all, but a mess of different enmeshed systems. Those of us who are fortunate to live amid plenty in wealthy countries are in a privileged position. I believe that brings with it a responsibility to be careful in our food choices. But there aren't easy answers. Eating local is not always better for the environment than eating from a huge farm at distance, but often it is. Food produced by a small farmer is not always healthier than that produced by a corporate, but it can be. Animal welfare may be handled better on small farms, but won't always be. Backyard gardens can provide useful food for the household, but aren't always the answer. Reducing meat consumption is a good idea for most Westerners, but not everyone. A vegan diet can be more environmentally friendly than an omnivorous diet, but won't always be. None of these things are true in all situations or at all times. There are always exceptions. It is difficult to navigate the morass of information and misinformation around food.

We are fortunate in Australia to have productive and reliable farms, despite our variable climate. The Australian National

University's Sustainable Farms project team considers Australian farmers to be among the most resilient and innovative in the world: 'Australian conditions create challenges quite unlike those anywhere else on Earth, and the nation's farmers produce food that carries an impression of wholesome goodness and integrity to overseas markets.' But I think in general we have dual and contrary views of farmers. They are both mythologised and demonised. If we strip away the fiction, farmers are businesspeople trying to run profitable businesses but they rely on social licence to continue to do so. But they are also motivated by lifestyle and social considerations not present in many other businesses.

Between them, Australia's 85,000-plus agricultural businesses manage just over half of the Australian land mass, and produce almost all of the food we eat. We non-farmers are right to be interested in what happens on farms. Farmers' decisions affect how our country looks and what we eat. But we need to be careful not to make unrealistic demands we are not prepared to pay for, or to blame farmers for things beyond their control. We want farmers to produce fabulous cheap food in great abundance and look after the environment while they do it. We want the farms of storybooks and the prices only scale and efficiency can deliver. As eaters, we have to remember that we too have responsibilities.

So, what to do? Or, more pertinently, what to eat? And does it matter? I think American author Michael Pollan was on the money when he wrote, 'Eat food. Not too much. Mostly plants.' But I have some principles and practices I use to navigate my way through the claims and counter-claims; my personal take on how to put food on my plate that I think nourishes me without overly damaging the environment or exploiting farmers.

I have made my peace with being an omnivore. I eat meat, but not a large amount, and I remain fussy about the meat I buy and eat.

I want livestock to have good lives and humane deaths. A lot of my meals are vegetarian. I like to try different fruit and vegetable varieties when I can – a new apple variety when I see one, or a pink or purple or yellow cauliflower from the farmers' market. I find buying at the farmers' market puts me in touch with the seasons. The blueberry seller is only there when her blueberries are in season, which is for a much shorter time than blueberries grace the shelves at the local supermarket. But I do also shop at supermarkets and appreciate the convenience and price. I shop at a variety of places. I think we need to encourage diversity in all forms in our food supply. When I shop in supermarkets, I tend to avoid the long-distance, out-of-season perishables. Except for bananas. We all have our weaknesses.

I grow food. Every day, I try to eat something from my garden – a handful of herbs chopped and added to dinner, a sandwich with fresh lettuce leaves for lunch. Again, it puts me in touch with the seasons and makes me value the effort of food production. And I enjoy it.

I try not to waste food. Not wasting food is, I think, likely more important than what we choose to buy. Most wastage in the developed world comes post purchase. Not buying excessively and storing food well are important. As is thinking about what to do with food that goes off. The problems it creates are diminished, but not entirely solved, if the waste doesn't end up in landfill.

I keep chooks. They are my answer to how to deal with kitchen waste and enable me to avoid buying eggs. At times when I find myself 'between' chooks, when one group of hens becomes old and the next is yet to be found, I compost food scraps and buy free-range or barn-laid eggs. I prefer having chooks. But chooks aren't for everyone.

I am careful what I ask for. We demand a type of perfection that only comes at the cost of great waste and boring uniformity. We demand mangoes in winter and cabbage in summer and eggs all year round. We want blemish-free apples and smooth washed potatoes. We need to accept imperfection more often.

I buy Australian, and more local if I can. I don't think food miles are necessarily a big deal (although all other things being equal, local will have a smaller footprint). More importantly, I think supporting and maintaining local food supplies is critical to food security. I don't think we should be importing food that competes on price with our local farmers and threatens to put them out of business. Especially when the production of that food may not be held to the same rigorous standards that we hold our farmers to.

I try to directly support farmers who I think are doing exceptional work. It's not that I doubt the good work of everyday commodity farmers nor the high quality of their products (I don't); it's that I worry that long supply chains don't always remunerate our farmers well enough. In *The Coming Famine*, Julian Cribb points out that farmers are currently paid in a way that exploits them and the planet, discouraging investment in more sustainable practices. He writes that when we underpay farmers, we risk our own future. Regrettably, higher retail food prices do not always translate to increases in farmers' incomes. I look for shorter supply chains, with closer connections to the people growing the food.

I avoid ultra-processed foods.

I cook from scratch. I'm still not a great cook, but I can cook. I think it's a life skill worth pursuing. I once listened to a guy talk about an environmental education program he was involved in somewhere in America. The program was called *Let's Grow Pizza* and the gist of it was this: a teacher told his class they were going to do some gardening and they would grow some food to eat. 'What should we grow?' the teacher asked.

'Pizza!' the kids replied.

'How do you grow pizza?' the teacher asked.

'From pizza seeds,' the kids answered.

'Where would we get them?'

'From a pizza shop.'

So the teacher took the kids on an excursion to a pizza shop. When the kids arrived and asked to buy pizza seeds, the shop owners told them they didn't have any, and they and the teacher talked to the kids about wheat and flour and pizza dough and tomatoes and tomato sauce. The kids left the pizza shop with some wheat grains and some tomato seeds. They grew the wheat and the tomatoes. They harvested the wheat and ground it into flour. It wasn't enough to make all the pizza dough they needed, but they got enough to understand where flour comes from. They made the tomatoes into tomato sauce. The teacher found a dairy that would send the kids some cheese and some videos of their cows and some information about the way cheese is made. After they'd done all these things, finally they made pizza. I reckon it was probably the best pizza the kids had ever eaten.

It's about three decades since I first heard that story and I still like it. I like it for the simplicity of its concept and the complexity of its message. Pizza doesn't come from pizza seeds and it doesn't just come from pizza shops. Sometimes, it's good to pull things right back to their constituent parts and see how they tick, see what is involved in bringing it to the table.

I have already said that I cook differently from how my grand-mothers and mother cooked. I embrace the international food cultures that have enriched our palates. I live and cook in a different time to my forebears. But still, I honour my own food traditions. I make Grandma Karridale's biscuits, Aunty Rosie's tomato relish, and pastry in the way Mum taught me. Our own individual food traditions, whatever they are, form our food history. When we keep alive our own little pieces of tradition, we help maintain the rich diversity of the world's food. I think that's important.

I don't have all the answers, so I keep asking questions. I want to know where my food comes from. I want to know who grew it and how it got to where I bought it. But I try to be neither obsessive nor self-righteous about it. I am thankful to have choices but I remind myself that none of us as individuals must solve it all. Food shouldn't be yet another source of angst and worry in our lives. Above all, food should nourish us.

Every night, whoever is in my household sits down to a meal together. The ritual of it is important to me. When my kids were little, we had a small ceremony we performed each night when we sat at the table. We would light a candle and say, 'For our food and our company, we are thankful.' It was a secular grace. Over the years, somewhere between the rush of football practice and gymnastics training and homework and deadlines, we dropped it from our daily routine. I'm sorry we did. Perhaps I will reinstate it. Some form of grace is common in many, if not all, of the world's religions; sitting down to a meal with appreciation. It's a good idea. Good to pause for a moment to acknowledge the privilege of being well fed, and the work that goes into getting food on the table. With gratitude, I eat.

Acknowledgements

T HIS BOOK IS unlikely to have ever seen the light of day were it
not for Sally Heath, commissioning editor at Thames & Hudson
Australia. From the moment I pitched the idea to her, Sally believed
in this book and also in my ability to write it. For that, I thank her
profusely. Thank you to my fellow author and friend Viki Cramer for
introducing me to Sally, and for support and encouragement along
the way. I'm glad we travelled the path to publication together. Thanks
also to my other writing buddies who have supported and encouraged
me along the way, especially Rashida Murphy, Rosemary Stevens,
Sally Hutchinson and Marie McLean, whose enthusiastic responses
to very early bits and pieces of this book pushed me onward.

Early readers provided valuable feedback, asking questions where
I had assumed too much prior knowledge and letting me know
where I had gone off track. Thanks to Helen Davey and Janet Paterson,
who both gave pertinent feedback on early drafts and provided much-
needed encouragement when I felt overwhelmed.

I met with and spoke to many farmers and researchers as I wrote
this book. Some of them are named within the text and their stories
bring it to life. I thank each of them for their generosity in sharing

their stories and work with me, and for allowing me to write about them. My gratitude also to the many others I have spoken to over the years and whose work has helped shape my ideas and knowledge. You are in here, too, between the lines and in the background, but no less important for your invisibility. Thank you.

The crew at Thames & Hudson Australia has been wonderful to work with. I couldn't have asked for a better team. I am humbled by the effort they have put into making this book the best it could be. Special thanks to copyeditor Fay Helfenbaum, whose attention to detail is superb. Thanks also to Sarina Rowell for running her very fine-toothed proofreading comb over my text. Thank you to Josh Durham for creating a cover by which I am proud to have my book judged.

And, as they say, last but by no means least: thank you to Rob, Toby and Lauren for being early readers, a sounding board and, most importantly, for your love and steadfast belief in me. Love you to the moon and back. This book is for you.

Endnotes

INTRODUCTION: SEVENTY-FIVE: TWELVE: FIVE
Page 3 'In *Out of the Scientist's Garden* ...' Richard Stirzaker, *Out of the Scientist's Garden*, CSIRO Publishing, 2010
Page 4 'Eating is an agricultural act.' Wendell Berry, *What are People for?*, Penguin Books, 2010
Page 5 '75 per cent of the world's food comes from...' United Nations Food and Agriculture Organization, 'What Is Happening To Agrobiodiversity?', *FAOSTAT*, 2022, <fao.org/3/y5609e/y5609e02.htm>

CHAPTER 1: TOMATOES
Page 9 'Chefs sing the praises ...' Tristan Lutze and Chynna Santos, 'When It Comes to Tinned Tomatoes, Aussie Chefs Prefer Italian Over the Local Stuff – But Why?' *Broadsheet*, 13 October 2020, <broadsheet.com.au/national/food-and-drink/article/tinned-tomatoe-aussie-chefs-prefer-italian-but-why>
Page 10 'These days, Italy processes ... globally each year' Pasquale Garofalo, Laura D'Andrea, Matteo Tomaiuolo, Accursio Venezia, Annamaria Castrignan, 'Environmental sustainability of agri-food supply chains in Italy: The case of the whole-peeled tomato production under life cycle assessment methodology', *Journal of Food Engineering*, vol. 200, 2017, pp. 1–12
Page 10 'In Australia, tomatoes come in second ...' Ausveg, 'Australian vegetable production statistics', *Ausveg*, <ausveg.com.au/resources/economics-statistics/australian-vegetable-production-statistics/>
Page 10 'The Australian tomato harvest is around 426,000 tonnes ...' ibid
Page 11 'SPC processes about 50,000 tonnes ...' Kagome, 'Product', *Kagome*, <kagome.com.au/product/>
Page 11 'According to Italian research ...' Pasquale Garofalo, et al 2017
Page 11 'An American study found ...' Sonja Brodt, Klaas Jan Kramer, Alissa Kendall, Gail Feenstra, 'Comparing environmental impacts of regional and national-scale food supply chains: A case study of processed tomatoes', *Food Policy*, vol. 42, 2013, pp. 106–114

Page 13 'As an example, Ridoutt and his colleagues …' Girija Page, Brad Ridoutt, Bill Bellotti (2012), 'Carbon and water footprint tradeoffs in fresh tomato production', *Journal of Cleaner Production*, vol. 32 pp. 219–226

Page 14 'A different study looked …' Alison Rothwell, Brad Ridoutt, Girija Page, William Bellotti, 'Environmental performance of local food: trade-offs and implications for climate resilience in a developed city', *Journal of Cleaner Production*, vol. 114, 2016, pp. 420–430

Page 17 'The Australia Institute reported …' Poppy Wise, *Grow your own: The potential value and impacts of residential and community food gardening*, The Australia Institute, 2014

Page 17 'At the start of the pandemic …' James Wong, 2020, 'Grow (just a bit of) your own', *New Scientist*, vol. 246(3278), 2020, p. 22

Page 17 'Before that there was the War Garden …' Janet Music, Erica Finch, Pallavi Gone, Sandra Toze, Sylvain Charlebois, Lisa Mullins 'Pandemic Victory Gardens: Potential for local land use policies', *Land Use Policy*, vol. 109, 2021

Page 17 'As Australian author Peter Timms …' Peter Timms, *Australia's Quarter Acre*, The Miegunyah Press, 2006, p. 129

Page 18 'Dr Sumita Ghosh from the University of Technology Sydney …' Sumita Ghosh, 'Urban agriculture potential of home gardens in residential land uses: A case study of regional City of Dubbo, Australia', *Land Use Policy*, vol. 109, 2021

Page 18 'In a survey of Hobart household vegetable gardeners …' Jamie B Kirkpatrick and Aidan Davison, 'Home-grown: Gardens, practices and motivations in urban domestic vegetable production', *Landscape and Urban Planning*, vol. 170, 2018, pp. 24–33

Page 19 'Canadian food researcher Dr Robin J Marles investigated …' RJ Marles, 'Mineral nutrient composition of vegetables, fruits and grains: The context of reports of apparent historical declines', *Journal of Food Composition and Analysis*, vol. 56, 2017, pp. 93–103

Page 19 'Then there's another study from environmental scientists …' IV Hume, DM Summers, TR Cavagnaro, 'Self-sufficiency through urban agriculture: Nice idea or plausible reality?', *Sustainable Cities and Society*, vol. 68, 2021

CHAPTER 2: WHEAT

Page 26 'The Australian national wheat harvest …' United States Department of Agriculture, 'Australian Wheat Production by Year', indexmundi, 2022, <indexmundi.com/agriculture/?country=au&commodity=wheat>

Page 26 '…around 2.7 million tonnes was produced in Western Australia … the harvest was close to 10 million tonnes.' https://www.agric.wa.gov.au/grains-research-development/western-australian-wheat-industry accessed 28 June 2019

Page 26 'The Australian wheat harvest …' Australian Export Grains Innovation Centre, 'Wheat', *Australian Export Grains Innovation Centre*, <aegic.org.au/australian-grains/wheat/>

Page 26 'The 700 or so million tonnes of wheat produced in … 60 per cent of the world's food calories.' Food and Agriculture Organization of the United Nations, 'Crops and Livestock Products', *Food and Agriculture Organization of the United Nations*, 17 February 2022, <https://www.fao.org/faostat/en/#data/QCL/visualize>

Page 26 'An alarmingly large amount ...' World Economic Forum, *'Meat: the Future'*, *World Economic Forum*, January 2019, <https://www3.weforum.org/docs/WEF_White_Paper_Roadmap_Protein.pdf>

Page 27 'A graph of rainfall averages ...' Meredith Guthrie, 'Climate change in the Cunderdin area Western Australia', *Department of Primary Industries and Regional Development*, 14 September 2021, <agric.wa.gov.au/climate-change/climate-change-cunderdin-area-western-australia>

Page 28 'By the turn of the century ...' Richard Stirzaker, *Out of the Scientist's Garden*, CSIRO, 2010, pp. 136–137

Page 28 'American agronomist Dr Norman Borlaug ...' The Nobel Prize, 'Norman Borlaug – Facts', *The Nobel Prize*, <nobelprize.org/prizes/peace/1970/borlaug/facts/> Originally published in *Nobel Lectures, Peace 1951–1970*, Editor Frederick W Haberman, Elsevier Publishing Company, Amsterdam, 1972

Page 31 'These days, over 90 per cent of Western Australian ...' The Western Australian No-tillage Farmers Association, 'About us', *The Western Australian No-tillage Farmers Association*, <wantfa.com.au/about-us/ >

Page 31 'Nationally, no-till is the most commonly used method ...' Australian Bureau of Statistics, 'Land Management and Farming in Australia', *Australian Bureau of Statistics*, 26 June 2018, <abs.gov.au/statistics/industry/agriculture/land-management-and-farming-australia/latest-release>

Page 33 'Once harvested, the majority of Australian wheat ...' Australian Export Grains Innovation Centre, 'Wheat', *Australian Export Grains Innovation Centre*, <aegic.org.au/australian-grains/wheat/>

Page 33 'Wheat is consistently Australia's tenth top export ...' Gregory O'Brien, 'Australia's Trade I Figures', *Parliament of Australia*, August 2016, <aph.gov.au/About_Parliament/Parliamentary_Departments/Parliamentary_Library/pubs/BriefingBook45p/AustraliaTrade>

Page 34 'protracted and complex history of domestication in wheat...' Alice Roberts, *Tamed: Ten species that changed our world*, Windmill Books, 2017, p. 62.

Page 34 'With 26.2 per cent of the market share ... spending around $8.20 each.' Andrea Hogan, 'Australians still eating plenty of bread, Roy Morgan Research', *Australian Food News*, 29 March 2017, <ausfoodnews.com.au/2017/03/29/australians-still-eating-plenty-of-bread-roy-morgan-research.html>

Page 34–35 'Between 1995 and 2018, average daily consumption ... overall carbohydrate levels in bread.' Sara Grafenauer and Felicity Curtain, 'An Audit of Australian Bread with a Focus on Loaf Breads and Whole Grain', *Nutrients*, vol. 10(8), 2018, <https://www.ncbi.nlm.nih.gov/pmc/articles/PMC6115933/>

Page 36 'A sourdough culture may contain more than ...' Luc De Vuyst and Patricia Neysens, 'The sourdough microflora: biodiversity and metabolic interactions', *Trends in Food Science & Technology*, vol. 16(1–3), 2005

Page 36 'It's the same species as brewer's yeast ...' Dan Saladino, *Eating to Extinction*, Penguin Random House, 2021

Page 36 'Sourdough bread, which does not use this type ...' Francesca Scazzina, Daniele Del Rio, Nicoletta Pellegrini and Furio Brighenti, 'Sourdough bread: Starch digestibility and postprandial glycemic response', *Journal of Cereal Science*, vol. 49(3), May 2009

Page 36 '… a few other desirable attributes.' Míriam Regina Canesin and Cínthia Baú Betim Cazarin, 'Nutritional quality and nutrient bioaccessibility in sourdough bread', *Current Opinion in Food Science*, vol. 40, August 2021

Page 38 'Making way for agriculture and creating the wheatbelt …' Tony Hughes-D'Aeth, *Like Nothing on This Earth*, UWA Press, 2017

Page 39 'Food production generally is now attributed …' Walter Willett et al, 'Food in the Anthropocene: the EAT-*Lancet* Commission on healthy diets from sustainable food systems', *The Lancet*, vol. 393, 2 February 2019, doi: 10.1016/S0140-6736(18)31788-4

Page 39 '… "a square mile of first class land would keep the farmer and his family in prosperous circumstances."', Reg Appleyard and Don Couper, *A History of Trayning*, UWAP, 2009

Page 40 'There were 13,106 farms in the Western Australian wheatbelt …' Neville Ellis, 'Where have the family farms gone? Climate change and farm loss in the Western Australian Wheatbelt', *Centre for Responsible Citizenship and Sustainability Working Paper,* vol. 2(1), 2016, pp. 1–30

Page 40 'The World Health Organization says that …' Hannah Ritchie and Max Roser, 'Urbanization', *Our World in Data*, September 2018, <https://ourworldindata.org/urbanization>

Page 41 'In 2021 there were thirteen.' Department of Education, 'Trayning Primary School (5440)', *Department of Education Western Australia*, 2021, <https://www.det.wa.edu.au/schoolsonline/student_current.do?schoolID=5440&pageID=SP01>

Page 41 'The shire population declined …' Reg Appleyard and Don Couper, *A History of Trayning*, 2009

Page 41 'By the 2016 census …' Australian Bureau of Statistics, 'Trayning, 2016 Census All persons QuickStats', *Australian Bureau of Statistics*, 2016, <https://quickstats.censusdata.abs.gov.au/census_services/getproduct/census/2016/quickstat/SSC51453>

Page 41 'The last meeting of the local football club …' Reg Appleyard and Don Couper, *A History of Trayning*, 2009

Page 41 'An analysis of the 2021 Australian Census data …' Erin Parke, 'A million homes sit empty, so where are they and can they help ease the housing crisis?', *ABC*, 20 July 2022, <https://www.abc.net.au/news/2022-07-20/homeless-crisis-million-homes-vacant-in-australia/101234424>

CHAPTER 3: POTATOES

Page 43 'Hort Innovation, a not-for-profit research and development organisation …' Hort Innovation, 'Australian Horticulture Statistics Handbook 2020/21', *Horticultural Innovation Australia Ltd*, 10 February 2022

Page 44 'It dropped by 20 per cent between 1995 and 2012.' Australian Bureau of Statistics figures quoted in: Katie Wood, John Carragher, Robbie Davis, 'Australian consumers' insights into potatoes – Nutritional knowledge, perceptions and beliefs', *Appetite*, vol. 114, 2017, pp. 169–174

Page 44 'Conversely, potato consumption in Africa and Asia is increasing …' Ramani Wijesinha-Bettoni and Béatrice Mouillé, 'The Contribution of Potatoes to Global

Food Security, Nutrition and Healthy Diets', *American Journal of Potato Research* vol. 96, 2019, pp. 139–149

Page 44 'A 2016 survey found Australian consumers …' Katie Wood, John Carragher, Robbie Davis, 'Australian consumers' insights into potatoes – Nutritional knowledge, perceptions and beliefs', 2017

Page 44 'But it turns out potatoes are loaded … 5 per cent of their magnesium.' Katherine A Beals, 'Potatoes, Nutrition and Health', *American Journal of Potato Research*, vol. 96, 2019, pp. 102–110

Page 44 'As University of Utah nutritionist Dr Katherine Beals writes …' ibid

Page 45 'If you take the water out of potatoes …' Janet C King and Joanne L Slavin, 'White Potatoes, Human Health, and Dietary Guidance', *Advances in Nutrition*, vol. 4(3), 2013, pp. 393S–401S

Page 45 'Potatoes have been associated with lowered …' Katherine A Beals, 'Potatoes, Nutrition and Health', 2019

Page 45 'They contain phytochemicals and antioxidants …' Mary Ellen Camire, Stan Kubow and Danielle J Donnelly, 'Potatoes and Human Health', *Critical Reviews in Food Science and Nutrition*, vol. 49(10), 2009, pp. 823–840

Page 45 'Those phytochemicals include lutein and zeaxanthin …' Umesh C Gupta and Subhas C Gupta, 'The Important Role of Potatoes, An Underrated Vegetable Food Crop in Human Health and Nutrition', *Current Nutrition & Food Science*, vol. 15(1), 2019, pp. 11–19

Page 45 'And potato peels have been shown to improve cholesterol …' Mary Ellen Camire, et al, 'Potatoes and Human Health', 2009

Page 45 'Potatoes are low in fat …' Umesh C Gupta and Subhas C Gupta, 'The Important Role of Potatoes, An Underrated Vegetable Food Crop in Human Health and Nutrition', 2019

Page 46 'According to Beals, previous studies …' Katherine A Beals, 'Potatoes, Nutrition and Health', 2019

Page 46 'Again in the US, University of Minnesota nutritionists …' Janet C King and Joanne L Slavin, 'White Potatoes, Human Health, and Dietary Guidance', 2013

Page 46 'Around two thirds of the potatoes grown in Australia …' Hort Innovation, 'Australian Horticulture Statistics Handbook 2020/21', 2022

Page 47 'McDonald's has almost a thousand restaurants in Australia …' McDonalds, 'Maccas Story', *McDonald's*, 2022, <mcdonalds.com.au/about-maccas/maccas-story>

Page 48 '… and over 14,000 restaurants in the US.' John O'Connell, 'McDonald's spent almost $136 million on Idaho ag products last year', *Idaho Farm Bureau Federation*, 26 August 2019, <idahofb.org/news-room/posts/mcdonald-s-spent-almost-136-million-on-idaho-ag-products-last-year/>

Page 48 'Worldwide, there are more than 36,000 McDonald's …' McDonald's, Maccas Story', 2022, <mcdonalds.com.au/about-maccas/maccas-story>

Page 48 'It doesn't matter if they offer promise …' John O'Connell, 'McDonald's spent almost $136 million on Idaho ag products last year', 2019

Page 48 'Shorter fries don't fit the machinery and packaging specifications …' Potato Pro, 'Europe's small potato a problem for McDonald's fries', *Potato Pro*,

30 September, 2018, <potatopro.com/news/2018/europes-small-potatoes-problem-mcdonalds-fries>

Page 49 'Preventing the recurrence of a modern-day disaster ... all global potato production.' Birgit Adolf et al., 'Oomycete, and Plasmodiophorid Diseases of Potato', *The Potato Crop*, 2020, pp. 307–350

Page 50 'In the 2020–21 survey, sixteen out of twenty foods ...' Department of Agriculture, Water and the Environment, *National Residue Survey 2020–21: Annual Summary*, Australian Government Department of Agriculture, Water and the Environment, 29 September 2021, <awe.gov.au/sites/default/files/documents/nrs-2020-21-summary.pdf>

Page 50 'When asked by *SBS News Australia* whether the list is relevant to Australia ...' Lauren Sams, 'Is your fruit and veg full of chemicals?' *SBS*, 28 April 2016, <sbs.com.au/food/article/2016/04/28/your-fruit-and-veg-full-chemicals>

Page 52 'An inquiry ordered by the then Western Australian Minister for Agriculture ...' Eric Kelly, *Inquiry into the levels of pesticides in meat*, Report to the Hon Monty House, MLA, Minister for Primary Industries, Western Australia, 5 May 1994

Page 55 'Things such as fuels, engine exhausts, organic solvents ... overall than the general population.' Ellie Darcey, Renee N Carey, Alison Reid, Tim Driscoll, Deborah C Glass, Geza P Benke, Susan Peters, Lin Fritschi, 'Prevalence of exposure to occupational carcinogens among farmers', *Rural and Remote Health*, vol. 18(3), 2018, 18: 4348, doi: 10.22605/RRJ4348

Page 55 'Australian agricultural workers have twice ... chronic low-dose exposure to pesticides.' Nufail Khan, Alison Kennedy, Jacqueline Cotton and Susan Brumby, 'A Pest to Mental Health? Exploring the Link between Exposure to Agrichemicals in Farmers and Mental Health', *International Journal of Environmental Research and Public Health*, vol. 16(8), 2019, doi:10.3390/ijerph16081327

Page 55–56 'This can happen when a farmer has direct contact ... mostly in developing countries.' Sienna Russell-Green, Jacqueline Cotton and Susan Brumby. 'Research Engagement Changes Attitudes and Behaviours Towards Agrichemical Safety in Australian Farmers', *Safety*, vol. 6(1), 2020, doi:10.3390/safety6010016

CHAPTER 4: SUGAR

Page 58 'Our bodies evolved feedback mechanisms ...' Amy Reichelt, 'Your brain on sugar: What the science actually says', *The Conversation*, 15 November 2019, <https://theconversation.com/your-brain-on-sugar-what-the-science-actually-says-126581>

Page 58 'This mechanism exists even in people ...' Vanessa Clarkson, *Sugar in Australia: A food system approach*, The George Institute for Global Health – global headquarters, 2020

Page 58 'Dopamine promotes learning and encourages us ...' Amy Reichelt, 'Your brain on sugar: What the science actually says', 2019

Page 59 'The value of its annual production is topped only ...' Food and Agriculture Organization of the United Nations, 'Production of Crops and Derived Products', *Statistical Yearbook: World Food and Agriculture 2020*, FAO, 2020, <fao.org/3/cb1329en/online/cb1329en.html#chapter-2_1>

Page 59 'In 2020, the global sugar industry ...' M Shahbandeh, 'Global market value of sugar manufacturing 2012–2022', *Statista*, 13 January 2022, <statista.com/statistics/1283819/global-sugar-manufacturing-market-value/>

Page 59 'Total commercial world production of sugar ...' Food and Agriculture Organization of the United Nations, 'Sugarcane', *Land & Water*, <fao.org/land-water/databases-and-software/crop-information/sugarcane/en/>

Page 59 'By volume, though, sugar cane outweighs ...' Vanessa Clarkson, *Sugar in Australia: A food system approach*, 2020

Page 59 'The world's refined sugar comes from ...' International Sugar Organization, 'About Sugar', *ISO*, 2022, <isosugar.org/sugarsector/sugar>

Page 59 'As with other species with a long history ... about 2500 years ago.' Mark Horton, Phillip Langton, R Alexander Bentley, 'A history of sugar – the food nobody needs but everyone craves', *The Conversation*, 31 October 2015, <theconversation.com/a-history-of-sugar-the-food-nobody-needs-but-everyone-craves-49823>

Page 59 'It arrived in Australia with the First Fleet ...' Queensland Sugar Corporation, 'Historical Events', *Australian Cane Farmers*, <acfa.com.au/sugar-industry/historical-events/>

Page 60 'According to historian Emeritus Professor Clive Moore ...' Clive Moore, *Hard Work: Australian South Sea Islander Bibliography with a select bibliography of the sugar industry and the Pacific labour trade*, Australian South Sea Islanders (Port Jackson) Limited (ASSIPJ), 2019,

Page 60 'Although not actually called slaves ... to which they had no immunity.' Sharon Verghis, '"A new form of slavery": The hidden history of Australia's sugar industry', *SBS*, 8 April 2020, <sbs.com.au/topics/voices/culture/article/2020/04/08/new-form-slavery-hidden-history-australias-sugar-industry>

Page 60 'In Australia, all our sugar comes from sugar cane ...' Department of Agriculture, Fisheries and Forestry, 'Senate inquiry into marketing arrangements', *Australian Government Department of Agriculture, Fisheries and Forestry*, 16 December 2021, <awe.gov.au/agriculture-land/farm-food-drought/crops/sugar#senate-inquiry-into-sugar-marketing-arrangements>

Page 60–61 'In that coastal strip, over 3000 farmers grow ... 30 million tonnes of sugar cane.' *Food, Fibre & Forestry Facts*, National Farmers' Federation, 2017

Page 61 'In 2018–19, sugar cane was the eighteenth most valuable ...' Vanessa Clarkson, *Sugar in Australia: A food systems approach*, 2020

Page 61 'Eighty per cent of the sugar produced in Australia ...' Department of Agriculture, Fisheries and Forestry, 'Senate inquiry into marketing arrangements', 2021

Page 62 'It ranges from a 1.2-fold increase up to a six-fold increase.' Queensland Government, 'Impacts of nutrient run-off', *Queensland Government*, 8 June 2022, https://www.qld.gov.au/environment/agriculture/sustainable-farming/reef/reef-regulations/about/nutrient-runoff

Page 63 'There are over 3000 farmers growing sugar cane ...' Vanessa Clarkson, *Sugar in Australia: A food system approach*, 2020

Page 63 'About 40 per cent of the domestic supply ...' ibid

Page 64 'Current average Australian daily consumption ... for Aboriginal and Torres Strait Islander people.' ibid

Page 64 'If we, as a nation, keep going on the current …' ibid

Page 64 'Dr Alan W Barclay from the Australian Diabetes Society Council …' Alan W Barclay and Jennie Brand-Miller, 'The Australian Paradox: A Substantial Decline in Sugars Intake over the Same Timeframe that Overweight and Obesity Have Increased', *Nutrients*, vol. 3(4), 2011, pp. 491–504, doi:10.3390/nu3040491

Page 65 'In their excellent book, *Eat Like the Animals* …' David Raubenheimer and Stephen J Simpson, *Eat Like the Animals*, Harper Collins, 2020, p. 135

Page 66 'The term 'ultra-processed' comes from … and many other types of product.'' CA Monteiro, G Cannon, M Lawrence, ML Costa Louzada and P Pereira Machado, 2019, *Ultra-processed foods, diet quality, and health using the NOVA classification system*, FAO, p. 8

Page 67 'It's a $104.2 billion industry in Australia … grocery industry.' Vanessa Clarkson, *Sugar in Australia: A food system approach*, 2020, p. 7

Page 67 'In 2018, 61 per cent of packaged foods for sale …' David Raubenheimer and Stephen J Simpson, *Eat Like the Animals*, 2020, p. 136

Page 67 'Raubenheimer and Simpson say ultra-processed products …' ibid

Page 68 'Research into Australian diets has shown …' Bradley Ridoutt, Kim Anastasiou, Danielle Baird, Javier Navarro Garcia and Gilly Hendrie, 'Cropland Footprints of Australian Dietary Choices', *Nutrients*, vol. 12, 2020, doi:10.3390/nu12051212

Page 68 'This might not sound like a huge percentage …' ibid

Page 68 'Not all land is of equal value …' ibid

Page 69 'Overall, the research found that around 45 per cent …' ibid

Page 69 'It would also likely reduce the number of overweight …' Olivia Willis, 'Australians living longer but with more chronic disease, COVID "excess deaths" jump national health report', *ABC News*, 8 July 2022, <abc.net.au/news/health/2022-07-07/health-australians-living-longer-but-with-more-chronic-disease/101213626>

Page 69–70 'In an illuminating series of experiments …' David Raubenheimer and Stephen J Simpson, *Eat Like the Animals*, 2020

Page 70 'In a detailed examination of a huge dataset …' ibid, p. 143

Page 70 'The Food and Agriculture Organization of the United Nations …' CA Monteiro et al, *Ultra-processed foods, diet quality, and health using the NOVA classification system*, 2019

CHAPTER 5: APPLES

Page 72 'The chances of getting something delicious …' Karen George, *John Cripps Interviewed by Karen George*, The Apples and Pears Oral History Project, Recorded 17 May 2010, <nla.gov.au/nla.obj-219220713/listen/0-5793>

Page 72 'The cultivation of sweet apples probably arose in China … recognised by plant scientists.' Riccardo Valesco, Andrey Zharkikh, Jason Affourtit et al, 'The genome of the domesticated apple (*Malus x domestica* Borkh.)', *Nature Genetics*, vol. 42, 29 August 2010, pp. 833–839, <nature.com/doifinder/10.1038/ng.654>

Page 72 'Most of the vast number of genes in the apples …' ibid

Page 72 '… huge apple trees in the Tian Shan Mountains.' Alice Roberts, *Tamed: Ten Species That Changed Our World*, 2017, p. 264

Page 72 'The apple trees grow up to 20 metres tall ...' Michael Pollan, *The Botany of Desire*, Bloomsbury, 2001, p. 12

Page 73 'According to the industry body Apple and Pear Australia Limited ...' Apple and Pear Australia Ltd, 'Imported Apples', *APAL*, 2019, <apal.org.au/consumer/consumer-faq/imported-apples/>

Page 73 'In 2015, a team of researchers ...' Matthew A Davis, Julie PW Bynum and Brenda E Sirovich, 'Association Between Apple Consumption and Physician Visits', *JAMA Internal Medicine*, 2015, vol. 175(5), pp. 777–783, <ncbi.nlm.nih.gov/pmc/articles/PMC4420713/>

Page 75 'The original Lady Williams still grows ...' Boronia Farm, 'Lady Williams Apple', *Boronia Farm*, 2022, <boroniafarm.com.au/lady-williams-apple/>

Page 75 'It is now thought that the Lady Williams ...' National Fruit Collection, 'Lady Williams', *NFC*, <nationalfruitcollection.org.uk/full2.php?id=3362&&fruit=apple>

Page 75 'Others suggest it is more likely to be ...' John Cripps, John and Eleanor Melvin-Carter, 'A tale of two ladies: Pink Lady and Sundowner', *Journal of the Department of Agriculture*, 1993, vol. 34(2), <researchlibrary.agric.wa.gov.au/journal_agriculture4/vol34/iss2/8>

Page 76 '"In 1959 I did do some cross-pollination and raised a few seedlings ...' Karen George, *John Cripps Interviewed by Karen George*, 2010, <nla.gov.au/nla.obj-219220713/listen/0-5670~0-5792>

Page 77 '"It came out of store in good condition ... so many people enjoy eating it."' Karen George, *John Cripps Interviewed by Karen George*, 2010, <nla.gov.au/nla.obj-219220713/listen/1-640~1-808>

Page 77 'The program that produced the Pink Lady ...' DPIRD Research Highlights 2021

Page 80 'John Cripps reckoned the mishandling ...' Karen George, *John Cripps Interviewed by Karen George*, 2010, <nla.gov.au/nla.obj-219220713/listen/>

Page 81 'Its high flavonoid levels appealed ...' Hon Alannah MacTiernan, 'One million more reasons to enjoy Bravo apples', *Government of Western Australia Media Statements*, 27 April 2021, <mediastatements.wa.gov.au/Pages/McGowan/2021/04/One-million-more-reasons-to-enjoy-Bravo-apples.aspx>

Page 81 'Dr Johanna Christensen says the pursuit of the flawless apple ...' JA Christensen, *Making the connection between history, agricultural diversity and place: the story of Victorian apples* [PhD thesis], The University of Melbourne, submitted March 2016, p. 132

Page 81 'There are 124 apples in the collection ...' ibid, p. 15

Page 82 'An apple grower interviewed by Christensen describes ...' 'Martha', January 2013, Yarra Valley, quoted in Christensen, p. 123

Page 84 'Breeding programs also influence variety selection and growers ...' ibid, p. 138

Page 84 'The direction is downward, because each decision ...' ibid, p. 141

Page 86 'Probably because you have to pay for ...' ibid, p. 142

Page 86 'Growing licensed varieties also ...' ibid, p. 143

Page 87 'Way back in 1862, American naturalist ...' Henry David Thoreau, 'Wild Apples: The History of the Apple-Tree', *The Atlantic*, November 1862

CHAPTER 6: SOY

Page 89 'In 1930, a Queensland newspaper ...' The Nambour Chronicle and North Coast Advertiser, 'A Rival of Butter', *The Nambour Chronicle and North Coast Advertiser*, 25 April 1930, <trove.nla.gov.au/newspaper/article/77300128>

Page 90 'It seems it was only ever a regionalism ...' Macquarie Dictionary, 'Australian Word Map: Peanut paste', *Macquarie Dictionary*, <macquariedictionary.com.au/resources/aus/word/map/search/word/peanut%20paste/Far%20North%20Qld/>

Page 90 '"Many of these products do not resemble ...' Dairy Australia, 'Why do you allow non-dairy milks (almond, soy etc) to still be called milk?', *Dairy Australia*, 2021, <dairy.com.au/dairy-matters/you-ask-we-answer/why-do-you-allow-non-dairy-milks-to-still-be-called-milk>

Page 90 'According to *ABC News* an Australian Government Senate Inquiry ...' Daniel Fitzgerald, 'Senate "fake meat" inquiry recommends overhaul of plant-based protein labelling laws', *ABC News*, 24 February 2022, <abc.net.au/news/rural/2022-02-24/definition-of-meat-inquiry-food-labelling/100855864>

Page 91 'In 2016, market research company Roy Morgan ... consumption of soy drinks had increased.' Roy Morgan, 'Soy drinks: dairy alternative or health elixir?', *Newsmaker*, 6 July 2016, <newsmaker.com.au/news/71279/soy-drinks-dairy-alternative-or-health-elixir#.Y3Q21C0Rpz8>

Page 91 'They reported consumption of energy and sports drinks ...' ibid

Page 93 'In 2019, the world used more than ... warming potential of carbon dioxide.' Michael Udvardi et al, 'A Research Road Map for Responsible Use of Agricultural Nitrogen', *Frontiers in Sustainable Food Systems*, 2021, vol. 5

Page 93 'In one of those clever, quirky things ...' Jill Griffiths, 'Rhizobia – the underground story', *Farming Ahead*, vol. 298, 2016

Page 94 'It is now one of the big-hitting plant species ... what it was in 1960.' Hannah Ritchie and Max Roser, 'Soy', *Our World in Data*, 2021, <ourworldindata.org/soy>

Page 94 'Soybeans are now grown across the world ...' M Shahbandeh, 'Leading soybean producing countries worldwide from 2012/13 to 2021/22', *Statista*, 11 February 2022, <statista.com/statistics/263926/soybean-production-in-selected-countries-since-1980/>

Page 94 'In a detailed analysis of global soy production, Our World in Data researchers Dr Hannah Ritchie and Dr Max Roser concluded ...' Hannah Ritchie and Max Roser, 'Soy', Our World in Data, 2021, <ourworldindata.org/soy>

Page 94 '... but soy production plays a significant role.' Hannah Ritchie and Max Roser, 'Forests and Deforestation', *Our World in Data*, 2021, <ourworldindata.org/forests-and-deforestation>

Page 95 'Since 1961 global yields increased by 150 per cent ...' Hannah Ritchie and Max Roser, 'Soy', 2021

Page 95 'Most Australian soybeans are grown in Queensland ...' Australian Oilseeds Federation Inc, 'Soybean Production', *Soy Australia*, <australianoilseeds.com/soy_australia/Soybean_Production>

Page 95 'Australia is a relatively small player ...' L Granwal, 'Volume of soybean crop production in Australia from 2012 to 2020 with a forecast until 2031', *Statista*, 24 August 2022, <tatista.com/statistics/631832/australia-volume-soybean-crop/>

Page 95 'In 2020, Australia exported $1.35 million worth of soy … the US and the Netherlands.' OEC, 'Soybeans in Australia', *OEC*, 2022, <oec.world/en/profile/bilateral-product/soybeans/reporter/aus#>

Page 95–6 'Overall, soybeans are considered to be …' Australian Oilseeds Federation Inc, 'Soybean Production'

Page 96 'Less than a fifth of the soy produced … raised for human consumption.' Hannah Ritchie and Max Roser, 'Soy', 2021

Page 96 'In 2012, only 9.7 per cent of Australians identified …' Roy Morgan, 'Rise in vegetarianism not halting the march of obesity', *Roy Morgan*, 12 April 2019, <roymorgan.com/findings/rise-in-vegetarianism-not-halting-the-march-of-obesity>

Page 98 'Looking at global figures for greenhouse gas emissions … and 25 kilograms CO_2e for beef.' Hannah Ritchie, 'Less meat is nearly always better than sustainable meat, to reduce your carbon footprint', *Our World in Data*, 4 February 2020, <ourworldindata.org/less-meat-or-sustainable-meat>

Page 98 'The government research organisation AgriFutures Australia …' Stephen Wiedemann, Eugene McGahan and Glenn Poad, *Using Life Cycle Assessment to Quantify the Environmental Impact of Chicken Meat Production*, Australian Government Rural Industries Research and Development Corporation, April 2012

Page 98 'The study points out that …' ibid, p. 8

Page 98 'The study also cautions that …' ibid

Page 98 'They attribute this to the lack of Australian market …' ibid, p. 10

Page 98 'Regardless of this, plant-based meat alternatives …' CSIRO, 'Future Protein', *CSIRO*, <csiro.au/en/about/challenges-missions/future-protein-mission>

Page 99 'Additionally, CSIRO sees a future export …' Jenna Daroczy, 'Innovating investment with Venture Science', *CSIRO*, 1 October 2019, <csiro.au/en/news/News-releases/2019/Innovating-investment-with-Venture-Science>

Page 99 'CSIRO is walking its talk as far as …' Tara Pereira, 'CSIRO and Jack Cowin partner to launch Australia's newest plant-based meat startup, v2food', *CSIRO*, 1 October 2019, <csiro.au/en/news/news-releases/2019/csiro-and-jack-cowin-launch-v2food>

Page 99 'With the help of the scientists …' , *v2*, <v2food.com/products>

Page 99 'They promise to "deliver on the flavour you love …"' v2, 'Our Products', *v2*, <v2food.com/products>

Page 100 '"Novel plant-based meat alternatives should … nutrients that impact human health."' Stephan van Vliet, Scott L Kronberg and Frederick D Provenza, 'Plant based meats, human health and climate change', *Frontiers in Sustainable Food Systems*, vol. 4 (128), October 2020

CHAPTER 7: CATTLE

Page 107 'Australian dairy cows usually receive …' Dairy Australia, 'Cows & Farms Data', *Dairy Australia*, <dairyaustralia.com.au/industry-statistics/cow-and-farms-data>

Page 108 'They are the most productive dairy cow …' Australia's Livestock Exporters, 'Cattle Breeds 101: Holstein Cow Characteristics', *ALE*, 18 June 2018, <australiaslivestockexporters.com/holstein-cow-characteristics.html>

Page 110 '"Unfortunately, not all male calves can be reared for beef ..."' Dairy Australia, 'What Happens to Male Calves?', *Dairy Australia*, 22 August 2019, <dairy.com.au/dairy-matters/you-ask-we-answer/what-happens-to-male-calves>

Page 111 'They encourage "farmers to raise calves ..."' RSPCA, 'Dairy cattle and bobby calves', *RSPCA*, <rspca.org.au/take-action/dairy-cattle-and-bobby-calves>

Page 111 'According to an article in *The Guardian* ...' Tom Levitt, 'Rise of ethical milk: "Mums ask when cows and their calves are separated"', *The Guardian*, 29 June 2019, <theguardian.com/environment/2019/jun/29/mums-ask-when-cows-and-their-calves-separated-rise-ethical-milk-vegan>

Page 116 'But it can also leach into food ...' Choice, 'Is plastic food packaging dangerous?', *Choice*, 7 August 2014, <choice.com.au/food-and-drink/food-warnings-and-safety/plastic/articles/plastics-and-food>

Page 116 'Ultimately, early in 2019, the supermarkets lifted the price ...' Australian Financial Review, 'The milk price war is over', *AFR*, 19 March 2019, <afr.com/companies/retail/the-milk-price-war-is-over-20190319-p515lc>

Page 118 'Livestock are responsible for 37 per cent ... 70 per cent of all agricultural land.' Livestock and Development Initiative (LEAD), *Livestock's Long Shadow – Environmental Issues and Options*, Food and Agriculture Organization, 2006

Page 118–199 Livestock are socially and politically significant ... focused on cows and climate.' ibid

Page 119 'One statement in particular raised ...' ibid, p. xxi

Page 119 'Only the so-called tail-pipe emissions ... transport emissions and livestock emissions.' Anne Mottet and Henning Steinfeld, 'Cars or livestock: which contribute more to climate change?', *Thomson Reuters Foundation*, 18 September 2018, <news.trust.org/item/20180918083629-d2wf0>

Page 120 'The facts remain that cows burp methane ...' M Shahbandeh, 'Number of cattle worldwide from 2012 to 2022', *Statista*, 18 July 2022, <statista.com/statistics/263979/global-cattle-population-since-1990/>

Page 120 'That's roughly one cow for every ...' Australian Bureau of Statistics, 'Agricultural Commodities, Australia', *ABS*, 26 July 2022, <abs.gov.au/statistics/industry/agriculture/agricultural-commodities-australia/latest-release#livestock>

Page 120 'But it's also because Australians ...' Meat & Livestock Australia, *State of the Industry Report 2021*, Meat & Livestock Australia

Page 120 'Over the past ten years ...' ibid

Page 122 'Asparagopsis is a seaweed that ... mix with non-treated animals.' John L Black, Thomas M Davison and Ilona Box, 'Methane Emissions from Ruminants in Australia: Mitigation Potential and Applicability of Mitigation Strategies', *Animals*, vol. 11(4), 2021, doi: 10.3390/ani11040951

Page 125 'American research suggests that beef raised ...' Stephan van Vliet, Scott L Kronberg and Frederick D Provenza, 'Plant based meats, human health and climate change', *Frontiers in Sustainable Food Systems*, vol. 4(128), October 2020

Page 126 '"An ecologically and socially enhancing agriculture ..."' Charles Massy, *Call of the Reed Warbler*, University of Queensland Press, 2017, p. 5

Page 128 'I visited his farm for a field walk on a sunny winter day.' Jill Griffiths, 'Bringing Back Biology', *Farming Ahead*, No. 344 September 2020

CHAPTER 8: CHICKENS

Page 132 'More than 20 billion chickens live …' Andrew Lawler, *How the Chicken Crossed the World*, Duckworth Overlook, 2015

Page 132 'By 2018, the global chicken population had risen …' Hannah Ritchie, Pablo Rosado and Max Roser, 'Meat and Dairy Production', *Our World in Data*, November 2019

Page 132 'They are the most important agricultural animal on the planet.' Alice Roberts, *Tamed: Ten Species That Changed Our World*, 2017

Page 132 'The Australian chicken meat industry …' Australian Chicken Meat Federation, 'The Chicken Family Tree', *ACMF*, 26 July 2016, <chicken.org.au/the-chicken-family-tree>

Page 132 'Chicken is Australia's favourite meat …' Australian Chicken Meat Federation, 'Time to Separate Fact from Fiction', *ACMF*, 10 March 2021, <chicken.org.au/time-to-separate-fact-from-fiction

Page 133 'The competition sought to find the …' Alice Roberts, *Tamed: Ten Species That Changed Our World*, 2017, p. 171

Page 133 'From those original Chicken of Tomorrow … in the chicken meat industry.' ibid, p. 173

Page 133 ''These fertile eggs are hatched out in quarantine …'' Australian Chicken Meat Federation, 'The Chicken Family Tree', 26 July 2016

Page 133 'In Australia, the two largest chicken meat companies … by smaller independent operators.''' Georgina Townsend, Michael Beer, Kylie Hewson and Chris Murphy, 2019, *AgriFutures Chicken Meat Program RD&E Plan 2019–22*, AgriFutures Australia, Australian Government 2019

Page 135 'Currently, about 78 per cent of Australian chicken …' Australian Chicken Meat Federation, 'Chicken Meat Production', *ACMF* <chicken.org.au/chicken-meat-production/>

Page 135 'As many as 60,000 birds per shed.' Australian Chicken Meat Federation, 'Video Library', *ACMF* <chicken.org.au/video-library>

Page 136 'Aviagen now says its breeding objectives are around …' Australian Chicken Meat Federation, 'Selective breeding – why is it important and what does it mean?', *ACMF*, 8 September 2015, <chicken.org.au/selective-breeding-why-is-it-important-and-what-does-it-mean>

Page 137 'Amazingly, they have eaten less than two kilograms …' Australian Chicken Meat Federation, 'Facts and Figures', *ACMF*, 2020, <chicken.org.au/facts-and-figures/#Efficiency_of_Chicken_Production>

Page 137 'As an example, the total greenhouse gas …' Stephen Wiedemann, Eugene McGahan and Glenn Poad, *Using Life Cycle Assessment to Quantify the Environmental Impact of Chicken Meat Production*, Rural Industries Research and Development Corporation, 2012, p. xi

Page 137 'Again, Weidemann and colleagues say …' ibid, p. xxii

Page 137 'Australian chickens have not been …' Wendy J. Umberger and Lenka Malek, 2021, *Market insights for Australia's chicken meat industry*, AgriFutures Australia

Page 138 'These aren't the only aspects of chicken meat …' ibid

Page 138 'When the broilers are ready …' Australian Chicken Meat Federation, 'Chicken Meat Production', *ACMF*

Page 138 '"Once at the abattoir, chickens are rested in their transport ..." RSPCA, 'How are meat chickens farmed in Australia?', *RSPCA Knowledge Base*, 24 November 2020, <kb.rspca.org.au/knowledge-base/how-are-meat-chickens-farmed-in-australia/>

Page 139 'American animal welfare researcher Dr Temple Grandin ...' Temple Grandin, *Animals Make us Human*, Mariner, 2009, p. 229

Page 139 'In Australia, over twenty million layers ...' Australian Eggs, 'Australian Egg Industry Overview', *Australian Eggs* <australianeggs.org.au/egg-industry>

Page 140 'The positives listed are mainly to do ... conflicting measures of animal welfare."' Australian Eggs, 'What Are Cage Eggs?', *Australian Eggs* <australianeggs.org.au/farming/cage-eggs>

Page 143 'CSIRO has reported mortality rates of ...' DLM Campbell, MS Bari, and JL Rault, 'Free-range egg production: its implications for hen welfare', *Animal Production Science*, vol. 61, 2021, pp. 848–855

Page 145 'Jenner predicts another outbreak of avian flu in Australia ... to be sold as free-range.' Department for Environment, Food & Rural Affairs and Animal and Plant Health Agency, 'Bird flu – Latest media updates: All poultry and captive birds must now be housed until further notice', *Gov.uk*, 7 November 2022, <gov.uk/government/news/bird-flu-latest-situation-avian-influenza-prevention-zone-declared-across-great-britain>

Page 146 'They argue that their use is ...' RSPCA, 'What is the RSPCA doing to get hens out of battery cages?', *RSPCA Knowledge Base*, 24 November 2020, <kb.rspca.org.au/knowledge-base/what-is-the-rspca-doing-to-get-hens-out-of-battery-cages/>

Page 146 'These behaviours include nesting, foraging, ground-scratching ...' RSPCA, 2016, The Welfare of Layer Hens in Cage and Cage-Free Housing Systems

Page 146 'There was talk of Australia introducing a ban ...' Amy Bainbridge and Alison Branley, 'Australia was planning to phase out caged eggs by 2036, but one state is threatening to derail that', *ABC News*, 4 November 2021, <abc.net.au/news/2021-11-04/australia-plans-to-phase-out-battery-hens-cage-eggs-at-risk/100566732>

Page 148 'In Australia, Hy-Line Browns (and another laying breed ...' Specialised Breeders Australia, 'Specialised Breeders Australia', *SBA*,

Page 149 'The CSIRO team developed a way of adding ...' TJ Doran, KR Morris, TG Wise, TE O'Neil, CA Cooper, KA Jenkins and MLV Tizard, 2016, 'Sex selection in layer chickens', *Animal Production Science*, vol. 58(3), 2016 doi: 10.1071/AN16785

Page 150 'But in mid-2022, Hendrix Genetics ...' Hendrix Genetics, 'New partnership to study innovative sex sorting technology for the egg laying industry', *Hendrix Genetics*, 30 June 2022, <layinghens.hendrix-genetics.com/en/news/new-partnership-to-study-innovative-sex-sorting-technology-for-the-egg-laying-industry/>

CHAPTER 9: PIGS

Page 160 'Once domesticated, they were spread by farmers ...' Amke Caliebe, Almut Nebel, Cheryl Makarewicz, Michael Krawczak, Ben Krause-Kyora, 'Insights into early pig domestication provided by ancient DNA analysis', *Scientific Reports*, vol. 7(44550), 2017 doi: 10.1038/srep44550

Page 160 'Yet in other cultures, such as some …' Marvin Harris, *Cows, Pigs, Wars and Witches: The Riddles of Culture*, Random House New York, 1974

Page 161 'This practice is now illegal in Australia …' Livestock Biosecurity, 'Pig feed: what you can and can't feed pigs (swill or prohibited pig feed)', *Agriculture and Food*, 26 August 2022, <agric.wa.gov.au/livestock-biosecurity/pig-feed-what-you-can-and-can%E2%80%99t-feed-pigs-swill>

Page 161 'At any given time, there are around 2.4 million …' Australian Pork, 'Industry facts', *Australian Pork* <australianpork.com.au/industry-facts>

Page 161 'I stress domestic in that sentence …' Business Queensland, 'Feral pig', *Queensland Government*, 6 September 2022, <business.qld.gov.au/industries/farms-fishing-forestry/agriculture/land-management/health-pests-weeds-diseases/pests/invasive-animals/restricted/feral-pig>

Page 162 'Between 1961 and 2014, global pork production …' K Watson, S Wiedemann, L Biggs, and E McGahan, *Trends in environmental impacts from the pork industry*, Australian Pork Limited and the Department of Agriculture and Water Resources, December 2018

Page 163 'Up to seventeen is fairly common …' Vincent ter Beek, '22 piglets at one sow and it is no problem', *Pig Progress*, 19 October 2018, <pigprogress.net/pigs/22-piglets-at-one-sow-and-it-is-no-problem/>

Page 163 'Manure releases greenhouse gases …' K Watson et al, 2018

Page 164 'Overall, the environmental performance of pork production …' ibid

Page 164 'They have a strong "seeking" behaviour …' Temple Grandin, *Animals Make us Human*, 2009

Page 164 'Sow stalls also allow sows to be protected … some farms are kept in.' Australian Pork, 'Housing', *Australian Pork* <australianpork.com.au/about-pig-farming/housing>

Page 164 'The American animal welfare researcher Dr Temple Grandin …' Cited in Dan Saladino, *Eating to Extinction*, Jonathan Cape London, 2021, p. 169

Page 164 'Australian Pork says, "Today, we aim to ensure sows …"' Australian Pork, 'Housing'

Page 165 'Grandin suggests that because modern pigs …' Temple Grandin, *Animals Make us Human*, 2009

Page 166 'Australian Pork has investigated alternatives …' Australian Pork, 'Housing'

Page 170 'He speaks eloquently on the topic …' Dr David Beggs (host), Episode 6, *RawAg* [Audio podcast], Te Mania Angus, 2020–present <temaniaangus.com/rawag>

Page 174 'Australian philosopher Professor Peter Singer argues …' Peter Singer, *Ethics in the Real World*, Text Publishing, 2016, p. 54

Page 174 'Singer, author of the 1975 book *Animal Liberation* …' Peter Singer, *Animal Liberation*, Harper Collins Publishers, 2009 (revised)

Page 174 '"The people who profit by exploiting large numbers …"' Peter Singer, *Animal Liberation*, 2009, p. 161

Page 174 '"Hence the need for each of us to stop buying the products of modern farming …"' ibid, p. 162

Page 174 'In a more recent book, *Ethics in the Real World* …' Peter Singer, *Ethics in the Real World*, 2016, p. 66

Page 174 'He writes that "*if* there is no serious ethical objection …"' ibid, p. 57

Page 174 '"Going vegan is a simpler choice …' ibid, p. 58

Page 174 'In *Animal Liberation*, Singer writes that …' Peter Singer, *Animal Liberation*, 2009, p. 97

Page 175 'Given what we know about human nature …' ibid, p. 229

CHAPTER 10: SHEEP

Page 181 '… research shows that around a fifth of lambs die between birth and weaning …' Jill Griffiths, 'Tailored approach essential to improve lamb losses', *Farming Ahead*, vol. 295, 2016

Page 182 '"To create life with the intention … work that cannot be overstated."' Anika Molesworth, *Our Sunburnt Country*, Pan Macmillan Australia, 2020, p. 36

Page 183 'If you have a couple of ewes … ewe and lamb mortality.' Jill Griffiths, 'Precision lambing brings rewards', *Farming Ahead*, vol. 320, September 2018

Page 183 'Still, Murdoch University research has shown …' Jill Griffiths, 'Looking closer at paternity', *Farming Ahead* January vol. 360, 2022

Page 185 'Flystrike is estimated to cost the Australian …' CSIRO, ' Managing flystrike and mulesing in sheep', *CSIRO* <csiro.au/en/research/animals/livestock/managing-flystrike-and-mulesing-in-sheep>

Page 185 'About thirty million of the forty million …' Meat & Livestock Australia Limited, 'Over 90% of producers to increase or maintain flock', *MLA*, 17 December 2020 https://www.mla.com.au/prices-markets/market-news/2020/whats-in-store-for-the-flock-in-2021/#

Page 186 'Australian Wool Innovation (AWI), the peak industry body …' Australian Wool Innovation Limited, 'Program Overview and Progress', *wool.com*, <wool.com/sheep/welfare/breech-flystrike/progress/>

Page 189 'I've spoken to Ludeman on many occasions …' Jill Griffiths, 'Behind the Headlines', *Farming Ahead*, vol. 358, November 2021

Page 189 '*The Australian* newspaper reported in May 2022 …' Sharri Markson, 'Activists hid live export footage payments,' in *The Australian*, May 5 2022

Page 189 'She is quoted on the Animals Australia …' Animals Australia team, 'Animals Australia's Lyn White honoured as a Member of the Order of Australia', *Animals Australia*, 9 June 20914, <animalsaustralia.org/latest-news/lyn-white-member-of-the-order-of-australia/>

Page 190 'Ludeman cites community attitude research …' Kieren Moffat, *Live Exports and the Australian Community 2019–2022*, LiveCorp, 2022, <livecorp.com.au/report/XZtizQCnhI3IoNJBqA5uh>

Page 190 'There are strict standards and regulations …' Animal Health Australia, *Australian Animal Welfare Standards and Guidelines — Land Transport of Livestock*, Australian Government Department of Agriculture, Fisheries and Forestry, 2012, <animalwelfarestandards.net.au/land-transport/>

Page 190 'There are strict standards and regulations ...' Department of Agriculture, Water and the Environment, *Australian Standards of Live Export*, Australian Government Department of Agriculture, Water and the Environment, 2020, <agriculture.gov.au/biosecurity-trade/export/controlled-goods/live-animals/livestock/australian-standards-livestock>

Page 190 'She says that although infrastructure varies ...' Department of Agriculture, Fisheries and Forestry, 'Exporter Supply Chain Assurance System (ESCAS)', *Australian Government Department of Agriculture, Fisheries and Forestry*, 8 November 2022, <agriculture.gov.au/biosecurity-trade/export/controlled-goods/live-animals/livestock/information-exporters-industry/escas>

Page 192 'The Australian Veterinary Association would like to see ...' Australian Veterinary Association, 'Humane slaughter', *AVA*, 7 December 2018, <ava.com.au/policy-advocacy/policies/euthanasia/humane-slaughter/>

CHAPTER 11: CANOLA

Page 201 'The case has been held up as everything from a ...' Australian Farm Institute, 'Getting the story right on the Marsh-Baxter GM case', *Australian Farm Institute*, 3 September 2015, <farminstitute.org.au/getting-the-story-right-on-the-marsh-baxter-gm-case/>

Page 201 'The latter because Monsanto, the patent owner ...' ABC News, 'Monsanto contributed to WA farmer Michael Baxter's legal costs in GM case', *ABC News*, 8 April 2015, <abc.net.au/news/2015-04-08/monsanto-contributed-to-michael-baxters-legal-costs/6377526>

Page 201 'Legal experts have suggested Marsh ...' Australian Farm Institute, 'Getting the story right on the Marsh-Baxter GM case', 2015, <farminstitute.org.au/getting-the-story-right-on-the-marsh-baxter-gm-case/>

Page 201 'In the Marsh v Baxter case ...' *Marsh v Baxter* [2014] WASC 187 (CIV 1561 of 2012) Judgement Summary

Page 201 'Monash University Associate Professor of Law Karinne Ludlow says ...' Karinne Ludlow, 'Growing Together: The Impact of the Regulation of Non-Innovative Activities on Agricultural Innovation Governance', *Journal of Environmental Law*, 2017, pp. 1–26 doi: 10.1093/jel/eqx021

Page 203 'Canola is now grown on almost three million Australian hectares ...' Australian Oilseeds Federation, Crop Report, Canola, November 2021

Page 203 'The EU market pays a premium for non-GM canola ...' CSIRO, *Maintaining access to EU markets for Australian canola*, July 2019

Page 204 'From when it was released in 1974 up until 2016 ...' Charles M Benbrook, 'Trends in glyphosate herbicide use in the United States and globally', *Environmental Sciences Europe*, vol. 28(3), 2016 doi: 10.1186/s12302-016-0070-0

Page 204 'Dr Matthew O'Mullane from APVMA said ... across the world' Jill Griffiths, 'Clearing up confusion over glyphosate safety', *Farming Ahead*, vol. 294, July 2016

Page 205 'TT canola was originally bred in Canada ...' Felicity Pritchard, *Herbicide tolerant canola in farming systems – a guide for growers*, Grains Research and Development Corporation, 2014

Page 205 'This can lead to herbicide-resistant weeds …' Felicity Pritchard, 2014, *Herbicide tolerant canola in farming systems – a guide for growers*, Grains Research and Development Corporation. GRDC Project Code: BWD00016

Page 206 'When it was approved by the Office of the Gene Technology Regulator …' Office of the Gene Technology Transfer, 'Twenty Years of the OGTR – timeline', *Australian Government Department of Health and Aged Care*, August 2021, <ogtr.gov.au/resources/publications/twenty-years-ogtr-timeline>

Page 206 'In Western Australia, which produces most of Australia's canola …' Standing Committee on Environment and Public Affair, presented by Hon Matthew Swinbourn MLC (Chairman), *Mechanisms for compensation for economic loss to farmers in Western Australia caused by contamination by genetically modified material*, Western Australia Legislative Council, Report 49, 2019

Page 206 'But cottonseed oil is extensively used …' Agricultural Biotechnology Council of Australia, *GM Cotton in Australia: A resource guide*, ABCA, 2012, <abca.com.au/wp-content/uploads/2012/09/ABCA_Resource_Guide_3_v2.pdf>

Page 206 'Long before GM crops were approved … land area sown to GM crops.' Standing Committee on Environment and Public Affair, *Mechanisms for compensation for economic loss to farmers in Western Australia caused by contamination by genetically modified material*, 2019

Page 207 ' … gene technology has not been shown to introduce any new or altered hazards …' Food Standards Australia New Zealand, 'Safety Assessments of GM Food', *FSANZ*, 2021, <foodstandards.gov.au/consumer/gmfood/safety/Pages/default.aspx page>

Page 207 'To date, the products of nine GM food crops are approved for sale …' Food Standards Australia New Zealand, 'GM Foods in Australia and New Zealand', *FSANZ*, 2021, <foodstandards.gov.au/consumer/gmfood/Documents/GM%20Foods%20in%20Australia%20and%20New%20Zealand.pdf>

Page 207 'He says he saw GM as humankind acquiring too much …' Mark Lynas, 'Lecture to Oxford Farming Conference' [video], *Oxford Farming Conference*, YouTube, 23 January 2013, <youtube.com/watch?v=vf86QYf4Suo&t=1901s>

Page 208 'Lynas writes that the "general level of public fear …' Mark Lynas, *Seeds of Science: Why we got it so wrong on GMOs*, Bloomsbury Sigma, 2020

Page 208 'Ghent University, Belgium, philosopher Stefaan Blancke writes …' Stefaan Blancke, 'Why People Oppose GMOs Even Though Science Says They Are Safe', *Scientific American*, 18 August 2015, <scientificamerican.com/article/why-people-oppose-gmos-even-though-science-says-they-are-safe/>

Page 208 'Lynas describes opposition to GM as being aesthetic …' Mark Lynas, Mark Lynas, 'Lecture to Oxford Farming Conference' [video], 2013

CHAPTER 12: BEES

Page 216 'As American writer Hannah Nordhaus describes …' Hannah Nordhaus, *The Beekeeper's Lament*, Harper Perennial, 2010, p. 57

Page 217 'The value of the surveillance system became apparent …' Minister for Agriculture and Western NSW, *Varroa mite incursion detected in NSW* [media release], New South Wales Government, 24 June 2022, <dpi.nsw.gov.au/about-us/media-centre/releases/2022/ministerial/varroa-mite-incursion-detected-in-nsw>

Page 217 'An immediate eradication plan was enforced ...' New South Wales Government, *NSW DPI varroa mite update* [media release], New South Wales Government, 8 July 2022, <dpi.nsw.gov.au/about-us/media-centre/releases/2022/general/nsw-dpi-varroa-mite-update>

Page 217 '"From almonds to avocados to the meat we eat ..."' AgriFutures, 'Honey Bee & Pollination', *AgriFutures Australia* <agrifutures.com.au/rural-industries/honey-bee-pollination/>

Page 217 'And around the world, two billion people ...' R Ponce-Reyes and BD Lessard, *Edible Insects: A roadmap for the strategic growth of an emerging Australian industry*, CSIRO 2021

Page 218 'Australia has around 62,000 native insect ...' ibid

Page 218 'Insects are high in protein, omega-3 fatty acids ...' ibid

Page 218 'Apparently, it's not aversion ...' Indee Hopkins, Asgar Farahnaky, Harsharn Gill, Lisa P. Newman, Jessica Danaher, 'Australians' experience, barriers and willingness towards consuming edible insects as an emerging protein source', *Appetite*, vol. 169, 1 February 2022 doi: 10.1016/j.appet.2021.105832

Page 218 'CSIRO sees it as the fastest-growing of a number of opportunities ... entomophagy is considered mainstream."' R Ponce-Reyes and BD Lessard, *Edible Insects: A roadmap for the strategic growth of an emerging Australian industry*, 2021

Page 219 'Food Standards Australia New Zealand (FSANZ) assessed three insect species ...' NSW Government Food Authority, 'Edible Insects', *Food Authority*, September 2021, <foodauthority.nsw.gov.au/sites/default/files/2020-10/edible-insects.pdf>

Page 219 'But an SBS article on entomophagy ...' Lucy Rennick, 'You could be accidentally eating 140,000 pieces of insect a year', *SBS*, 8 August 2017, <sbs.com.au/food/article/2017/07/26/you-could-be-accidentally-eating-140000-pieces-insect-year>

Page 220 'RMIT researchers found insect-based flour was the insect-based food ...' Indee Hopkins, Asgar Farahnaky, Harsharn Gill, Lisa P. Newman, Jessica Danaher, 'Australians' experience, barriers and willingness towards consuming edible insects as an emerging protein source', 2022

Page 221 'Fight Food Waste Cooperative Research Centre is working with ...' Fight Food Waste, 'Optimising And Industrialising Black Soldier Fly (BSF) Production – Redirecting Food Waste To Livestock Feed Production Using Insects', *Fight Food Waste*, 2021, <fightfoodwastecrc.com.au/project/optimising-and-industrialising-black-soldier-fly-bsf-production-redirecting-food-waste-to-livestock-feed-production-using-insects/>

Page 221 'As Goterra puts it on their website ...' Goterra, 'Insect Products', *Goterra* <goterra.com.au/insect-protein-products/>

Page 222 'Australians throw out 20 per cent ...' Climate Council, 'From Farm To Plate To The Atmosphere: Food-Related Emissions', *Climate Council*, 16 October 2016, <climatecouncil.org.au/from-farm-to-plate-to-the-atmosphere-reducing-your-food-related-emissions>

Page 222 'Figures from the World Resources Institute show that ...' Katie Flanagan, Kai Robertson and Craig Hanson, 'Reducing Food Loss and Waste: Setting a Global Action Agenda', *World Resources Institute* <files.wri.org/d8/s3fs-public/reducing-food-loss-waste-global-action-agenda-executive-summary.pdf>

Page 223 'For example, it is estimated that 3.5 per cent ...' Fight Food Waste, 'Consumer Fridge Behaviour And Waste Reduction Of Red Meat', *Fight Food Waste*, 2021, <fightfoodwastecrc.com.au/project/consumer-fridge-behaviour-and-waste-reduction-of-red-meat/>

CHAPTER 13: SALMON

Page 224 'The biggest is Tassal, which produces ...' Brad Thompson, 'Canadian suitor lands Tassal with $1.1b offer', *Australian Financial Review*, 16 August 2021, <afr.com/companies/agriculture/canadian-suitor-lands-tassal-with-1-1b-takeover-offer-20220816-p5ba6x>

Page 224 'Petuna, with a workforce of around 300 ...' Petuna, 'About Petuna', *Petuna*, <petuna.com.au/who-we-are/about>

Page 225 'Huon Aquaculture was started by the Bender family ...' Huon Aquaculture, 'Our Operations', *Huon Aquaculture*, 2022, <huonaqua.com.au/our-approach/our-operations/>

Page 225 'JBS Australia claims to be the ...' JBS Australia, 'Australia', *JBS Foods*, 2022, <jbsfoodsgroup.com/locations/australia>

Page 225 'Research from US organisation The Center for Food Integrity shows ...' Charlie Arnot, 'Earning Consumer Trust Through Shared Values' [conference paper], *LambEx 2018 Conference*, Perth, 5–8 August 2018

Page 225 'In her enlightening book *Farm (and Other F Words)* ... and great businesspeople.'" Sarah K Mock, *Farm and Other F Words*, New Degree Press, 2021, pp. 180–2

Page 226 'Ironically, and sadly, at the same time ... inside underwater cages.' Dan Saladino, *Eating to Extinction*, Jonathan Cape London, 2021, p. 190

Page 227 'Tasmanian writer Richard Flanagan has also drawn ... and profit big business.'" Richard Flanagan, *Toxic: The Rotting Underbelly of the Tasmanian Salmon Industry*, Penguin Random House Australia, 202, p. 77

Page 227 'A piece by veterinarian Dr Steve Percival ...' Steve Percival, 'The Importance of Balanced Information', *Huon Aquaculture*, 9 June 2021, <huonaqua.com.au/the-importance-of-balanced-information/>

Page 228 '"In 2019 Tassal used 62.28 grams of antibiotics ..."' Richard Flanagan, *Toxic: The Rotting Underbelly of the Tasmanian Salmon Industry*, p. 71

Page 228 'It does sound like a lot of antibiotics ...' One Health, 'Combating Antimicrobial Resistance in People and Animals: A One Health Approach', *Centers for Disease Control and Prevention*, 11 March 2022, <cdc.gov/onehealth/in-action/index.html>

Page 228 'The NGO Environment Tasmania rates all three ...' Salmon.org, *A Fresh Approach: Tasmanian Salmon Consumers Guide*, Environment Tasmania, <d3n8a8pro7vhmx.cloudfront.net/marine/pages/2155/attachments/original/1574374357/ET_consumers_guideFINAL_CORRECT_LOGO_%281%29.pdf?1574374357>

Page 228 'In the marine food web, omega-3 fatty acids …' CSIRO, 'Omega-3 canola', *CSIRO*, 7 January 2021, < csiro.au/en/research/plants/crops/Oil-crops/Omega-3-canola>

Page 228 'For example, cattle and sheep that graze pasture …' Hannah Davis, Amelia Magistrali, Gillian Butler and Sokratis Stergiadis, 'Nutritional Benefits from Fatty Acids in Organic and Grass-Fed Beef', *Foods*, vol. 11(5), 2022, p. 646, doi: 10.3390/foods11050646

Page 229 'But a Belgian study found most consumers …' Wim Verbeke, Isabelle Sioen, Karen Brunsø, Stefaan de Henauw and John Van Camp, 'Consumer perception versus scientific evidence of farmed and wild fish: exploratory insights from Belgium', *Aquaculture International*, vol. 15, pp. 121–136, doi: 10.1007/s10499-007-9072-7

Page 229 'On the other hand, a UK study found some evidence …' M Sprague, S Fawcett, MB Betancor, W Struthers and DR Tocher, 'Variation in the nutritional composition of farmed Atlantic salmon (*Salmo salar* L.) fillets with emphasis on EPA and DHA contents', *Journal of Food Composition and Analysis*, vol. 94, 2020, doi: 10.1016/j.jfca.2020.103618

Page 230 'Noting this, a group of researchers looked at dietary guidelines …' Anna K. Farmery, Gilly A. Hendrie, Gabrielle O'Kane, Alexandra McManus and Bridget S. Green , 'Sociodemographic Variation in Consumption Patterns of Sustainable and Nutritious Seafood in Australia', *Frontiers in Nutrition*, Volume 5(118), December 2018

Page 230 'Tassal says they use 0.7 kilograms of wild fish …' Tassal, 'How We Care', *Tassal*, <tassal.com.au/sustainability/>

Page 231 'A 2018 survey found 78 per cent of Australians had eaten … more than eight million square kilometres.' Fisheries Research and Development Corporation, *Annual Report 2018–2019*, Australian Government, <transparency.gov.au/annual-reports/fisheries-research-and-development-corporation/reporting-year/2018-2019-22>

Page 232 'In 2021, the *Fisheries Status Reports* (which is produced by ABARES …' Seafood Industry Australia, 'A testament to industry': Australian seafood given sustainability tick for eighth consecutive year', *Seafood Industry Australia*, 14 October 2021, <seafoodindustryaustralia.com.au/a-testament-to-industry-australian-seafood-given-sustainability-tick-for-eighth-consecutive-year/>

Page 232 'The reports investigated the status of 100 species …' Australian Bureau of Agricultural and Resource Economics and Sciences, *Fishery status reports 2021*, Australian Government Department of Agriculture, Water and the Environment, 2021

Page 232 'CSIRO researchers Dr Aysha Fleming and Dr Ingrid van Putten …' Aysha Fleming and Ingrid van Putten, 'There aren't plenty of fish in the sea, so let's eat all that we catch', *The Conversation*, 21 December 2021, <theconversation.com/there-arent-plenty-of-fish-in-the-sea-so-lets-eat-all-that-we-catch-104329>

Page 232 'Fleming and van Putten say 8 per cent …' ibid

Page 232 'WWF Australia says …' WWF Australia, 'Bycatch', *WWF Australia*, <wwf.org.au/what-we-do/oceans/bycatch#gs.3jxdtv>

Page 232 '"In Australia, most people tend to dislike 'fishy' flavours ..."' researchers Dr Aysha Fleming and Dr Ingrid van Putten ...' Aysha Fleming and Ingrid van Putten, 'There aren't plenty of fish in the sea, so let's eat all that we catch', 2021

Page 233 'According to the Good Fish Guide ...' GoodFish, 'Barramundi', *GoodFish*, <goodfish.org.au/species/barramundi/>

Page 234 'In his book *Eat Like a Fish*, Smith details ... 40 million pounds of seaweeds.' Bren Smith, *Eat Like a Fish*, Murdoch Books, 2019

CHAPTER 14: MACADAMIA

Page 237 'The food now produced annually in Australia ...' Bill Bellotti, 'How many people can Australia feed?' *The Conversation*, 13 July 2017, <theconversation.com/how-many-people-can-australia-feed-76460>

Page 237 'Each Australian farmer feeds ... food consumed here is produced here.' Entegra Signature Structures, 'How Many People are Fed by Australian Farmers?' *Entegra*, 24 January 2022, <entegra.com.au/how-many-people-are-fed-by-australian-farmers/>

Page 238 'The nuts are high in oil ...' Nutrition Data, 'Nuts, macadamia nuts, raw', *Nutrition Data*, 25 May 2018, <nutritiondata.self.com/facts/nut-and-seed-products/3123/2>

Page 238 'Australia, fittingly, produces most of ...' Australian Macadamia Society, 'About', *Australian Macadamia Society*, <australianmacadamias.org/industry/about>

Page 238 'Commercial cultivation began in the late 1800s ...' Roger D. Norton, *The Competitiveness of Tropical Agriculture*, Academic Press, 2017

Page 238 'In Australia, the first commercial macadamia ... fourth largest horticultural export.' Australian Macadamia Society, 'About'

Page 239 'Almonds, table grapes and oranges ...' Hort Innovation, *Australian Horticulture Statistics Handbook 2018–19*, Hort Innovation, 2019

Page 239 'The macadamia industry has a current annual turnover ...' AgriFutures Australia, *New Opportunities 2020: The next wave in new & emerging agricultural industries in Australia (Stage 1)*, 2020 Rural Industries Research and Development Corporation, November 2020

Page 239 'The Federal Government agency AgriFutures Australia says ...' ibid

Page 239 'According to AgriFutures, some native plants ...' ibid

Page 239 'Put simply, "most Australian flora and fauna ..."' ibid

Page 239 'There are only thirteen Australian native foods ...' ibid

Page 239 'As AgriFutures puts it: "The sector is high profile ..."' ibid

CHAPTER 15: ENOUGH

Page 252 'A British study confirms ...' Theresa M Marteau, Gareth J Hollands, Ian Shemilt, Susan A Jebb, 'Downsizing: policy options to reduce portion sizes to help tackle obesity', *British Medical Journal*, vol. 351, 2015, doi: 10.1136/bmj.h5863

Page 252 'The 2016 *Trolley Trends* study ...' Bernard Salt, 'Foreword', Woolworths *Trolley Trends 2013*, Woolworths, 2013, <scribd.com/document/228626115/Woolworths-Trolley-Trends-2013-28-8-13>

Page 253 'As Dan Saladino writes in *Eating to Extinction* …' Dan Saladino, *Eating to Extinction*, Jonathan Cape London, 2021

Page 254 'The International Food Policy Research Institute reports that between 1974 and 2005 …' Cited in Julian Cribb, *The Coming Famine*, CSIRO Publishing, 2010, p. 169

Page 254 'In 2022, it rose above 1975 levels …' Food and Agriculture Organization of the United Nations, 'FAO Food Price Index', *Food and Agriculture Organization of the United Nations*, 12 December 2022, <fao.org/worldfoodsituation/foodpricesindex/en/>

Page 254 'The Australian Bureau of Statistics reported the price of food …' Australian Bureau of Statistics, 'Consumer Price Index, Australia', *ABS website*, 26 October 2022, <abs.gov.au/statistics/economy/price-indexes-and-inflation/consumer-price-index-australia/latest-release>

Page 254 'But the ABS also reported a 2 per cent decline …' Australian Bureau of Statistics, 'Australian National Accounts: National Income, Expenditure and Product' *ABS website*, 7 September 2022, <abs.gov.au/statistics/economy/national-accounts/australian-national-accounts-national-income-expenditure-and-product/latest-release>

Page 255 'US figures indicate Americans spent less …' USDA Economic Research Services, 'Total food budget share increased from 9.4 percent of disposable income to 10.3 percent in 2021', *USDA*, 15 July 2022, <ers.usda.gov/data-products/chart-gallery/gallery/chart-detail/?chartId=76967>

Page 255 'According to University of Melbourne researchers … food relief from charities jumping by 47 per cent.' Rachel Carey and Maureen Murphy, 'Australia's New Government Must Tackle Food Insecurity', *Pursuit*, <pursuit.unimelb.edu.au/articles/australia-s-new-government-must-tackle-food-insecurity>

Page 255 'Ironically, access to fresh, healthy food … obesity rates outside of metropolitan areas.' Jill Whelan, Lynne Millar, Colin Bell, Cherie Russell, Felicity Grainger, Steven Allender, Penelope Love, 'You Can't Find Healthy Food in the Bush: Poor Accessibility, Availability and Adequacy of Food in Rural Australia', *International Journal of Environmental Research and Public Health*, 2018, vol. 15(10), p. 2316

Page 255 'The *EAT-Lancet Commission on healthy diets from sustainable systems* …' Walter Willett et al, 'Food in the Anthropocene: the EAT-*Lancet* Commission on healthy diets from sustainable food systems', doi: 10.1016/S0140-6736(18)31788-4

Page 256 'Australian science journalist Julian Cribb …' Julian Cribb, *The Coming Famine*, p. 103

Page 256 'He writes that, at the start of the twenty-first century …' ibid, p. 105

Page 256 'He contrasts this with the $1.5 trillion …' ibid, p. 106

Page 257–258 'The Australian National University's Sustainable Farms project team considers …' David B Lindenmayer, Suzannah M MacBeth, David G Smith, Michelle L Young, *Natural Asset Farming*, CSIRO Publishing, 2022, p. xi

Page 258 '"Eat food. Not too much. Mostly plants."' Michael Pollan, *In Defence of Food*, Penguin Books, 2008, p. 1

Page 260 'In *The Coming Famine*, Julian Cribb points out …' Julian Cribb, *The Coming Famine*, p. 201

Index